Carole Galloway
Montreal 1995

The MIT Press
Cambridge, Massachusetts
London, England

Reading the French Garden: Story and History

DENISE LE DANTEC and JEAN-PIERRE LE DANTEC

translated by Jessica Levine

First MIT Press paperback edition, 1993

This book was set in Galliard by DEKR Corporation
and printed and bound in the United States of America.

Library of Congress Cataloging-in-Publication Data

Le Dantec, Denise.
[Roman des jardins de France. English]
Reading the French garden: story and history/Denise
Le Dantec and Jean-Pierre Le Dantec; translated
by Jessica Levine.
    p. cm.
Translation of: Le roman des jardins de France.
ISBN 0-262-12144-1 (HB), 0-262-62087-1 (PB)
1. Gardens--France--History. 2. Gardening--France--
History.
I. Le Dantec, Jean-Pierre, 1943-   II. Title.
SB451.36.F8L413   1990
712'.0944--dc20   89-13363
                                              CIP

The history of art is the history of the human spirit in forms.

HENRI FOCILLON

And yet, periodization is not entirely artificial. It matters little that the chronological limits of periods are vague and even overlapping; from a certain distance, the distinctions seem more or less clear; and men of the same era do have a certain family resemblance.

ALEXANDRE KOYRÉ

History is a true novel.

PAUL VEYNE

CONTENTS

Reading the French Garden: Story and History

At that time, bramble and lentisk were swallowing up marbles and colonnades relentlessly. Nettle was growing over the pavement, couch grass between the mosaics, and the ancient topiary decoration was vanishing in the confused growth of the unpruned cypresses among the shaggy boxwood. The water beneath the duckweed was stagnant, the beehives and aviaries empty. Near the caved-in pools, the tangled vinebranch and laburnum indicated that in a world now destroyed men had once built arbors and bowers. But the forest was triumphing. It seemed as though the very idea of the garden had fled, erased from memory by violent turmoil.

It was the seventh century of our era, in a Gaul where villas were no more.

In the year of our Lord 650, let us say.

A man and a young girl are following the path that Colomban[1] first took through the barbarian forest and working their way toward the city of Meaux, whose bishop is Faron, a friend of the Scots. From the man's tonsure, shaped like a half-moon, and the long mane of hair falling down on his shoulders, we know he is a pilgrim from Ireland.

His name is Fiachra,[2] and he is the son of a king of Erin. He wears a long gray alb that one can see used to be white, and leans on a curved cane called a *cambutte*: a flask swings from his belt alongside a bag full of liturgical books, and the bronze capsules on his chest, near his heart, are held solidly in place by leather straps. They contain his only treasure: sacred relics and consecrated hosts. As for the young girl, who is also dressed in white as a sign of her virginity and carries a bag made of hide, she would seem an elf if not for the fierce determination in her eyes: she is Fiachra's sister and her name is Sira.

The two walk in the forest, unescorted, gaunt in their tattered clothes, their bodies covered with scratches and tick bites, and yet they are happy, confident they are enough within the God who guides them not to fear the wild creatures, be they men or beasts, that might attack them at any moment. Clouds of flies, bugs, and bats swirl down from the dark foliage hanging over their heads. Furtive movements often stir the forest undergrowth as their naked feet sink into the bramble. Is that trembling in the copse a rabbit or a knot of vipers? And that hoarse cry coming from the pond, is it a wolf, a bandit, or a stag? . . . It makes no difference to the pilgrims. Their bodies do not feel, their ears do not hear, and their eyes, wide with fever, are blind to the world and entirely turned within, where they gaze, wide open, upon the soul.

They walk and sing:

The wind is coming up, a horrible rain beats upon us
But the monks dominate and brave the storm with their solidarity and strength.
Hey ho! And a bellowing echo answers our cries: hey ho!
Faced with our steadfastness, rain and thunder give way!
Our confidence, our repeated efforts master all obstacles.
Hey ho! And a bellowing echo answers our cries: hey ho!
Continue your struggle, ensure your success
Oh you who have suffered the gravest dangers,
God will grant you an end to your fears.
Hey ho! And a bellowing echo answers our cries: hey ho! . . .

They sing Colomban's heroic hymn and go, never looking back. Their mission is so great, so burdensome. In Bangor, where for many years Fiachra was a monk, one of a throng of brothers and novices immersed in study and prayer, his teachers did in fact repeat every day: "It is our lot, as Scots, to become God's pilgrims! To go to sea as Brendan the navigator did, or to spread out in Gaul, in Germany, and in Italy, just like Colomban! We have received our mission to take the divine Word everywhere, to the north as well as the south, and to conquer the horrendous pagan night in deep forests and icy lands, in the depth of fertile valleys and on rugged mountain slopes! And in order not to fail in this sacred task that our Savior has entrusted us, we must establish our iron rule everywhere:

Benchuir, bona regula
Recta atque divina
Stricta, sancta, sedula
Summa, justa et mira."

A descendant of the great kings of Ireland, Fiachra did not hesitate: "He who flees the pleasures of this world will be so fulfilled by the heavenly Father that he could desire no more," says Scripture. With his sister he crossed the sea, indifferent to its storms, and now they are walking in the hostile forest, their hearts filled with joy and their souls unworried by dark forces.

They go forward, these two pilgrims, and never look back, greeting the charcoal carriers they pass only to make sure they are Christians. Soon the forest thins out as they approach its edge.

They have reached the valley. Not the prosperous space of ancient Roman *Gallia* where, in a carefully cultivated countryside, one might have encountered some rich *villa* surrounded by cypresses and an artfully designed garden. No fields of wheat stretching to the horizon; no porticoes; no *diaetae* with lovely arbors or basins with marble copings; no groves where an eager Dionysos might lie in wait for a dancing Io or a thoughtful Athena. . . . The civilized *ager* has retreated before the virgin *saltus*. One can barely make out a few sparse fields where skinny, lowing cows graze, a patch of wheat, a strip of barley, a flock of pigs led by children, and, at the end of the road, nestled below, a ghost of a town.

For, instead of the powerful city one might expect of the seat of a bishopric, Meaux is a country village, poorly protected by a wooden fence and crossed by three barely passable dirt roads. The huts stand in a circle; their cob wall, for lack of regular repair, reveals the bare, poorly joined wattling. Women come and go, and clusters of children, who have been trained to beg, wander about. In the center, framing a square of clay, are the buildings of the bishop's palace: rising much higher than the rest, they are topped with new thatch and firmly planted on walls with stone foundations.

The two pilgrims present themselves. And, as soon as he learns they are Scots, Faron appears with a joyful expression. The reason is that this bishop has hardly any opportunity to speak, and even less to engage in worthwhile conversation in his diocese where there are only two or three priests who can call themselves learned. "An Irishman!" he cries enthusiastically. "A man of God, come from the holy island, who was not afraid to face the trials of the Ocean! A servant of Jesus Christ able to calm demons and to make the monks, my brothers, lie down on the ground most humbly, so that we may all enter into the glory of the Lord! This is a man worth meeting."[3]

Faron approaches along with his bowing monks. Fiachra enters the abbey with his sister. Faron exhibits his treasures and relics: reliquaries, missals, crosses, censers, and priestly vestments heavy with sards. The clasps are open, and a few amethysts, topazes, and jaspers are seen sparkling. Fiachra is silent. Then, when they have sung the service for the canonical hours and the bell has rung, the abbot and all his monks accompany the visitors outside. "The thirty-five of us who inhabit this place," says Faron, "have come from various parts of the country, with God's help, by the Very Great Love that we bear for him." He explains how long they have been there and who brings them supplies and by what dangerous means. After embracing Fiachra and his sister, he leads them to the refectory where they are served some thick soup, white bread, pears, and a full glass of wine. But the monk from Ireland seems to have little appetite, while Sira, marveling at the feast, swallows mouthful after mouthful so eagerly that her cheeks become as red as peonies.

"I am very thankful to you, my father, for this food," says Fiachra. "But now let me ask you a great favor: could you place me in some remote spot so that I might apply myself to the evangelical task that has brought me this far?"

"You will not be lacking for work!" the bishop exclaims, licking his bowl. "These parts have reverted to so much vile paganism that my energy alone is not sufficient to contain it. But what about your sister?"

They resolve the matter in this way: Sira will be a nun and join Faron's sister in a nearby convent. As for the monk, since his deepest desire is to be a hermit, he will go live in Breuil, a terribly wild place that has never been cleared but has a flowing spring. It is located not more than a league's distance from Meaux.

It is a clear afternoon when they all come out of nones. And it is a long embrace that brother and sister exchange, in the foreign manner, like two lovers parting.

"May heaven grant you success in your mission," the young girl murmurs.

"And may heaven keep you from temptation," says the future hermit, crying.

This is the way important enterprises begin, when the path has been marked by Providence.

Fiachra is soon in Breuil, busily making a hut of branches when, between prayers, he realizes that his body is in need of food. Aware that *gula*, like *luxuria*, is a capital sin, he contents himself with wild berries and boiled roots. He prays. He meditates. He is counting on the example he intends to give, hoping that God will, through him, unfold miracles capable of breaking the pagan night. Did the Almighty not manifest himself in this way in order to help Patrick in his mission to Ireland?

Often, when solitude has brought him near despair at the end of a fruitless day, Fiachra comforts himself by reading the saint's miracles as related by Tirechan, the chronicler.

One day at sunrise, when Patrick was praying by a spring near Cruachan, Loegaire's daughters, Ethne the fair and Feldelm the redhead, came to bathe.

Now, when these two saw the assembled clerics in their white robes, they thought they were ghosts and cried out:

"Where are you from, where do you come from?"

To which Patrick answered: "It is better to believe in God than to inquire about our race."

Then the eldest of the daughters asked: "Who is God? Where is he? Where does he live? Does he have sons and daughters, gold and silver? Is he still living? Is he handsome? Were there many people who raised his son? Are his daughters kind and loved by the men of this world? Is he in heaven or on earth, in the sea, the rivers, or the mountains? How does one love him? How does one find him?" And Patrick, filled with the Holy Spirit, answered: "Our God is the God of all men, the God of heaven and earth, of land and water, of the sun and moon, the God of tall mountains and deep valleys. He inspires, He gives life, He surpasses and supports all things. He kindles the light of the sun and spreads the darkness of night. He creates springs in the desert and dry islands in the middle of the sea, and the stars He placed in the sky serve as great lights. He has a Son, also eternal, who resembles him in all things, and the Son is not younger than the Father, and the Father is not older than the Son. And the Holy Spirit breathes through them, and the Father, the Son, and the Holy Ghost are not separate. And I, Patrick who have come to you to teach you His Word, I wish to unite you to the heavenly King, since you are daughters of an earthly King." And Loegaire's daughters spoke as though with one mouth and one heart: "Teach us to believe in the heavenly King, show us how to see him face to face, and as you command us, we shall do." And Patrick said: "Do you believe that the sin of your father and mother is redeemed through baptism?" "We do," they answered. "Do you believe in repentance after sin?" "We do." "Do you believe in life after death and resurrection on the day of judgment?" "We do." "Do you believe in the unity of the Church?" "We do."

And Patrick baptized them and placed a white veil upon their heads. And the saint said to them: "You cannot see the face of Christ without first tasting death and taking communion." At which they cried out: "Give us communion, then, so that we may see the Son, our husband, face to face." And they received the Eucharist and fell asleep in death. And they were placed on a bed, and covered with their clothes. Their friends came from all over to weep over them, and even the druids came, who had raised them in ignorance of the true God. The druids came to cry over them, and Patrick preached to them, and they believed in Him . . .

Fiachra raises his clasped hands to the sky and, alone and lost in hope, repeats this glorious story to himself.

A faith bright as the spring sun lights up his soul and transports his entire body. And what light bathes all living things! How many blessings! Counting them, Fiachra cries out joyously before breaking into tears as new and frank as the child within him.

And the miracle of conversion is soon revealed. The pilgrims come by the dozens, curious about this man's saintliness, which is already reputed to be perfect and is quickly becoming known outside the Meaux diocese. Although this influx of visitors pleases the holy man—since it gives him the opportunity for many baptisms and communions—it also presents a new concern.

How, he asks himself, am I to restore all these people whose bodies, often exhausted by long walking, need more than spiritual nourishment? He has confidence not only in himself, but even more in the Virgin to whom he has dedicated his shrine. He knows he can quench the thirst of anxious souls, even perform a few modest cures. But what about the reasonable hunger of empty stomachs? That too is a creation of nature, he tells himself, and therefore is also the will of God—at least insofar as ordinary men are concerned, for they have not been called upon to serve *Him* in everything.

Fiachra makes a resolution. He will have a garden, since that is what Heaven commands. Yes, but how? And does he have the right? The land belongs to Faron who only gave him the right to use its surface for an ascetic way of life. Faced with such an important dilemma, Fiachra does not hesitate: he abandons his retreat for a day, runs to the bishop, and confides in him both his project and his scruples. A man who serves God without forgetting his own interests, Faron answers that, why not, he will gladly give the hermit as much of the Breuil as he can surround with a ditch in one day. Given the difficulties involved, he calculates that this generous gift will not ruin him; the height of the trees and the thickness of the bushes are bound to guarantee his fief.

The hermit, however, is not offended by these conditions. Not grasping the irony of the gift, or its pettiness, he goes back and, grasping his stick, puts it to work.

Miracle! the cane does its job; oaks fall before it and their roots are laid bare while the earth opens up like a block of butter carved with a spoon, creating a ditch that seems to proceed by itself! A little surprised perhaps, but not more than is suitable for a man of faith, Fiachra is overjoyed by the vastness of his new domain: "I will have enough so that I can let one part rest while the other produces," he thinks. And for a moment he remembers the exodus from Egypt and lets himself compare his ditch with the rift open in the heart of the Red Sea!

But a woman passing by—a pagan creature called La Becnaude—has neither his faith nor his candor. "It's witchcraft!" she hollers, pointing to the enclosure. "No Christian trick could work where my magic has failed!" Her words unmask her and prove that, when it comes to wondrous acts, it is she who is in league with Satan.

The saint does not hear her. He is already dreaming of seeds, manure, and carefully traced paths. And, while the shrew runs to get the bishop, he sits down sweetly as can be on a big stone in order to think the matter over. Now—this is what witnesses of the miracle maintain—all of a sudden the stone he is sitting on undergoes an astonishing transformation. No longer hard and bumpy, it sinks softly under the hermit's backside and takes the shape of a chair.

The miracle cannot be denied and satisfies the bishop as soon as he reaches Breuil. "One can doubt everything," he cries, "except for a Scot's rear!" His outburst proves—if one thinks how emaciated a hermit's buttocks are—that the prelate deserved to be a bishop, given how knowledgeable he was about miracles and that he was able to overcome his disappointment by noting that an insignificant weight, by itself, could not hollow out granite.

The bishop, however, did not know that the stone the holy hermit had taken for his seat was the one he had chosen for his altar and that, given its appropriate, eastern orientation, it was the sacred center establishing, like Jacob's stone, communication between the different *stages of the world*, and the *seat* of the presence of Yahweh.

Meanwhile, the young hermit tears up a tall oak with one motion and replaces it with the Cross. Then, with astonishing strength, he pulls up rushes, nettle, and broom, using neither felling axe nor billhook nor sickle. He even uproots two other tall trees as though they were fennel, dill, or danewort. No longer sterile, the soil is made to carry wheat. The strength of nourishing plants is wonderful to see. Here grow squash, rape, cabbages, and cardoons. There, propped up against the forest, the vine stocks are neatly lined up. In the middle of the river, where the froth laps over the water lilies and gladiolas, trout, perch, and salmon frisk about, slapping the fresh bunches of cress with their tails. Further on all kinds of medicinal herbs grow: bistort, rosemary, borage, dittany, black bryony, elderberry, bilberry, broom, and chaste tree.

Thus can one see how different kinds of plants have come to grow upon a *repulsive* earth, while up in the trees hundreds of hives drip with honey and small birds hop about gaily.

Fiachra works unceasingly, telling himself that the Promised Land will be destroyed if nothing comes to help him prosper. The sun completes three revolutions and then three more, and still the monk's back is bent over the earth. Finally his work is done and the hermit allows himself to rest. Lying in the grass with his eyes fixed on the sky, he listens to the birds sing compline, then he falls asleep after commending his soul to the Lord, the Virgin, and to Jesus Christ.

As soon as the cock crows, he recites matins and goes back to work. And soon, from all points in the forest, the poor, the hungry, and the ragged arrive.

"All of you come here, by God, because you will be able to eat!" cries the hermit as soon as he sees them in the distance.

What was said is done. And, from dawn till dusk, each one was well seated as though in a royal court, and there was much laughing and smiling at the banquet because, when hunger and cold have spread their empire everywhere, it is not a sin against God to eat well.

But here comes Becnaude, who hates nothing more than simple and deserved joy, once again stepping over the cemetery gate to visit Breuil. Wolfsbane, black nightshade, and red bryony stick out of her beggar's pouch.

"Witchcraft!" she cries out in rage when her red eyes see the miracle of the freshly raked earth and the joyous banquet.

She knows—the evil one—that her future depends on Breuil. Not only her own future, but that of her pagan magic. And so, seeing that her fuss has no effect upon the assembled beggars who are singing with Fiachra, she rushes to Meaux in order to bait Faron.

"You're being robbed!" she cries. "Your land is being eaten up, and the land of the holy Church! All the beggars are in Breuil, stuffing themselves along with that foreigner!"

As concerned as Faron may be about his goods, he is still a holy man, and so he answers sharply: "Get back to your spinning, Becnaude, and let us true believers pray in peace!"

The golden legend is perpetuated in *mirabilia*, marvels, and miracles. Fantastic cures; the miracle of the leprosy that covered Fiachra's face so that he could dismiss an emissary from Ireland who had come to make him king of Erin; the meeting with Killian who, although a saint, does not seem to have given his compatriot gardener the attention he deserved; and finally, Fiachra's edifying death on August 30 of 670.

This hagiography spread far and wide, destined as it was to found the sainthood of a hermit who, under the name of Fiacre, became a very popular saint—as a flourishing toponymy and many statues in the countryside indicate today.

For example, if one considers Brittany only, one finds a *Saint-Fiac* in Maroué, a *Liffiac* in Trégomeur in the Côtes-du-Nord, and a *Men-Fiac* in Plouescat in the Finistère. There is also a *Lan-Fiac* in Mahabon which, according to Jean Loth, "might be a faulty written form."[4] "Popular" magic and "learned" supernaturalism are combined as Saint Fiacre is placed in a simple, static, and good imaginary world.[5]

Escaping extravagance, he stands discreetly today in the small chapel of the peaceful village of *Saint-Fiachra-en-Brie*, whose rectangular plaza, called *le Breuil*, and *Becnaude's stone* remind us of the history of this saint whose church is only open on the day of his Pardon.

Carrying spade, this holy Scottish gardener stands in a niche over the porch of this country church, and seems so resolute, so intent upon using all his time to work the earth, that his gesture, immutable and paradoxical, seems to freeze in the indolent atmosphere of the leisurely life around him, sometimes troubled by the distant hum of a tractor drowning out the singing birds. As for the place that the gardener saint occupies in edifying literature, it is modest; few ancient texts, but allusions, which sometimes support and other times contradict each other, dispersed in the *Lives* written by Faron, bishop of Meaux in the seventh century of our era, or in the work by Killian; scholarly studies[6] gathered in the *Actes* of a colloquium held in Meaux on the occasion of the thirteen-hundredth birthday of the worthy hermit.

It was only later that the corporation of master gardeners chose Fiachra as their patron saint. These, ranked in five classes according to their specialty—*courtilliers, préoliers, verdiers, treillageurs, maraîchers*—the *floresses* being separate, since they were women—demanded however a statute comparable to that of other corporations.[7]

So that in 1599 King Henry IV, friend of earthly works, had the good inspiration to grant them such a statute, in order that the brotherhood might take on all the attributes necessary to its rank: an office on the rue des Rosiers; a chapel at Saint-Nicolas-des-Champs, a coat of arms made of "sable, with three garden lilies of silver, with branches and leaves of sinople, two placed in chief and one in center point, and an azure chief bearing a sun of gold," but, above all, a patron saint for whom the spade had replaced the stick—sign of wise concern with practical matters: Fiachra from Ireland, who was most deserving of this honor.

"Open or closed, the medieval *hortus*," engravings from the *Speculum humanae salvationis*, circa 1435. Photo © Bibliothèque Nationale, Paris.

Allée One

*At the top of a mountain of pure gold stands the
wall enclosing the flowers of Paradise.*
BENEDEIT, The Voyage of Saint Brendan

Fiachra's work ushered in the renaissance of the Western garden. Not that the "garden" of
Breuil could be compared to the beautiful works designed by Gallo-Roman culture and
described by Pliny the Elder, Pliny the Younger, Ovid, Palladius, Vitruvius, or Sidonius, or to
the virtuous compositions that were being built in China and in Persia in the same period.
But the West of that time had fallen so low and had forgotten so much that even a modest
enclosure seemed a step forward. And a step that was all the more significant in the case of
Fiachra's garden in that, besides its conventional character, the legend concentrates traits that
were in the image of the challenge that would soon be launched by the Carolingian
renaissance.

On the one hand there was the great obstacle: the triumph of ignorance, represented by the
dominating forest. At the opposite extreme the little bit of humanity that had saved its faith:
those monks who held on to their beliefs obstinately and fashioned them with the greatest
constraint, knowing that only strict rule could hold firm against barbarism. In the center,
obscure and seductive, stood the temptation of paganism.

Let us summarize the drama: Forest, Fiachra, and Becnaude, with a sword as referee. For it
was only the monk's alliance with Faron, here a figure more temporal than spiritual, that
made the new development possible—so true is it that Christian culture has always required
two supports in order to make progress: the support of faith on the one hand and of power
on the other.

The renewal remained fragile, however. Another wave of disturbances could have annulled
it. Perhaps Pierre Riché's argument will prove true,[1] that the barbarian invasions did not have
the brutal and destructive consequences that romantic history has enjoyed describing, but
that there was instead a slow decay of the ancient Christianized Roman culture, then a
resurgence of a new type of Christian West by means of an ascetic, Irish "replenishing in the

desert." The fact remains, however, that toward the year 1000 this resurgence, given the classical name of "Carolingian renaissance," underwent a painful passage the breadth of which has been described by Georges Duby: the geniuses Alcuin, Scotus Erigena and—why not?—Fiachra (if one understands that when we speak of gardens we are asking "how shall we feed ourselves?") almost disappeared without leaving any descendants.[2]

Nonetheless, the impulse indicated by the legend of Fiachra was too irresistible and too many broad-minded men decided to follow suit.

Thus, Childebert III, king of Neustria, Burgundy, and Austrasia, spent his days "loafing" in his garden, abandoning without regrets the leadership of the kingdom to the mayor of the palace, Pepin the Young, often considered the precursor of the Carolingian line. Thus, the capitularies promulgated by Charlemagne, especially the *Capitulare de villis vel curtis imperii*, concern horticulture, enumerating the list of the "seventy-three" plants and fruit trees that should be grown in the entire empire. Finally, the monks of many abbeys devoted their time not taken up with prayer to building groups of beds composed of a *hortus* or vegetable garden, a *herbularius* reserved for medicinal plants, a flower garden, and an orchard: the whole necessarily comprising these four parts, according to the rule established by the Edict of Milan in 313, which was founded on the necessity, for the monks, to heal themselves, to drink, and to take nourishment, as well as to adorn the altars with flowers.

It is consequently not surprising that, shortly before the middle of the ninth century, a practical poem appeared testifying to these efforts: our first "modern" manual of gardening, a work by brother Walahfrid Strabus, monk of Reichnau, addressed to Grimald, abbot of St. Gall.[3]

The figure of Strabus has fascinated many experts in monasticism, beginning with the novelist J.-K. Huysmans who, in *The Oblate*, made him one of his hero's favorite obsessions:

"But, by the way, who is this Strabo you've been harping on for months on end?"
"Strabo or Strabus, which means 'the squint-eyed,' is the name or rather nickname of a monk, the disciple of Rabanus Maurus, who was in the ninth century abbot of the monastery of Reichnau on an island in Lake Constance. He wrote a number of works including two saints' lives in verse, the life of Saint Blatmaic and of Saint Mammes; but only one of his

poems has survived, the *Hortulus*, in which, in fact, he describes the garden of his abbey—to which, by the way, I owe a memorable phrase spoken by Philigone Miné when I asked him to explain the virtues of the various plants mentioned by Strabo: that author would have been completely forgotten if he had written only religious poems and liturgical studies, for he owes his fame to his pharmaceutical poem alone."

The *Hortulus* by Strabus—the complete title of which is *Liber de cultura hortorum*, that is to say *Book Concerning the Cultivation of Gardens*—is charming in spite of its edifying intentions. Following the rules of Latin metrics, it begins, after a few Virgilian reflections upon the tranquility of horticultural life—as well as the painstaking work that it implies—with a question that, several centuries later, a Russian revolutionary would answer in a way that would surely have astonished the peaceful monk from Reichnau: *Quid facerem?* he asked himself. *What should I do?* The answer to this breathtaking question comes immediately thereafter: to break the thick tangle of nettle roots with an ax and to do it repeatedly—in other words, to clear and then cultivate the land.

The rest of Strabus's poem is bucolic, naive in its rusticity: "Having cleared the ground," he explains, "we try small vegetables, shoots taken either from seedlings or from older plants whose first youth we try to restore. The first growth is then sprinkled by the rain of spring, then the moon caresses the tender shoots with her gentle warmth." But, adds the holy man, "when excessively dry weather refuses to help with dew, my love of gardening and my fear that the frail fibers will succumb to thirst push me to hard work, and I make sure to provide a flow of pure water, which I bring in large casks and let run from the hollow of my own hands, drop by drop, as I am afraid that if I pour it too rapidly, it will fall in torrents and carry away the seeds I have sown."

One can imagine this touching scene: the monk kneeling on the ground with his tunic spread wide as the water falls through his fingers in drops, like rosary beads, bringing nourishment to the rescue of the precious seedlings. He imagines he has tapped the fountain of youth; it may even be holy water that he sprinkles. The poem's twenty-two stanzas constitute a pharmacopoeia. Few flowers or vegetables, only the iris, rose, and lily on the one hand—the latter two being liturgical symbols[4]—and pumpkin, melon, and horseradish on the other.

It is mainly a collection of medicinal herbs, of which catnip, lovage, betony, mint, agrimony, tansy, poppies, horehound, cerfolium, and wormwood were the most interesting from a pharmacological point of view.

Thus, with the conscientiousness and caring typical of the botanist monks—and supported by the profane desire of the powerful—our garden hero pursued his garden growth.

Meant to be a medicinal as well as a kitchen garden, and almost always enclosed within the cloister, the garden became the *hortus conclusus* irrigated by a central source usually branching out into two channels forming a cross, so as to figure the rivers of Paradise.

For in that era nothing was truly innocent, neither Strabus's naive ardor nor the holy space of a monastery.[5] Every layout had a meaning, and every orientation referred back to a model that—although not the imagined one of the "Ancients" that became the rule during the Renaissance—was even more tightly rigorous: the original Eden and the Temple imposed their canons, ruled by the *logia*, and whoever dared challenge them only revealed his own ignorance or dark impiety.

The image of Paradise also dictated in its own way the disposition of secular gardens, the *vergiers* that were soon flourishing around castles or within their protecting walls. Surely, their style was freer than those of the monasteries. But their enclosure was not only meant as a protection against thieves: isolating Paradise from the fallen world, it referred back to the melodious verse of the Song of Songs: "A garden locked is my sister, my bride, / a garden locked, a fountain sealed."[6] And if their geometry remained repetitive, evoking the image of the checkerboard, it also revealed other influences.[7]

First of all, the reference to the Celtic meadow, carpeted with flowers of the kind the old druids might have used to adorn the forehead of nubile young girls with braids or crowns at the time of the pagan feast of Samhain: a persisting imaginary insists on seeing it enclosed in the air, away from inquiring eyes, for the simple reason that it was to be reserved for love— to be a place apart where Lancelot and Guinevere, Tristan and Iseult, Erec and Enide, the galant *laostic* in the lay by Marie de France, and all true lovers could frolic about without any impediment or Christian restraint, with the total joy of bodies delivered from marriage.

Then, from the *pays d'oc*, came the refined system of the southern "courts of love."

That the initiatory path followed by the ritual of *fin'amor*, with all its expected trials, seems to have drawn its inspiration more from heresy than any Christian tradition—this much, if nothing else, we will grant Denis de Rougemont. The lascivious presence of an Orientalism come by way of Spain is evident,[8] if only in the flavor of the music of Jaufré Rudel and Bernard de Ventadorn, rendered sublime by the vertiginous Manichaeism of Cathar perfection, which was radically opposed to marriage and to the idea of procreation.

So that there is no *topos* more revealing of courtly sensibility than the medieval *vergier* or garden. It combines north and south, the dominating Christianity—which first had the tone of Hellenic culture, then of Asian communities—the old Gnostic background, a barely dominated nature, and a strong desire to break with the ruling coarseness. And if today we no longer have tangible evidence about these gardens—with the exception of a few images and miniatures[9]—we can imagine them without much difficulty, for no spot was more frequently described in the literature of the Middle Ages.

Let us begin with the book that sums up everything—the *Romance of the Rose*—and its description of the garden of the God of Love.

It is in the first part of the *Romance*, written by Guillaume de Lorris in the thirteenth century, that we find, besides the allegory of the Rose that represents the ideal *Amye* or Beloved, the most beautiful and precise descriptions of the medieval *hortus conclusus*.

When the poet, Amant, after having risen in a dream to cross the spring countryside, runs into the Garden of Love, home of the Rose, a decorated wall comes to his attention:

When I'd advanced a space along the bank
I saw a garden, large and fair, enclosed
With battlemented wall, sculptured without
With many a figure and inscription neat.[10]

The wall, described in all its symbolic splendor, asks to be climbed over. The temptation becomes all the more pressing when the hero begins to suspect, because of the sumptuous decoration he has just discovered and the marvelous bird songs he hears from the other side of the enclosure, that destiny, or rather the possibility of love, is calling him. A small and narrow gate is opened on his request by a very attractive maiden by the name of Idleness,[11] whose apparition indicates that entry into the garden, for courtly thought, implies an encounter with the mystery of femininity.

Beauty lies everywhere in this garden of love. The grass is fresh and undulating, the little path that the poet follows abounds with fennel and mint, and in a small corner he finds the rarest spices:[12]

Licorice and gillyflower cloves,
A malagueta pepper tree, whose fruit
Is given the name of Grains of Paradise[13] *. . .*
Zodary,[14] *anise seed, and cinnamon . . .* [p. 27]

As for the trees, which stand five to six fathoms apart—their branches long and high enough "for defense against the heat"—they exude many exotic scents,[15] and Idleness explains that it is Mirth, "a genteel beau,"

Who owns this garden planted full of trees
That he had brought especially for him
From that fair land where live the Saracens.[16] [p. 13]

The home of many animals, such as deer, roebuck, rabbits, and squirrels, the garden presents the astonished hero with a vision of Paradise before he reaches the enchanting rosebush:

When once I was inside, my joyful heart
Was filled with happiness and sweet content.
You may right well believe I thought the place
Was truly a terrestrial paradise . . . [p. 14]

The *Romance*, however, was truly a dream—in spite of the poet's protests—and as such imitated the *Dream of Scipio*.[17] And, as for the *vergier* it describes, it is not a real garden, but the courtly ideal of one. Everything in it is allegory, not only its characters—Mirth, Fair Welcome, Danger, etc.—who are presented as such. The Rose itself, heart of the vegetable system, represents the ideal Beloved, unattainable according to the gallant Guillaume de Lorris, but which the poet-philosopher Jean de Meung, who detested pretense and made no mistakes about the vigorous appeal of the flesh, did not hesitate to reduce to the explicit image of virginity.[18]

Is this to say that it is consequently inappropriate to consider this *vergier* the model of the aristocratic garden of the thirteenth century? Such a conclusion would undoubtedly be premature. Not that the real *vergiers* of that period equaled in splendor the Garden of Love; but what is the art of gardens if not—as Jean de Meung suggested—the reaching for an ideal dependent upon the work of man and the corruptible contingency of Nature?[19] And the product of this reaching, in its material manifestation of garden beds, paths, bushes, meadows, and fountains, is it not allegory from beginning to end, since it is an artifice sustained by a cultural code that makes it a garden and not natural nature? If, throughout the ages, nature has been called the true model, that nature, as we know, has never revealed itself naturally: always, beyond the variations of intellectual circumstance, it has been produced by the mind, attesting that it is a conception of the world. However, the courtly ideal was obviously one of the better realized of these conceptions.

The proof is the permanence of the *vergier* in the medieval imaginary and its insistent presence after the *Romance of the Rose* in the literature of the thirteenth, fourteenth, and fifteenth centuries. If—motivated by our love of storytelling—we have chosen to illustrate it with a narrative that seems to take us away from these allegorical gardens, the reason is that Guillaume de Machaut's adventure seems the appropriate expression of a gap we find amusing: the one separating the convention of the real from the concrete place of gardens in the extravagant amorous intrigue experienced by an older poet who had opened his rhetorical career with a reworking of *The Romance of the Rose* called *Le Dit dou vergier*.

One fine afternoon in the summer of 1360, Guillaume de Machaut was taking a siesta in his country garden near the city of Reims. Lying in the grass in the shade of an apple tree with his amice spread wide over his face so that the "sweet heat of the sun would harm neither body nor eye," the poet dozed, sweetly digesting his noontime meal and dreaming of melodies to ornament his next ballades. All around him summer was making the cypress boughs crack and the crickets sing in the colored wattling of the fence. From the *herbularius* rose a perfume of basil and fennel that blended with the tart odor of the still green grapes on the vine. In the meadow dotted with a thousand wild flowers, in the image of those tapestries that one can now admire in the Cluny Museum or at the Hospices of Beaune, bees hummed with pleasure as they attended to their honey. A spring of clear water sung below, its refreshing babble making music with the amorous trills of the thrushes.

The poet was resting with his neck propped up against a canopy of green and his pearl-gray tunic tucked up above his knees. He rested with his mouth open as though trying to better breathe in the heat. His face bore an expression of such serene abandon that, if not for the wrinkles engraved upon his sleeping face and the white hair sticking out of his priestly cowl, one might have thought him a young knight, tired from wine or an excess of love, who had stretched out here, in a paradise arranged for his pleasure only.

But here comes a visitor to the garden gate. Ignoring daisies, buttercups, cornflowers, poppies, violets, and honeysuckle, he briskly crosses the *préau*, as a flowered meadow was then called, and leans over the sleeper.

"Wake up, master Guillaume. I come from Armentières bearing a letter for you."

"Well, well!" cried the poet, rubbing his eyes. "Is it really you, master Henry! So many years have passed since our last meeting . . . "

"Most certainly, my good friend. Not everyone has the good fortune that you have had, to serve a prince as powerful as Jean de Luxembourg. And even less to obtain an office as noble as yours."

"No bitter words," Guillaume answered. "Did you not know how to manage your career yourself? The canonry of Reims, which I exercise, is a heavy burden. And if it were not for my poems . . ."

"Indeed. And it is the poet I am visiting today. The poet that people are already calling Orpheus, Arethusa, or Alpheus. He who penned the *Dit dou vergier* and not the author of the *Messe Nostre Dame*. Now read what my mistress has written you."

Guillaume de Machaut cannot restrain a disappointed frown. To have his siesta disturbed for this kind of *pensum*! A request for a recommendation, or perhaps a packet of mediocre verse.

"I would read her letter more willingly if not for this devilish gout eating at my knees. But since you are the messenger . . ."

The letter almost falls from his hands. It is a rondel, and well wrought.

She who has never seen you
And who loves you faithfully
Makes you a present of all her heart
And says she does not live as she likes
When she cannot see you often,
She who has never seen you
And who loves you faithfully.
Because for all the good things
Everyone says of you
You have completely won her over.
She who has never seen you
And loves you faithfully
Makes you a present of all her heart.

"And you pretend that a maiden wrote this rondel!" exclaims the poet in astonishment. "Ah, you are part of this farce, Henry! Admit it, so that I may forgive you!"

"I assure you, master Guillaume. On my word . . ."

"Enough of these jokes! Who would believe that a girl of sixteen years could fall in love with my old bones! . . . These things only happen in stories and foolish tales!"

"Well, it has happened now," says the visitor, getting annoyed. "You have written so many absurd stories that they have started to come true . . . And with Guillaume de Machaut here, and your garden romances there . . . You have made my young mistress's head spin . . . To the point that, moved by a year's worth of sighs, I gave in. I explained to her that I have known you for a long time and, so as to stop her tears . . ."

Henry bowed his head and then continued:

"She is so adorable, my lovely mistress! . . . And well read. One cannot refuse her anything."

"And you say she is only seventeen years old? And that she is alone in the world?"

"Not completely alone. But as good as. Her mother, who was Dame d'Unchair, took the sire of Conflans as her second husband. So that she no longer has any time for this first daughter, whom she lets go her own way. But for this the mother is not to be blamed . . . Péronnelle is temperamental, but her conduct is straight as can be."

Guillaume de Machaut sinks back into the grass, and is absorbed by the dance of bees.

"Péronnelle . . ." he muses, eyeing the liveliest dancer, whose mouth and legs are dripping with honey. "Péronnelle . . . Quite a lovely name, if truth be told . . . It sings on the tongue and lends itself to rhyme . . . All the same, I never would have thought . . ." Then, suddenly collecting his thoughts: "Let us be kind to your mistress, my good Henry. I would not give her a pretext to reprimand you for having come for nothing."

He takes up a pen and parchment and writes in one go:

Great-Beauty, nothing pleases me
Nor gives me peace or relief
But you whose servant I am.
When I do not see your beauty
And your lovely body, which beautify all poetry
Great-Beauty, nothing pleases me
Nor gives me peace or relief,

And your sweetness which sweetens
My illness and heals me sweetly
Is truly too far away.
Great-Beauty, nothing pleases me
Nor gives me peace or relief
But you whose servant I am.

This exchange of rondels constitutes the charming beginning of the *Livre* that recounts the love of an aging poet and a maiden who was undoubtedly more taken with poetry than with a person she did not know at all. Although this adventure was in no way unique—a similar passion would unite the aged Goethe with Bettina five centuries later—it possesses the singular feature of having been reported by the poet himself in a kind of novel of letters that mixes poetry and narrative and bears the title *Voir-Dit*. *Voir* . . . At the time the word meant *vrai* or "true," which alone might make one suspect that it is autobiography.

It was only at the end of the nineteenth century, however, that someone gave a complete interpretation of it. In 1875 a scholar with a great love of medieval literature, Paulin Paris, worked through the manuscript, comparing various versions and pursuing his research until he was able to decipher the anagrams woven through the text.

In short, he established that the Great-Beauty of the *Voir-Dit* existed without a doubt, that her name was Péronnelle d'Armentières, and that the amorous intrigue reported by Machaut was most likely not a fiction, but the literary treatment of a real adventure.

The enigma is puzzling indeed, but let us return to our two lovers, who have been using the obliging Henry to send one another passionate epistles in which ballades and virelais alternate with rondels.

They do not see each other and the fact that the pen, for many long months, is their only means of connection causes them to dream of each other all the more ardently.

They do eventually meet, however, and, for the mature canon who is always counting his ailments, the world is turned inside out. Great-Beauty, with her long, slender, and graceful body, leads him to her garden as is expected, while the "noble rhetorician," who has so often meditated upon the subject, feels as though this time his heart were really bursting.

Seeking a shady spot, the two lovers sit under a cherry tree that, he tells us, is "round as an apple." A grassy bench has been made there, supported by wattling from the fence woven around the tree trunk. Thyme, summer savory, and wild mint grow in the fine grass; honeysuckle shoots across it in all directions, turning the canopy into a bed of flowers; and surely there is a nightingale in this scene, casting its amorous trills around the retreat where Guillaume and his friend have sat down to talk.

The heat of an early spring, the perfume of flowers, the singing of birds: Beauty soon lets herself sink onto the lap of her friend and falls asleep. Or pretends to, as is so often the way of young women with timid sweethearts. At this moment Machaut's secretary, more resourceful than his master, has a real inspiration. Picking a leaf from the tree, he places it cautiously over Péronnelle's mouth and says: "Kiss this leaf, master."

The poet blushes, hesitates: "Look at her sleeping. Doesn't she look like an angel?"

"You will not be kissing the lips of a maid, master Guillaume, but a leaf from a cherry tree on the mouth of an angel."

How can he resist such a charming invitation? Great-Beauty seems to be dozing, and Desire knocks at the door so insistently! But a mischievous breeze comes at that very moment to blow it aside, and it is "an amorous touch . . . nonetheless on the sweet mouth" that the poet places, to his own dismay, near his Beloved's proffered lips.

"Oh, Guillaume, how dare you!" she protests slyly, pretending to wake up.

But her reproach ends with such a tender, charming smile that the poet is amazed.

Thus it happens that Péronnelle is the one to take the initiative. Not only during that first week when she whispers in the lovestruck poet's ear the hour of their evening rendezvous in her garden, but even more when, later on, the time comes to go further.

According to a happy coincidence, the young girl had vowed to make a pilgrimage to Saint-Denis. And, in matters of religion, what could be more necessary than the presence of a canon? Machaut will therefore travel with her two chaperones: Péronnelle's younger sister and a neighbor they are calling a cousin in order to better allay suspicion.

The *Lendit* was at the time a well-attended fair. The merchants' stalls sided with religious banners, and the secular festivities were no less splendid than the pious ceremonies. Between one mass and the next people strolled about, haggling with the clothiers and icon vendors, dancing, and feasting in the inns. It was a garland of pleasures unfolding in a sunny countryside full of dust and fragrant grass, for the feast took place in mid-June and fields, meadows, and woods extended over several leagues between Saint-Denis and Paris.

Our four friends, after a day full of laughter and prayer, of romping joyously and exchanging tender looks, decide to go dine

> *In a city that people*
> *In all of Paris call La Chapelle.*

But in that place

> *. . . there was such a number*
> *Of folks, that there was no shade*
> *Where one might well shelter*
> *A shepherd's body and his dog.*

By chance, a sergeant who has imbibed much of the "good wine of Saint-Pourçain" becomes friendly with them and leads them to a friend who, without any fuss, places at their disposal a room with two beds and a floor covered—as was customary—with freshly cut grass.

Péronnelle's younger sister lies down on the first bed, Péronnelle and her false cousin Guillemette take the second: Guillaume, who finds himself without a bed, is told to sleep outside or make himself comfortable on the hay spread over the beaten earth.

Who has not, at some point in his life, suffered from such a disappointment? But who has also been faced with such seductive temptation? It was a more common affair, long ago, as travelers were crowded more tightly in bed than today.

The canon, in spite of his age, is still a vigorous man whose natural desires seek satisfaction. And this fresh body, lying almost naked within his reach, makes his stomach quiver and the blood beat in his veins. Oh! how insipid courtly convention seems now, when it is no longer a matter of arguing with Desire, or with some other rhetorical figure, but of grappling with Ardor that ignites his loins and burns his brain! How devoid of meaning seem all those rules of restraint that claim to make the delights of *fin'amor*! Especially when Péronnelle, who can play the ingenue as well as she fashions verse, innocently proposes:

"Come here, my love. The space is very narrow, but you can lie close by me."

Here is Guillaume now in the arms of his beauty, all his limbs trembling, but bound to chastity. Certainly he has the right to a bit of fondling, to those kinds of embraces that enervate desire, instead of exhausting it. So he spends an agitated night, without sleep or satisfaction.

Morning is cruel. He wakes up, an old man who can barely conceal his headache or the horrible aches and pains knotting his back, to face three young graceful girls having a good time, splashing each other as they wash, chirruping as they dress, and dreaming out loud of the pleasures they expect that morning. By evening, however, his pains have dissipated. A merry group has gathered around Péronnelle, Guillemette, and the younger sister whose name is unknown. And it is amid the exhilaration of joyous games and songs that the little troup unanimously agrees to sit down to supper

> *In a garden, whose sweetness*
> *Well resembles the lovely paradise*
> *That Eve and Adam had long ago.*

The feast, according to the *Voir-Dit*, lasts seven days. Seven days and seven nights by the end of which the poet, having jousted with indefatigable youth and received nothing in return but a migraine and enervated senses, has grown pale. He drags his feet, the poor "rhetorician," becoming more and more "sad, mournful and tearful" as the end of the trip approaches. God, how cruel they are, he thinks, those rules that I made myself and continue to celebrate every day, in lays, ballades, and rondels!

The issue of the matter is at hand, however—the triumph that will make him master of a pleasure that has been escaping him. The morning of their departure, he opens the window to awaken his friend—as she asked him to do at bedtime—and finds that her very bed has become a garden. Fresh grass, leaves, and flowers, in fragrant armfuls plucked during the night, ornament his beloved's bed. Irises here, a cherry branch there, and peonies and daisy chains . . . Above the flowering bed, in a heavenly sky where anemones, violets, and cornflowers have been woven into a background of boughs, an arbor exhaling a thousand perfumes has been built. But the most superb flower of them all, the rose of roses, gracious and trembling in her springtime shrine, is the royal nudity of his mistress, fully exposed to the June light: an offering.

Whatever happened that morning, in an inn of La Chapelle, between the old Guillaume and the very young Péronnelle, exceeds our knowledge.

For his part, the poet lets us understand in rather convoluted verse that all his desires were fulfilled without his Lady's honor having been affected in any way. An enigma that one can interpret either as a virtuous lie meant to protect his beauty, or as a confession that the lovers' joust came to its conclusion prematurely, or finally as the enactment of practices that, although they may have led the two lovers to shared ecstasy—as the poet maintains—cannot be described in a gallant *Dit*, restrained as it is by courtly rhetoric.

At this point in Machaut's narrative we are only half way through the poem. We leave it at this time, however, not out of some timid sense of propriety, but because the *Voir-Dit* begins to falter here. As though the two lovers, having consummated the act—or having merely sketched it—found themselves drained of desire. The intrigue continues, and the letters, and the rondels. But it smacks of convention. Great-Beauty is now sighing for more substantial loves, and pursues her gallant correspondence only in order to collect epistles that flatter her vanity. As for Machaut, whose already failing vigor is ebbing day by day, he is not upset about returning to allegory with his pen rather than his penis. In short, the torrent dies down, and the knot of love is untied, leaving on the one hand an old man who, walking in his garden amid falling leaves, will soon only be thinking about his soul's salvation, and, on the other hand, a woman in search of a husband.

"So it goes for many men and women," as another poet, François Villon, would say a century later.

Allée Two

Know that I am not displeased, but rather pleased
that you will have to plow rosebushes, guard violets,
and make hats.

LE MÉNAGIER DE PARIS

The courtly garden, a symbolic theater where, behind high walls, a learned aristocracy played the ideal comedy of ordering passions, is a far cry from Fiachra's kitchen garden or Walahfrid Strabus's *herbularius*. These closed spaces, thoroughly artificial in their conception, have no apparent utility: in them we do not witness one nature, recomposed in the style of literary and alchemical fiction, battling with another, brute one; nature is the cultivation of deliberate speech, and the blade of grass as well as the fountain are elements of a language as precise as that of a poem or a scholastic treatise. So that one is justified in seeing here the Western matrix of the learned garden, an intellectual and concrete adventure whose path we shall soon follow in Colonna, Mlle. de Scudéry, Milton, Rousseau, Flaubert, Ruskin, and Michel Serres, as well as in Palissy's rock gardens, Boyceau's embroideries, Le Nôtre's perspectives, the "arcadias" of the marquis de Girardin, the attractions of the didactic Promenades, the city gardens of suburbia, all the way up to the cinematic "follies" staged at La Villette by Bernard Tschumi.

But if we measure our hero solely within the context of the learned garden, we will not do justice to his polymorphic genius. His history—modest, but not without attraction or beauty—presents his humble acceptance of the constraints of living and doing, which we can better appreciate by merely considering the title the medieval period gave to botanical treatises: *Libris de simplici medicina* or *Books of simples*, "simples" being medicinal plants found in nature that have undergone no pharmaceutical treatment and may be used to deal with the worst ailments if need be.[1]

After the dreadful epidemics of bubonic plague that ravaged Gaul until the eighth century—the consequence, according to Gregory of Tours, of catastrophic floods[2]—and the terrible famines of the year one thousand, regular economic growth, aided by the rediscovery of Aristotelianism through contact with Islam and Judaism, brought the sweet gifts of mores, emotions, and new "countrysides" (*campagnes*) to the twelfth century. The fact remains, however, that malnutrition and endemic illnesses presented a permanent menace to a prosperity that remained relative.

For most of the population, the nutritional basics remained cereals suitable for bread making, root vegetables, and leguminous plants[3] cultivated in rustic kitchen gardens. Moreover, the fourteenth century saw the explosion of a new epidemic of plague, which provoked in turn a violent resurgence of anti-Semitism[4] leading to a financial crisis in the economic sector. This is to say that the garden, except for the few individuals who took refuge there, as in the *Decameron*, had a utilitarian rather than a recreational function during this period: it was a source of food and medicine. And we should add that it demanded constant attention: endless work was needed to manipulate a nature that was undoubtedly generous, but difficult to tame.

To manipulate, to tame . . . We use these verbs on purpose. For, before the advent of modern science, nothing would have been more foreign to those who worked in gardens than the image of nature as a mechanical system subject to laws, that is to say controllable.

This idea would only come into being later on, with Galileo, Descartes, and Newton. For the men of the Middle Ages, including the most learned and the most skillful, one dealt with divine creation by means of an art related to faith or magic, so that one might sometimes receive its favors and other times its condemnations. And the tools they used,[5] although complex and developed (and those drawn in Villard de Honnecourt's *Notebooks* indicate the style), were conceived as instruments not so much of domination as of "machination," which might trick nature into taking man's side. Machines, consequently—in the first sense of the word *machinate*.

So that, when it came to shaping a real garden, and not to painting an allegory of it, the resulting artifice should be understood as a diversion from what was, and not as the creation of a subject fashioning an object: a grassy space was not a lawn, but the reconstitution of a meadow; a spurt of water was not a fountain, in the sense that Palissy and Boyceau would understand it, but the rerouting of a beneficial stream; and the planted trees, flowers, and vegetables would for a long time be considered carefully acclimated rather than domesticated. This conception did not mean, however, a servile submission to the resources at hand, or an absence of creative daring: in gardening as in architecture, the fervor guiding medieval society was strong enough to convince it that it was capable of miracles.[6] The miracle of the cathedrals, of course, but also the miracle of gardens—the ones that the immense figures of twelfth- and thirteenth-century Christianity, Herrade of Landsberg[7] and Albertus Magnus, did not hesitate to classify as divine works in their descriptions of the botany, methods of development, and rules of correct composition used in these gardens.

"The garden will include first a lawn of fine grass, carefully weeded and trod upon, a true carpet of greenery where nothing will grow up beyond the uniform surface. . . . At one of its extremities, to the south, the trees will stand: pear, apple, and pomegranate trees, laurels, cypresses, and others of this kind, where vines will climb and their foliage will to some degree protect the lawn and provide a pleasant and fresh shade. . . . Behind the lawn will be planted a number of aromatic and medicinal herbs, for example rue, sage, and basil, the perfume of which will delight the sense of smell, then flowers such as violets, columbines, lilies, roses, and other similar ones, which by their diversity charm the eye and excite admiration." So wrote Albertus Magnus. And the famous Dominican, who was Saint Thomas Aquinas's teacher, concluded this passage of his *De naturis rerum* (undertaken, he tells us, "upon the request of his brothers so as to make Aristotle's wisdom more accessible") with this recommendation: "It would be suitable to raise the ground so as to make a verdant and flowering seat where one can sit down and gently rest the spirit."[8]

This description, although edifying and learned, was certainly not written by a practician, but came from a mind curious about everything and desiring to embrace all knowledge in an encyclopedic and Christian perspective. It seems faithful to its model, however, as it has been confirmed by other entirely secular descriptions presented by "bourgeois" chroniclers reporting the delights gardens have brought them.[9] So that a scholar of the late nineteenth century, Charles Joret, to whom we owe a staggering compilation of minutiae, *La Rose dans l'Antiquité et au Moyen Age*, did not hesitate to make the following connection:

If one limits Albertus Magnus' garden to the area planted with aromatic herbs and flowers, adding a few vegetables, onions, leeks, garlic, beets, melons, cucumbers, and others (list drawn from *De naturis rerum*, book II, chap. 166), one will have the garden of a thirteenth-century bourgeois, such as the garden of John of Garland, and, more or less, at the end of the following century, the one of the author of the *Ménagier de Paris*—who, besides the few flowers already mentioned, also cultivated lavender and stocks, plants unknown before him, but that can now be found in all gardens.[10]

Although the garden is one of the most fragile products of human endeavor—and we have already indicated that there remains no evidence of the medieval gardens, besides a few reconstitutions such as the one at Angers—the *hortus conclusus,* as far as we can tell today, had a very real existence alongside its allegorical figure. This doubling should not be surprising, given that it was in its way the translation of that dual culture of the Middle Ages: on the one hand, there was the culture of the clerks taken with scholasticism and/or the courtly ideal; on the other, the culture of a practical world composed of peasants, craftsmen, and merchants, whose effervescence and vigor have been described in the works of Mikhail Bakhtin.[11] But this doubling does not imply separation, as the comparison between the gardens of Albertus Magnus and John of Garland might suggest. On the contrary, everything leads one to see a web of connections, something like the marriage that, with Suger channeling the tremendous energy of the "low" (of bourgeois, stonemasons, and carpenters), gave rise to the fabulous "work in progress" of the Gothic cathedral. A model that was, in fact, learned in its essence, but constantly reshaped by its concrete genius: as though immanence were ceaselessly reworking and remodeling transcendence to the point of vertigo.

To the point of vertigo. That is to say to an impasse, or an exit. The impasse of infinite complication, having no other object besides its own pursuit, or the exit toward something else: a new world.

The adventure of our garden does not escape this dilemma. Everything we know about it during the fifteenth century leads us to think that, at least in its learned version, the Gothic garden reached its limits in undergoing the test of sophistication that afflicted scholasticism and courtly rhetoric.

Take, for example, the story of Alain Chartier, Guillaume de Machaut's successor two centuries later: exiled with the dauphin to the small court of Bourges—a place made all the more contemptible by the fact that its courtiers thought themselves very refined—he attempted to write a great poem that today stands as the last spasm of a dying art. He records, in fact, that one day, after a melancholy ride in the country, he reached, according to the conventions established by the *Romance of the Rose*, a "tranquil and private" garden where a joyous feast was taking place. There, however, in spite of the general jubilation, his heart could not open up to pleasure so that, tired of war, he withdrew

. . . behind an arbor
Wonderfully overgrown with leaves,
Intertwined with green willows,
So that no one, because of the thick leaves
Could see me through them.

Hidden in his shelter, he witnessed a lady and her sweetheart having a lover's quarrel. The tale so far is banal, except for the poet's retreat, which announces his departure from convention. But the quarrel, which began in accordance with courtly ritual, soon took a different turn: while the suitor did nothing but awkwardly sigh about his love, his beauty adroitly manipulated rhetoric in order to preserve her freedom. So that at the end the theater became real, the simulacrum of coded emotions was broken, and while the Belle Dame sans Mercy went back to dance in the garden, her suitor really died of love.

The fable is brilliant. Grouped in a *Cour amoureuse*, the upholders of tradition went so far as to organize "countertrials" in order to invalidate a verdict they considered against the rules. But the poet's vision was correct. The courtly masks had lost their magic, and the era had had enough of wearing them.

Bawdier games, moreover, were becoming more and more popular; they added to the old "gardens of love"[12] some of the ribald *joyeusetés* (merriments) that the court of Burgundy had introduced into France—a vogue that would continue, in a more or less risqué form, into the baroque period. What were these games like? The order that Philip the Good addressed in 1432 to Collard the Thief, his "valet and painter," provides us with such a detailed description that it makes us regret we do not have an equivalent document concerning the surrounding park and garden, which covered ten hectares overlooking the valley of the Cauche, the summer residence of the dukes of Burgundy in Hesdin-le-Vieux.[13] Involved was a "device to wet ladies from underneath"—which, a priori, does not seem at all courtly. Another device "should come hit in the face those who are underneath and dirty them"; and yet another was such that "all those who pass through will be struck and beaten with big balls on their heads and shoulders."

And so on and so forth. The description of these "childish mystifications"[14] takes up several pages.[15] The bourgeois minds of the nineteenth century were so shocked by the list that men like Alphand and Édouard André considered them "proof" that the gardens of the Middle Ages were only a jumble of vulgarities. The list is however all the more significant in that it had been drawn up upon the express request of the sovereign of the "luxurious" court of Burgundy, the splendor and wealth of which had been as yet unequaled in the West and were a kind of prefiguration of the Versailles of Louis XIV.[16] This new luxury was a sign that the simplicity of the *vergiers* of yesteryear was no longer capable of satisfying the appetites of an era that would from then on aspire to divert itself with surprising inventions in new gardens subject to artifice.

This change, it goes without saying, did not come from nowhere. It had deep roots in Spain, Italy, and the Orient.

Thus the creation of the domain of Hesdin, between 1295 and 1302, had been commanded by Robert d'Artois (1250–1302), who had accompanied his uncle Saint Louis on the Crusade of 1270 and was named regent in 1285 of the Kingdom of Naples: there he was able to admire the Sicilian gardens established by Frederick of Hohenstaufen with the help of Moslem mechanics. Did he bring back from that distant place a few Oriental technicians capable of creating automatons for him? The fact is that the account books published by Monsignor Dehaisnes mention various pavilions and devices that Robert d'Artois ordered for Hesdin, including a *gloriette* and a *gayole*, which were two kinds of aviaries, the first of which contained a tree and artificial birds spouting water—an apparently sophisticated automaton, since the display included, among other things, a king sitting among a group of singing birds.

Moreover, while we should remember that the *Romance of the Rose* mentions certain trees that came from Saracen lands, it is appropriate to note, as does Charles Joret, that "horticulture had made important progress since the first centuries of the Middle Ages; the expeditions to the Orient had revealed the existence of plant species unknown in the West before then, a few of which were imported. It is said, in particular, that Thibault IV, count of Champagne, brought back from Syria the rose of Provins cultivated until recently in the city and the vicinity."[17]

Finally, not only had the primitive geometry of the garden—that of the checkerboard—become more flexible and complex, but its very syntax had solidified, by means of the diversification of gardening tasks as well as the circulation of an important treatise from Italy. This was the *Opus ruralium commodorum* by Pietro de' Crescenzi, a theological work written at the beginning of the fourteenth century upon the request of Charles II of Anjou, king of Sicily, and translated into French upon the order of Charles V.

It is in no way astonishing that it was under the reign of this very wise and learned king, who knew how to use Du Guesclin and how to attract the greatest minds of his age—beginning with Nicole Oresme, his private tutor—that one can situate the peak of the Gothic garden, which Sauval has painted for us in this precious description:

In his [Charles V's] time all the royal gardens ordinarily consisted of meadows called *préaux*, or vines, and of *tonnelles*. The meadows and each garden were surrounded by hedges covered with trellises, intertwined, and laid out in lozenges, which are the *tonnelles*; and these *tonnelles* connected at the two ends with pavilions constructed as they were, and not only were there pavilions in every corner of the gardens and *préaux*, but also in the middle, and even other *tonnelles* that traversed them, and divided them into compartments; in the meadows there was hay, which was reaped at times. The vines were planted at the end of the big garden, often in the park, and cultivated so well that good wine was gathered from it every year. The pavilions were round or square, or one and the other alternately; inside all around were seats made of turf, raised up on steps of the same; the trellises that surrounded them finished in crenels, or in fleurs-de-lis; the crenels ended in tabernacles, a little like a bell tower crowned with a large apple, out of which stuck a weather vane with France's coat of arms painted upon it. As for the lozenges of the trellises, they were ordinarily filled with fleurs-de-lis and sometimes folded so that they represented the coats of arms of France and of the princes of royal blood. In the middle of the garden one could often see, instead of the *préau*, a fountain in a basin of stone or marble, which spouted water through the mouth of a lion, or some other wild beast.[18]

Pavilions that turn into grass-covered seats; seats surrounded by trellises ending in crenels, which in turn are transformed into tabernacles: the Gothic spirit is fully present in these extraverted devices, nested one in the other, each exhausting itself in the next up to the sky. . . . But our description so far has been too general, and deserves to be detailed.

At the heart of the little hotels forming the Hostel Saint-Pol, in fact—the "solemn site of the great games," whose layout, less severe than that of the Louvre, seems to have been appreciated by the monarch—eight gardens had been organized upon the request of Charles V. They were not, Saint-Foix tells us, "planted with yews and linden trees, but with apple and pear trees, vines, and cherry trees. One saw lavender there, and rosemary, peas, broad beans, long trellises, and beautiful bowers. The farmyards were flanked by dovecotes and the king's domains were filled with fowl that the farmers of the king's lands and domains were supposed to send him, and that were fattened for his table and his dining companions."[19]

Other authors, especially Sauval, mention that strawberries were also cultivated there in abundance; and there was also a menagerie containing boars, parrots, and several lions, large and small, whose roars terrified the gardeners working nearby.

The fact remains that this marvel, like the sumptuous creations of "King René" in Angers or in Aix-en-Provence,[20] announced a decline. Barely a century later, the Hostel Saint-Pol was falling in ruins and Francis I sold it piece by piece to Jacques de Genouillac, grand master of the artillery who would establish there the beginnings of the Arsenal. Of the gardens that had filled the Gothic world with ecstasy nothing was left except a memory that subsisted in a few street names: the rue aux Lions for the menagerie, the rue de la Cerisaie (Street of the Cherry Orchard), which Charles VI had enlarged by over a thousand plants, it has been suggested),[21] rue de Beautreillis. Suffice it to say that by the fifteenth century the Gothic garden was throwing its dying sparks, surviving against the background of its own exhaustion.[22] An exhaustion that merely reflected the state of a society weakened by a hundred years of sporadic wars; with its points of reference and convictions lost, it became "feminine"—the word Osip Mandelstam used in his lovely essay on François Villon[23]—that is to say seductive, desirable like a languid beauty accepting her conqueror, but unable to give a start and even more incapable of revolt, for lack of vigor.

The factors of renewal thus came from elsewhere. From an elsewhere charged with an energy stemming from the rediscovery of ancient beauty and virtue: the *Hypnerotomachia*, or *Dream of Poliphilo*, was the key book of this new esthetic, which would reorient the history of the learned garden.

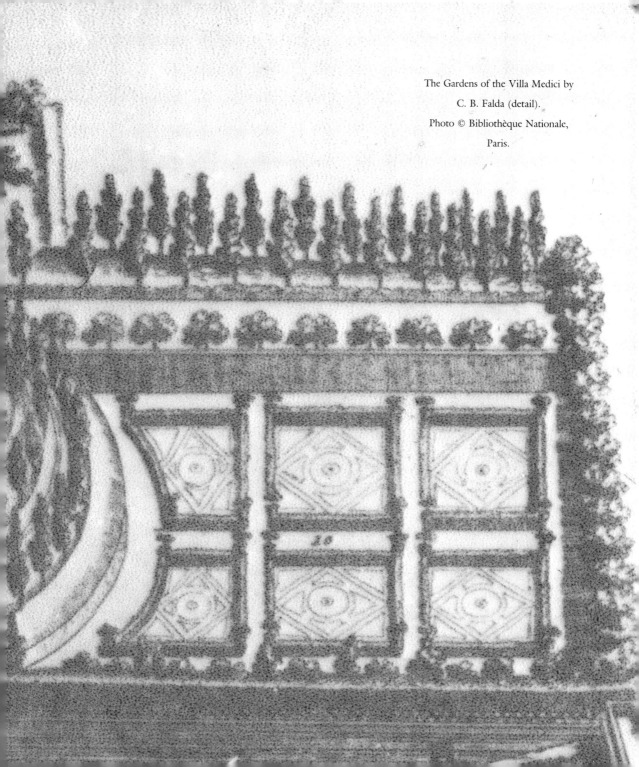

The Gardens of the Villa Medici by
C. B. Falda (detail).
Photo © Bibliothèque Nationale,
Paris.

"And why should I receive this monk, Basileo? You know very well that Aldus Manutius's presses will not debase themselves by printing ordinary writings. The only ones we consider are of the highest order, and those are brought to me by scholars I know."

"But master Manutius, he insists upon seeing you! He says he is a Dominican from San Nicolo of Treviso and that he was master of arts in the very learned and powerful city of Padua."

"A lot of good may it do him. What did you say his name was? Francesco Colonna? No, I have never heard of him."

In Venice, on this autumn morning of 1495, the sun, still brilliant, gilds the sparkling domes. The large jade shadows floating on the canals are agitated only by the wakes of the small boats speeding toward the noisy markets of San Gerolamo and Santa Maria Formosa. Sometimes, coming from Torcello or some other island in the lagoon, a gust of moist heat slides into the courtyards, bringing in putrid fumes from the swamps. Rain would help. It would also help if summer came to an end, and the clouds of mosquitoes accompanying it.

In Aldus Manutius's workshop, where about thirty craftsmen are working, the air is heavy, almost suffocating. The casters have started up the oven again. They mix lead, antimony, and tin together in correct proportion. This mixture, placed in an ovenproof urn in the middle of the furnace, will provide them with the alloy they need to cast those roman and italic characters that have made their master famous. There is not a single Gothic letter in their press, they explain proudly, for they have always rejected the barbaric practices and odious tastes of the North. Here they assemble in tight lines, along the composing sticks and chases, only characters worthy of the texts, most of them ancient, that are being printed in translations chiseled by the best humanists of the Renaissance.

Basileo, however, returns with the visitor's request.

"Nothing doing. This Trevisan is stubborn as a mule. He pretends he can give Leonardo Grasso as a reference and several other people whose names he won't mention. The greatest minds of Italy, or so he says."

Aldus's curiosity is piqued. After all, this monk may have his reasons. Even if Venice remains independent, free of the climate of inquisition that has fallen over most Italian cities, the era dictates caution. Long gone, by now, are the times of the enlightened popes, when Nicholas V, then Pius II brought to the Roman Curia the freest thinkers of the Quattrocento: Poggio, Valla, Manetti, Alberti, Aurispa, Tortello, and Decumbrio—not to mention titular cardinals such as Bessarione and Nicholas of Cusa. The times have taken a turn for the worse for free thought. Rodrigo Lenzol Borgia has seized Saint Peter's throne by means of bloody crimes and simony, and is chasing the humanists down.

But the name of Colonna is sweet to the printer's ears. Could this Fra Francesco Colonna of Treviso be related to the great Prospero Colonna, the powerful cardinal who—until his death, which occurred in conditions as suspicious as those that surrounded the deaths of Lorenzo the Magnificent, Politian, and Pico della Mirandola—opposed the fiendish intrigues of the sinister Borgia with all his might?

Seized by curiosity, Aldus asks not to be disturbed under any circumstance, and opens his door to the visitor.

The monk sits down with an air of contentment. Through the half-open window looking over the lagoon, sounds of cheerful activity come into the room. Gondolas loaded with fruit, spices, and fabrics are moving up and down the Grand Canal ceaselessly. People are hailing, shouting, and insulting each other from one boat to another. Venice will continue her long-standing expansion as long as knowledge is not brutally asphyxiated.

Aldus, who takes joy in the view from his window, contemplates his visitor with interest. He is a tall, somewhat portly man. Above a rather pronounced, but well-drawn mouth, his lively eyes shine with intelligence.

"Forgive the secretiveness and fuss," the monk begins. "But in these times . . ."

He draws out of his pouch a thick manuscript out of which fall a number of drawings.

"I have rewritten the text according to the instructions of its first author who finished it in 1467, and I have rectified the plates with my own hand. In spite of the macaronic language with which I have surrounded the argument, and the overdone rigidity I thought wise to give the illustrations, I am sure you will recognize it as a fundamental work, the testament of a school condemned today, although it remains the pride of the century and of our Italy. I will say no more. You will understand yourself what *tall column* supports the entire book, and why Poliphilo must watch over Polia, the lovely and most wise who is menaced by the *fierce jealousy* of you know who."

Aldus restrains himself from consulting the manuscript immediately. He already knows, from a certain discussion he had with Pico and Politian during their last stay in Venice in the winter of 1491, that an important heritage must be saved. A great effort must be made to return to sources in order for the future to be imaginable—an enterprise led by the initiated, who had decided to realize the program defined around the year one thousand by Gerbert d'Aurillac, the pope whose formation took place in Spain, through contacts with Jewish and Arab scholars: "To fuse in a single and coherent doctrine all that can be learned from pagans and Christians." But, if this Dominican is not lying, if what he has taken out of his pouch is really the hermetic manual that Pico and Politian told him about, he will have the chance to print the actual state of this research, today proscribed.

The prospect does not prevent him from feigning ignorance:

"You can imagine, Francesco, that I cannot take you on your word. There are so many impostors these days . . . Besides, my schedule is already full, and I am under very tight financial constraints. I am in need of success, like all my competitors. And if the writing of your book is as obscure as you say, I am afraid that . . ."

"I will pay, or rather we will pay whatever is necessary," answers the monk, without getting flustered. "The publishing of such a work has no price, and only you can give it the shape that it requires."

At this rate the matter was soon settled, and four years later, that is to say a week before the new century began, the *Hypnerotomachia Poliphili* came off the Aldine press. *Hypnerotomachia Poliphili*: the title itself is enigmatic, to the point that it had to be expanded, in the edition of 1546, to *Hypnerotomachia di Poliphilo, cioè pugna d'amore in sogno*, which may be roughly translated as: "The battle of love fought by Poliphilo in a dream." With this important comment: the hero's name must not be written *Polyphilo*, with a *y*, which would mean "he who has many loves," but *Poliphilo*, with an *i*, which means "the lover of Polia."

This fascinating book, which in France has been called *Songe de Poliphile* since Kerver published Jean Martin's translation of it in 1545, thus saw the light in Venice in December 1499, when a little snow was covering the Piazza San Marco and laughing children were getting ready for Christmas. It was such a commercial failure that one of Aldus's collaborators remarked humorously: *Non habi potuto quelli mandar fuori per altre urgente cause essi non si a reussito.*[1]

Moreover, the printer's attitude was strange. For almost four years he had applied himself to making the *Dream of Poliphilo* his masterpiece, overseeing the choice of each character and multiplying the proofs for the plates. And now that the book was completed, as sublime in the beauty of its composition as in the perfection of its engraving, he was losing interest in it. Ostensibly. As though, once this work for which he had been generously paid had been completed, he gave in without resistance to the opinion of his employees who, during the book's fabrication, had continually made fun of the Trevisan monk's amphigoric language, which smattered here of Venetian dialect, there of faulty Latin, and also bore traces of Greek and Hebrew.

In fact, Aldus was trying to allay suspicions, for he did not want anyone to guess the secret content of his book. He was especially concerned about his glaring failure as he was convinced that he had staked all his talent on an initiated future audience rather than his blind contemporaries.

He was not mistaken. The *Dream* would soon become a book of capital importance, one of those works that, ignored by the majority before being recognized by scholars, are nonetheless meditated upon obsessively by those who consider themselves its depositaries. It was a posthumous triumph that demands a look back to the era of its first composition.

One spring afternoon in 1463, the famous Leon Battista Alberti, who was at the time abbreviator of the Vatican chancellery and member of the Vitruvian Academy founded by his old protector and friend, the powerful cardinal Prospero Colonna, was meditating in the gardens of a Roman villa.

The gardens had not yet been finished, nor had the villa, which was being built at the same time. However, everything there already spoke a language of a strange and new beauty. And Alberti, the glorious *uomo universale* of the Italian Renaissance, was filled with wonder as he walked around this domain conceived according to plans that he himself had been employed to theorize. In accordance with his recommendations, the villa had been planted upon a hill so as to provide the pleasure of a double perspective: the windows, which opened at regular intervals in well-proportioned walls, looked out upon "a large city, other cities, the sea, a large plain, and the tops of a few known hills and mountains." But when, reciprocally, one climbed the paths leading to this dwelling in an "imperceptible ascension," it first seemed hidden, then all of a sudden revealed its splendor and the "vast perspectives" surrounding it.

Alberti found the terrace particularly ravishing; it was built lengthwise as an extension of the façade and bordered by a row of green pines. Also lovely was the small mountain built in the middle of the checkerboard flower beds. He often lingered on this belvedere, placing his elbows on the stone copings, his mind far from the many quarrels of his century; his gaze would drift down the steps and wander along the paths bordered by regular rows of cypresses, or it might settle on a mossy cave, an Egyptian obelisk, a fountain where Neptune was surrounded by gracious naiads, dolphins, and tritons, or perhaps on the marble statue of some ancient god, such as the twin figures of the old Terminus that guarded the staircase at the foot of the artificial mountain.

"To think that all this beauty could disappear," mused the pontifical abbreviator.

Several years earlier, he had been powerfully impressed by the discovery of the ruins at Palestrina during the restoration works on the temple of Fortune he had undertaken upon the request of Prince Stefano Colonna, cousin of Prospero and father of a young boy bearing the same name as our Trevisan monk: Francesco Colonna. In a short time, after barely eleven years of neglect following the ravages of Eugenius IV's militia, the site had suffered irreparable damage. Although brambles had grown between the stones, ruining forever the fabulous building, the site was still magnificent. As superb as this description in the *Dream* suggests:

There I found a colonnade so noble in form, design, and matter that it is impossible to represent it. One part of it was broken, one ruined part remained in place, another was intact with architraves and capitals of superior invention and superb sculpture. Cornices, friezes, arched bays, enormous basins, conches and vases of Numidian marble, of porphyry, or of different ornamented marbles, large bowls, aqueducts, and other immense fragments, of a lovely sculptural appearance although hardly recognizable and almost reduced to their rudimentary state—all this lay here and there scattered on the ground. Wild plants were putting forth shoots and creeping among these ruins, mainly bean clover, difficult to break with its faceted pods, and also lentisk, oursine, couch grass, asafetida, common morning glories, centaury, and many other plants that grow among ruins. The steep walls were covered with pellitory, hanging cymbalaria, and thorny wild damsons. Among these plants, on these walls covered with vegetation, crept certain lizards, which often, in these deserted and silent places, came in a first movement right up to me, leaving me completely startled and afraid.

Yes, the spectacle was still sumptuous, although distressing. Here, in a work meant to defy the passage of time, one could see the ruins produced by the hatred of knowledge and ambition.

Alberti's bitter reflections were disturbed by the joyous cries of a group of gardeners. A few steps below him, taking care not to fall down the steep slope, around ten young people were bustling about under a foreman's direction, their pants rolled up above their knees and kerchiefs on their heads. Their energy was pleasant to witness, especially since their task turned out to be difficult. They had to plant, on the slopes of the artificial mountain, a regular sequence of cypresses so as to form around the mount a geometric spiral following the path's precise course. Besides the fact that this exercise required a laborious survey, the still loose earth often slipped out from under the feet of one or the other who, losing his balance all of a sudden, found himself tumbling down the hill with cries of joy or terror, and was then forced to climb up once again in order to continue with his work, like an industrious ant that no disaster can stop.

"I certainly must speak to Giovanni Bessarione," Alberti murmured, witnessing this display of determination. "Our cause has not yet been defeated! We too can climb up the slope! . . . If I can manage to convince the old cardinal to return to the Curia, nothing proves that that Spanish devil will get his creature, that miserable Pietro Barbo, elected. If only Prospero and Cusanus were still alive!"

But this renewal of hope, taking place in an already aged scholar in an unfinished garden warmed by a spring sun, remained vain. Cardinal Bessarione, undoubtedly worried that he too might contract the "gout," as Prospero Colonna and Nicholas of Cusa had, kept his distance from the Roman Curia, and Pietro Barbo was elected under the name of Paul II. This was the same Paul who hastened to dissolve the college of abbreviators of which Alberti was a member, and to replace it, under the pretext that it was more economical, with the single position of *Prefetto dei Brevi*—a task he confided to his friend Lenzol Borgia—before launching against the humanists a frontal attack that would culminate, in 1468, in the trial of the Castel San Angelo.

But, in the meantime, Leon Battista Alberti took refuge in Florence at Lorenzo de Medici's. By his side he undertook, under the discreet guise of a symbolic tale, the task of shaping that essential vision that, beyond his theoretical work on architecture, painting, and domestic economy,[2] and beyond his practical work in the area of geometry, cartography, and architecture, had oriented both his efforts and those of his friends of the former Roman Academy: his aim was to discover, or rather to find again, the thread of a *prisca enarratio theologica*, that primordial wisdom common to all ancient religions, those founded explicitly on the Book as well as those, either earlier or parallel, of Pharaonic Egypt and of the Greece of the Eleusinian mysteries. In other words: *Polia*. Alberti, in his new Tuscan home, found assistance and friendship for this task in the Neoplatonic Academy supported by Lorenzo, with whom he sealed his alliance in 1468 at the "discussions" of Camaldoli: after that he was frequently seen attending the lectures of Marsilio Ficino until his death in Rome in 1472.

Our novel thus joins the ranks of those works that for decades have been attempting to unravel the mysteries of the *Hypnerotomachia*. We are suggesting that Leon Battista Alberti was its principal writer—a thesis that has been defended somewhat confusedly, albeit with enthusiasm, by Emanuela Kretzulesco-Quaranta,[3] and that has been opposed, with the weight of university authority, by less imaginative scholars who attribute to the Trevisan monk alone— reveler, womanizer, and spendthrift that he was—the authorship of a book that he may simply have backdated to increase its effect.[4] But our thesis, besides being seductively romanesque, is intellectually solid in that it takes the *text* of the *Poliphilo* seriously, while the two Swiss scholars demonstrate obvious contempt for it and attribute importance to the engravings only. Although we admit that, when it comes to hermetic writings and the occult sciences, wild interpretations are legion, it is worth noting that the *Poliphilo's* growing audience was not composed of ignoramuses. And that, even if it has not been demonstrated that Alberti was the writer of the first version of the *Dream*, or that Mantegna, Botticelli, Raphael, or Bellini drew its sketches (as some researchers once held), it is clear that only a humanist of broad learning could have played so expertly with linguistics, precise architectural knowledge, hermetic symbolism, and the Neoplatonic themes of Cusanus's *On Learned Ignorance*. An exceptional humanist for whom the repression of the learned circles he moved in was such a tragedy that he placed it in danger:

> *Muse, who is the author of this work?*
> *I myself, with my eight sisters.*
> *You? Why does the title attribute it to Poliphilo?*
> *Because he deserves well of us, the student of us all.*
> *But I beg of you, who is Poliphilo, what is his real name?*
> *We do not want you to know.*
> *Why?*
> *It is better to be foresighted, in order to prevent divine things*
> *From being devoured by fierce jealousy.*
> *Excuse me, but who is he?*
> *It must not be known.*
> *But all the same?*
> *We prefer not to call Poliphilo by his real name.*
>
> *Oh Polia, happier than all mortals,*
> *Though you are dead, you live, more living than ever.*
> *Poliphilo, plunged in his vision, watches over you*
> *Through the learned men who celebrate you.*[5]

Having given this warning to the impatient reader who follows us into terrain he believes well established, let us return to our narrative. We have left the *Hypnerotomachia* in its first, apparently Latin, version in the hands of Alberti, whose death was drawing near. But the author of the *De re aedificatoria* remains anxious. He knows that his argument, although cloaked in the dream of a hero running through gardens in search of his Beauty, runs the risk of being found out, which would prevent him from receiving the imprimatur. So he imagines a subterfuge. He will disguise his work using the kind of literary joke he had practiced in his youth. Did he not once write a *Philodoxeus* that, for fun, he presented as an unpublished manuscript of Lepidus? And wasn't the farce so successful that he subsequently found it difficult to convince his readers of their mistake? I only have to proceed in an analogous fashion, the old Alberti says to himself. To make the reading of the *Dream* difficult and to scramble the paths leading to its author.

But he feels too old to undertake this revision of an already written work. Too old, and especially too busy to devote his last days to such a tedious work. He has so much to learn in Florence, so many new ideas to learn from Marsilio Ficino, and so little time left to live.

It is decided. He will entrust his unknown masterpiece to a man in whom he has complete confidence, a man learned enough to transcribe it into a hermetic language, and powerful enough to impose it when the time comes: Francesco Colonna. Not the obscure Dominican from Treviso whom, in fact, he does not even know, but Prospero's grandnephew, the young man whom he used to bounce on his knees ten years ago when he was directing the restoration of the Palestrina domain. Studious since childhood, this fortunate adolescent has already been introduced to the big questions.

Francesco is not easily convinced.

"How," he exclaims, showing his old teacher the domain he will inherit, "how can I see two such difficult tasks through to a successful conclusion? Look at this garden. Bramble and bindweed, wasps and snakes, ruins and lentisks . . . And you would have me rebuild it and reformulate your work at the same time? It is impossible. I would fail at one task, and then the other."

Alberti sees the situation differently. He is attached to his project, the fruit of long meditation.

"If I ask this of you, Francesco, it is because I know you are capable of it. A garden does not take shape in one day, no more than a literary work does. There is an outline, an initial conception. But unlike Ficino, I do not think that the work of creation can be stopped . . . It enters into a new phase in order to confront form, held by matter. Words, stones, plants—what difference does it make! Nothing is coarse in them, only our inability to adjust them well. And, as for the message that we wish to transmit, what will remain of it without an appropriate form? The *skéma* without *morphé* remains empty."

"That is to say?"

"You understand what I am saying. Gardens, even if drawn according to Vitruvius's plans, cannot survive unless they are inhabited. Unless the soul that wanders through them is one always in quest. In search of the Wisdom I have called Polia."

Alberti looks at Francesco tenderly, then, sliding his arm under his, continues: "It is thus a *single* project I am giving to your life. To rebuild the temple of the Fortuna Primigenia, to return the Aedes Fortunae to its primitive form, to re-establish the approach ramps, the *nicchioni sovraposti,* and the roaring Medusas that ought to decorate it. But also, with equal determination, to become Poliphilo and watch over Polia. In other words, to learn; not to relinquish knowledge, and thus to guarantee your freedom as a man. And to accomplish this there is no better way than to apply yourself to reforming my book."

Francesco Colonna was faithful to the mission Alberti had entrusted him. He completed the restoration of the Palestrina ruins, put the *Hypnerotomachia* in hermetic form, and resisted the tortures of the Inquisition.

But who then was the Trevisan monk? The man who brought Aldus Manutius the definitive manuscript? One last wrong track, and a signature.

A supporter of Sixtus IV against the Aragons in the war of 1483, Francesco Colonna, who had become prince of Palestrina, had been the target of the excommunication that Alexander Borgia pronounced against his family in the bull of September 17, 1501. To have appeared publicly as the second father of the *Dream* would thus have been a provocation. A gesture of vanity that would have entailed the condemnation of a book that was the repository of the hermetic message of humanism. Francesco Colonna thus had the idea, which both protected and signed the *Hypnerotomachia*, to find among his last allies, the Dominicans of Venery, someone bearing his name,[6] and then to disappear.

Thus it was that Fra Francesco Colonna of Treviso, one morning in the fall of 1495 . . .

Allée Three

Oh sweet glances, oh eyes full of beauty
Small gardens, full of amorous flowers
Where the arrows of love are dangerous. . . .
LOUISE LABÉ, Sonnets

The gardens of the *Dream of Poliphilo* have kept some of the features of the medieval *ver-giers*. Thus, they are always enclosed, protected by walls or tall hedges of tangled trees whose growth has been forced in such a way as to produce artificial twists in the trunks and branches: a development against nature making the screen of greenery more opaque, while offering the visitor the means to scale it. Likewise, they contain a "flowered meadow" similar to the ones described by Albertus Magnus and the courtly poets.

"A field sprinkled with sparse greenery, mixed with all medicinal herbs such as celery of all species, absinthe, rosemary, birthwort and apple of earth, common mandrake, woodbine or bindweed, melilot, fumitary, celandine, sumac, betony, hypericum or perfoliate Saint-John's-wort, nightshade, peony, and other simples. The same goes for all those used for eating, such as cabbages, lettuces, spinach, sorrel, roquette, chervil, parsnip, asparagus, artichokes, rampion, peas, beans, purslane, salad burnet, anise, melons, winter squash, cucumbers, licorice, cress, and similar."

This kinship demonstrates that while the humanism of the Quattrocento—far from having been a cultural meteorite, as it used to be described—had deep roots in the Gothic period, it was nonetheless accompanied by evident ruptures signaling, in their own way, the epistemological break inscribed in Western history that Foucault has taught us to see.

The first break, which imposes itself upon a reading of both the text and the engravings, is the insistent presence of ruins—ancient ruins, of course. Since Italy in that period was covered with the evidence of ancient Roman power, this presence might seem banal; it is, however, quite the contrary. For ruins had previously been part of the countryside: they were a source of stones not unlike the openly available quarries, and in them stonemasons took lessons in line and equipment—but people did not look at the ruins themselves. Or if they did, it was with horror. In them, in the decay of their broken splendor, the hand of God was only present in destruction, the razing of an impious world the vestiges of which subsisted only to teach Christian souls to fear punishment. But, by reintegrating these ruins into the space of the garden of love and wisdom, by turning them into objects of plastic admiration and essential places for initiatory meditation, the *Dream of Poliphilo* effected a complete shift in vision. The ancient world rediscovered its place in the history of men. Better yet, it became the guiding reference and principal object of reflection. And not this time in the exclusive field of the rediscovery of texts, but in the field of the visible, with the rereading of Vitruvius making the junction. True, the Roman architect's famous *Treatise* in ten books had been known for a long time—Jean Gimpel, an analyst of medieval technique, has remarked that, contrary to the once accepted thesis of a complete rediscovery of the manuscript of Vitruvius by Poggio in 1414, this text had been recopied many times in the medieval scriptoria, and that Charlemagne's "architect," Einhard, already owned a copy. Nevertheless, the fact remained that its importance, over time, had been neglected[1] and that the plates supposed to have accompanied it had disappeared. But those of the *Hypnerotomachia Poliphilo* hoped to do nothing less than to fill this lacuna by offering a reconstitution that would be completely legible, in spite of the ruins, for a man in the profession.

The second clear rupture in the *Dream* has to do with the deliberate appeal to "antinatural" artifice. We have mentioned that the trees in it are twisted according to the will of man when they are destined to form hedges. But they are also sculpted at will. Thus the text of the *Hypnerotomachia*, as well as one of its engravings, presents a giant carved in greenery; not a vague silhouette, but a precise image elaborated with a stunning precision and complexity of form. Indeed, the giant, solidly planted on the scissors of his legs above an ornate cornice, holds a castle in each hand, but these, in turn, join above his head in a new motif with an openwork design that forms a second cornice. Some of the flower beds, on the other hand, break with the tradition of the "flowered meadow" in order to imitate embroideries representing, for example, an emblazoned eagle. Moreover, a number of trompe-l'oeils are present, not through tricks of perspective or anamorphosis, but by means of painted galleries forming a transition with the mineral architecture and including colored birds fluttering around in the boughs. Finally, the supreme artifacts, which surely continue the magical landscapes of the medieval tales like the amusing machines of the Oriental, Sicilian, and Hesdin gardens,[2] are a large number of elements composing the gardens subsequently discovered by Poliphilo, fantastic forgeries of "nature" elaborated in precious materials: fake plants made of silver, silk bushes, trees of spun glass, roses woven from golden thread.

As for the third break, undoubtedly less evident but perhaps the most significant of all, it consists in the insertion of sculpture into gardens. Until then, in fact, at least in the Christian West, this art had been consubstantially linked to religious architecture. Medieval statuary had no decorative intention, at least in the sense that it is understood today, but a function that was primarily theophanic. It was not only a celebration of the divine presence in the shape of sumptuous offerings (this was Suger's explicit aim, for example), but also, and especially, the sculpted form of the emanations of the Most-High: a thoroughly edifying preoccupation consequently, doubled by the representation of the hideousness attached to His negation. Statuary, which was thus completely commanded by God, was attached to His consecrated spaces, included in their capitals, walls, porches, rood lofts, or riveted to their niches. It was absolutely unmovable[3] and sometimes even invisible, though not by Him. For if the craftsman's hand had sculpted it "from the outside" by releasing its shape from wood or chalk, it was another hand in truth that had accomplished this miracle, modeling the faces "from the inside" or placing the draperies around the bodies of stone, because only the light from heaven could animate the soul whose visible exterior, as beautiful as it might be (and it had to be beautiful) was appearance. Certainly, a less "pure" movement had gradually pervaded the great art of the Middle Ages, attuned to the competition between cities and to the priests' temporal desire for power. But the basic principle had never been placed in question. The *Dream*, however, proposed a usage of statuary in which the sculpted visible detached itself from its religious space and multiplied itself, once again tying into the ancient tradition.

Not that it was already the *object* it has become today, that is to say a plastic creation that can be moved around at will, its position determined only by the need for adequate lighting in an exhibit hall or the practical marking-out of a "public space": on the contrary, each statue was part of a spatial and symbolic code that inscribed it into a constraining web aimed at releasing a meaning. But once it was no longer theophanic, statuary was freed from its support; it entered into the garden to which it gave rhythm and significance; it became part of an initiatory discourse designating a new path to perfection, which tapped the polytheist language of a hermetic antiquity even more freely when the medieval cosmological points of reference entered a state of crisis.

For—and here is the major break, the one commanding all preceding ones—the ideal path indicated by the complex organization of the gardens of the *Dream of Poliphilo* was no longer that of the servant of God as understood by Fiachra, nor even the one, magnetized by a gnostic vision, of the courtly lover. The chosen one of the *Hypnerotomachia*, although still having a foot in the medieval space, is already firmly engaged in a "modern" course in which the enchantment of the world tends not to depend any longer on Creation, but on the possible mastery one may acquire over it. "Acting" no longer follows from "being," as the ancient scholastic thesis stated, but, on the contrary, the being of man results from his action. And if, in order to take place, this reversal needs a spiritual space that strikes him a priori as opposite—because it does not belong to a clearly enunciated rational discourse, but to Neoplatonic hermeticism—this paradox, today, no longer surprises us: since Cassirer and Koyré—and also, by contrast and homology, since the appearance of Corbin and Jambet's works on Persian Neoplatonism—we know through what displacement inside this "imaginal" space the advent of man developed, a man open to the infinity of the world because he is installed in a radical separation from it.

This, therefore, is the message that Poliphilo delivers us in his passionate quest for Polia-Sophia through the gardens that are the landscape of his soul. A soul very close to the one that Pico della Mirandola celebrated in his *Discourse on the Dignity of Man*: "As for you, you are limited by no barrier, it is according to your own will, in whose power I have placed you, that you will determine your nature."

If one follows this interpretation of the *Hypnerotomachia Poliphili*, the ultimate fate of the work is made clear. To begin with, its enthusiastic reception by humanist—that is to say mainly Huguenot—circles of the French Renaissance. These knew, in fact, how to read its hidden message in the French translation[4] that the "Notice to the Reader" presented as reduced "from a more than Asian prolixity . . . to a French brevity." And the message, beyond the precise theories of Luther or Calvin, seemed to contain the initial spirit of the Reform: the Church must watch over souls, but it does not have the mission to rule over man's attempt to think and know, for this attempt is the very expression of his liberty. If it seems curious that Calvinist austerity should turn up in a text celebrating pagan beauty and in luxuriously decorated engravings, one of which explicitly represents the cult of Priapus, let us remember that those belonging to the first reformed milieux in France were neither killjoys nor prudish; Henry IV stood among them, and Marot and Rabelais were not far off.

The original "French channel" of the *Hypnerotomachia* was Catholic, however, and connected to the family that, for more than a century, would incarnate radical opposition to the Reform: the Medici.

The *Dream*'s publication had passed almost unnoticed in Venice. But Francis I brought back a copy from his Italian expeditions, proof that this book was already considered important in the learned artistocracy and artistic milieux on the other side of the Alps. In addition, following his return, the "noble king François" celebrated by Janequin would make sure that the esotericism of the gardens of the *Dream* would be the secret rule of his domain at Fontaine-bleau.[5] The Medici family, moreover, which could rightfully claim itself the princely heir of the Florentine Academy, would shoot its strongest branches right into the court of France, so that it was natural that Marie de Medici should at the beginning of the seventeenth century order the famous Jacques Boyceau de La Baraudière to create a garden for the Luxembourg inspired by the *Hypnerotomachia*; and that this book, which was already more than a century old, was one of the bases of the education that Mazarin gave the young Louis XIV (who would draw inspiration from it for the symbolic layout of Versailles).

But the edition of the *Dream* published by Kerver in 1546 went far beyond this royal sphere. Not only in the splendor of its plates, which were engraved with a multitude of new details by a workshop near Jean Goujon[6] and inspired a quantity of fabulous feasts and plastic motifs in the painting, sculpture, architecture, or decoration of gardens, but also in the intellectual influence—which set the *Hypnerotomachia* apart from the other "best-sellers" of the period, adorned though they may have been by descriptions of marvelous gardens—that it exerted on men of genius as different as Maurice Scève, Rabelais, Goujon, Marot, and Bernard Palissy. There they found, in addition to the spirit of reform that animated them—and which was at first an appetite for truth unfettered by any spiritual policing—a climate that was fantastic, joyously sensual, impregnated with the craziest oddities, but anxious nonetheless. It brought them close to that vertigo that the religious wars were bound to open in their thoughts. "Where one sees that all human things are only a dream," the *Hypnerotomachia* announces already in the subtitle, an already baroque theme that would soon appear in Calderón, Shakespeare, and Corneille.

This is the explanation for the singular genius of the *Poliphilo*, a Janus-like work that drew its vigor from the innocent hope of Renaissance humanism, and announced at the same time the exalted disequilibrium that the religious crisis of the Reform would pour over Europe like whitewash.

It would be an exaggeration, however, to see the *Dream* as the sole model of the learned gardens of the sixteenth and seventeenth centuries. It is true that the monstrous oddities of the Villa Orsini at Bomarzo, the sumptuous layouts of the Primatice (that of Gaillon in particular, as we can imagine it through the engraving by Androuet du Cerceau), the vignettes of Thomas Hill's *Most Briefe and Pleasaunt Treatyse*, the strange machineries of Salomon de Caus, the hypnerotomachic decors conceived by Jean Goujon for Henry III's entry into Paris, and the grottoes and ceramic basins built by Bernard Palissy in the gardens of the Louvre[7] all bear the mark of gardens imagined by the *Dream*; nonetheless, the fact remains that these works also bear the traces of many other influences:

Those that continue the medieval imaginary through the interminable *Amadis des Gaules* in which one can see the matrix of the *esprit précieux*, and of the *Carte du Tendre* connected to it.

Those tied to the direct encounter with Italian art that Paolo Mercogliano at Amboise and Gerolamo da Napoli and Serlio at Ancy-le-Franc would import to France following the Italian expeditions, during which Charles VIII and his companions experienced ecstatic transports.[8]

Those going back to the passionate discovery of the biblical text. Marot's version of the Psalms, for example, constituted the explicit reference of the ideal garden described by Palissy.[9]

Those of an Orient revealed by so many travel narratives, one of the strangest of which is Jean de Mandeville's, which combines a rather precise description of Palestine with the phantasmagories of a supposed expedition to China through a series of increasingly fabulous "islands" with astonishingly rich vegetation and numbers of bizarre creatures that undoubtedly influenced Rabelais.[10]

Those of the Utopias, providing the perfect and complicated geometry irrigating Dürer's checkerboards, Filarete's stars, the radioconcentric crescents described by Thomas More, as well as the labyrinths of Gaillon, of the first Versailles, and of the English gardens of the period.[11]

Those, finally, proceeding from the effective discovery of new worlds that, enlarging both botanical science and vision, would engender an order of gardens dedicated to scholarly classifications through a graft onto the ancient medicinal *Herbularius*.

But a concern of a different kind was taking shape at the same time. A concern that was contradictory in appearance because it associated a desire for separation—between pleasure and utility—with an interest in expanding the practice of gardening to the entire cultivatable area.

The "rural" dimension was already present in the treatise by Crescenzi, translated upon the request of Charles V under the unambiguous title *Rustican de labeur des champs* (1373), as it was in the later works inspired by it, such as the one by Charles d'Estienne (*Praedium rustican*, 1554, revised in 1583 by his nephew Jean Liébard), or in the one by Augustino Gallo translated from the Italian in 1571 (*Secrets de la vraye agriculture*).

But what was happening here, rather than a broadening of horticultural concerns, was the development of agrarian "theory" in the space of the garden itself. If the medieval imaginary had in fact dreamed (and sometimes conceived) of courtly enclosures separated from country gardens, its practical economy—and this also applies to the Hostel Saint-Pol—had led it most often to make no distinction between the pleasant and the useful. Instead it combined orchard, vegetable garden, farmyard, and leisure garden in a single "rustic" space: moreover, the term agriculture designated both gardening as we understand it and field work. One of the most original features of Crescenzi's work consequently had to do with its repeatedly stated project to separate the different registers combined at the heart of the profane garden by assigning one part to *utilitas* and another to *voluptas*.

But parallel to this desire to draw an internal distinction was a movement turned toward the "exterior" and completing Crescenzi's approach, which was but a facet of modernity. For, in setting himself the goal of importing horticultural techniques into ordinary rural economy,[12] he invented agronomy and facilitated the emergence of the notion of "landscape" according to the triple mode that is familiar to us today: deliberate artistic creation; the domestic countryside the historian-poet Gaston Roupnel has celebrated so marvelously; and the natural site, even though it was for a long time detested as the crude expression of pagan savagery.[13]

This movement of the *hortus* toward the countryside had already been the subject of a genius as practical as Bernard, who had made himself its bard in an implicit fashion during his "tour de France" as a journeyman-surveyor. This took him from Saintonge to Provence and from the Vosges to Brittany; his travel diary is full of observations on the nature of soils, the variety of climates, and the possible extent of cultures.

But it was another Huguenot, Olivier de Serres, who deserves credit for having thought of the country as a possible extension of the garden—a *Theater of Agriculture* as he called it himself, which might fuse the economic project formulated by Sully and the "plastic ambition" brought back from Italy.[14]

The Beautiful Gardener (La Belle Jardinière), plate by Bernard Palissy. Photo © Giraudon.

A gentle wind is blowing in the Cévennes today. The harsh line of greenhouses where the snow is beginning to melt is etched against the horizon.

Located in the middle of the triangle constituted by Villeneuve-de-Berg, Aubenas, and Privas, the domain measures two hundred hectares. Coming to it by way of the large meadow called the Pradel, one crosses a ditch bordered by an enclosing wall: in this season, that is to say spring, the water rises about two meters. The wall, which carries a covered way and a sentry box, is broad and, like the house and the adjacent farm buildings, built of basalt—a heavy molten stone, rich in iron and dark yellow. The main door faces north and has a porch with shutters made of heart of oak.

The main building, in the shape of an imposing quadrilateral, rests on vaults covering the cowsheds, stables, sheep pens, henhouses, and wine cellars. Climb up to the second floor and you enter a kitchen lit by two large corner windows that provide a downward view of the farmyard and a *vue de surveillance*, or survey view, toward three cardinal points over the domain. There are cabinets for provisions, a brick furnace, and a monumental vaulted chimney with stone benches called a *chauffoir*. Farther on, the great hall with its ceiling of sculpted beams and its luxurious furniture with inlaid work, an ancient pulpit and a ceremonial bed. A small vaulted room, another immense chamber, and, finally, the "obscure chamber" with no windows. Above, under the roof timbers, two vast "high chambers," one of which occasionally serves as an attic.

On going back down, you find, outside but connected to the house, the barn, stables, storeroom, and the shepherd and herdsmen's house opening onto the great courtyard and facing the shelter containing the carts, coaches, plowshares, plows, and all the agricultural material. There are also two paved places near the stables where the manure is piling up; the gardener-coachman's small house with its small adjoining garden; and, to the south, a terrace running lengthwise where the first cherries are drying.

Next to the house there is a garden consisting of an enclosure of four or five ares in the shape of a rectangle running along the eastern wall. A low wall of dried stones separates it from the Pradel meadow to the west: vegetables, medicinal herbs, flowers, and "exquisite curiosities." At the foot of the garden wall, there is the orchard and two long nurseries sparkling in the southern sun. To the west, bordering the Gazel from which rises a screen of blue mist, the rather stony ground of the "Couderc." Then the vines, and the large Pradel meadow surrounded by a lovely oak grove and crossed by a meager brook. At the bottom of the domain, near the mills of Brialas, the brook joins the Claduègne in a deep gully that climbs back up the fields and meadows along the edge; next, the Mauberte with its bright grass and, to the northeast, the Plaine with its deep and heavy earth.

We are in April 1584. April, "The honor of woods / And months . . . The sweet hope / Of fruits that, under the cotton / Of the bud, / Nourish their young childhood."

And, in the west of the domain, a man pushes his swing plow across the rocky earth of the "Couderc." He does not know that what he has undertaken and will pursue for the rest of his life will be so fruitful that he will go down in history as a man of his time, the sixteenth century, and also, in the eyes of the French, the "father of agriculture."

Born around 1539 in the province of Vivarais, at Villeneuve-de-Berg, Olivier de Serres was an example of those rural gentlemen who, unlike the nobleman and his "officers," was both the financial owner of his land and its plowman. Unlike these new farmers, however, he not only transformed certain agricultural techniques, but was also artful enough to record them for his contemporaries.

The mid-sixteenth century was marked by an effort at theorization that integrated both the heritage of the past and the novelties of the time. But, whereas the treatise by Charles Éstienne and Jean Liébault—as well as a number of other treatises that were plagiaries published under another name—added nothing new to Crescenzi's work, the *Theater of the Fields* (*Théâtre des champs*), published in 1600 and reprinted around twenty times during the seventeenth century, founded modern agronomy by combining experience and science.

Responding, on the one hand, to Sully's famous saying—"Pasturage and plowing are the two breasts nursing France"—and, on the other hand, to the taste for knowledge demonstrated by King Henry IV, who affixed his arms upon it when it was published, Olivier de Serres's work was widely successful beginning in his own time.

Olivier de Serres's distant ancestors came from the Berg region with its stony hills, rivers, small valleys and, to the north of the great plain with the black soil, rich volcanic detritus from the Coiron massif. Monks of the earth, companions of the abbot of Mazan, they had come from the neighboring mountains that, with their fang-shaped ridges, stood tall and somber against the horizon; they were called "those from the Serres" or Desserres. The son of Jacques and Louise de Leyris, who both belonged to the urban, merchant bourgeoisie, Olivier divided his early childhood between the sheet shop located on the corner of the two most traveled streets of an extremely prosperous commercial center, his father's garden on the path of Saint-Jean-le-Centenier, and, outside the city, the wheat- and fruit-bearing lands cultivated by his father's tenant farmers.

In this period small farms were in crisis, and lands were being sold and "gathered," usually bought up by bourgeois who were later ennobled. In this context, Jacques de Serres, first magistrate of the city, had to arbitrate conflicts constantly, a task made all the more delicate by the fact that, in this era of religious crisis, he had openly chosen to side with the Reform. He was, however, satisfying everyone with his recognized integrity when he suddenly died, leaving his wife and three young sons, Olivier, Jean, and Raymond, to fend for themselves right in the middle of a civil war, the Wars of Religion.

While Jean entered the university of Lausanne with the fervent desire to be a pastor, Olivier left his old humanist instructor and went to study for five years in Toulouse and Valence, then in Switzerland and Italy. There he took courses in law, medicine, and botanical science, but subsequently returned without any diploma. At the age of eighteen he bought from Pastel the mill of Brialas and the lands surrounding it along the Claduègne and, a few months later, from M. de Pampelonne who had just acquired it without having paid it off entirely, the "domain of Pradel for the price of: 3,828 livres," in exchange for the sale of various scattered lots inherited from his father.

Olivier de Serres thus became the owner of the Pradel, thereby obeying one of the first principles of his *Theater of the Fields*—that the best way of being a friend to the earth is to be its owner, since the most beautiful domains "become ugly and hideous as though dressed in mourning, for the absence of their masters." Furthermore, by selling scattered domains in order to replace them with an estate all of one piece and near the mills, Olivier de Serres became the first to support the regrouping of lands.

The seigniorial domain was extremely broken up because of the inheritance partitions that had multiplied and parceled out the land into a multitude of poorly maintained fiefs with real concurrent rights coexisting on the same lot. Nonetheless, a "reconstructed" seigniorial domain emerged through a regrouping of lands, permitting coherent farming as well as the restoration of socioeconomic unities in which self-sufficiency was the ideal. Olivier de Serres and his wife Marguerite, who belonged to the same social class, formed the lively and harmonious cell that would manage (*mesnagier*) "their common affairs with perfect friendship and intelligence." Seven children would come from their union. A portrait of Daniel, their oldest son who would continue their work after them, can still be found in the Pradel: the child is two or three years old and holds a cherry and a small bird in his hands. His father, Olivier, painted the portrait himself.

It was the middle of spring, and there was a certain softness in the air. Olivier was driving the swing plow with his bare arms. Marguerite, the child Daniel, and Olivier's mother, Louise, were with Ranc, a tenant farmer, in the great courtyard. The two women sat picking over the bale of wild grasses, some medicinal and others harmful, that Olivier had gathered at dawn.

Against the horizon rose the black escarpments of the basaltic Coiron. And, nearby, one could hear the dull sound of civil war, rumbling as it did when Jacques was dying and before Olivier's marriage.

It was in vain that Michel de L'Hospital, who was Catherine de Medici's chancellor, appealed for tolerance during the convention of the Estates General. And it was also in vain that the colloquy of Poissy proclaimed the edict of Saint-Germain, the first charter proclaiming freedom of conscience and worship. The carnage at Vassy wreaked by the duc de Guise and his men was deeply disturbing. And that winter Olivier, who had been made deacon and was reformed like his father and younger brother Jean, went with a mission to Calvin in Geneva in order to request a pastor for Villeneuve. With the help of his companion Tichet, he crossed the ridges and icy passes of the Alps; he was received by Calvin himself in his house on the rue des Chanoines, and he attended several of his famous sermons. This confirmed him even further in his convictions and, in a characteristic gesture of fervent generosity, he housed the new pastor and his family for several months and bought the pulpit for the hall reserved for religious services.

But the atrocities of war grew in number: Largentière, Viviers, Saint-Agrève, Bourg-Saint-Andéol, and Annonay, where his brother Jean was seriously wounded, were all besieged, ransomed, or razed. There was rape and murder everywhere. Alone in this area, Villeneuve-de-Berg was protected thanks to an agreement between the Protestants and Catholics of the city: it was Olivier de Serres who was asked to keep in his home the sacred deposit for the religious articles used in Catholic worship.

On May 25, 1563, when Calvin died in Geneva, Catherine de Medici, Michel de L'Hospital, and the young king Charles IX, crossing France province by province in a gesture of reconciliation, were traveling along the Rhône, near Villeneuve-de-Berg.

During the respites from war, Olivier, who had refused to lease out the Pradel, visited it as often as he could and became acquainted with his lands and their soil. He studied Hesiod, Palladius, and the famous Columella, author of *De re rustica*, and also his Italian contemporaries, Tarello, Augustino Gallo, Pietro de' Crescenzi, Gorgole de Corne, who had just been translated into French. But his favorite book was one written by the French Protestant Bernard Palissy, *True formula according to which all men of France will be able to learn how to multiply and increase their treasures (Recette véritable par laquelle tous les hommes de la France pourront apprendre à multiplier et augmenter leurs thrésors)*, in which Palissy, deploring the routine practice of agriculture, gives insights into the study of soils and the way to improve them.

In the meantime, the Wars of Religion had started again with terrifying violence: Olivier continued to carry a sword and pistol during three painful years of wandering.

A captain now, he had abandoned, after the massacre of Saint Bartholomew, "domain, provisions, and patrimony" to three farmers. He then conducted a military campaign with the object of retaking Villeneuve-de-Berg, which was in the hands of the Catholics. The city was liberated as a consequence. But cadavers continued floating down the Rhône and, suddenly, as though the sight of the atrocities of war had horrified him, Olivier decided to retreat with his family to the Pradel. One could certainly still find his name attached either to concerns providing aid and welfare, or to the direction of "security groups" against the looters that the violent disturbances would continue producing for a long time, but from then on Olivier, who was almost forty, would live as a plowman and direct the management of the fields.

The preceding year, in the middle of the torments of war, the baron of the Astars had transferred to Olivier his seigniorial rights over the entire domain of the Pradel in exchange for an annual and perpetual rent of five *setiers* (a unit containing between 150 and 300 liters) of wheat to be taken from the emphyteuta of Saint-Jean-le-Centenier. At stake were the rights to command (to issue the *ban* or decree indicating the opening of the furnace, grape harvests, mill, and wine press); to nominate the rural officials and to supervise the fields; to administer high, middle, and low justice, both civil and repressive, and even to judge crimes punishable by death. As a consequence, Olivier officially became "noble Olivier de Serres, lord of Pradel." His coat of arms and seal would bear three eagle talons (*serres*), and his mottoes were *Cuncta in tempore* and *Sordida quaeque fugit*.

The first years were a time of grueling work involving first the renovation of the strong house of the Pradel, then of its lands.

Inspired by his reading of Bernard Palissy, Olivier de Serres had already had marl transported onto two fields deficient in lime. He had also tried using green fertilizers. Then he decided to pave over the ground in front of the cowsheds in order to pile up there the manure, the fat of which would enrich the large parcel of land located in the northeast of the domain, called La Plaine, whose earth, although dark and fertilized by detritus from the Coiron, had not produced enough; stubbles would also be buried there so that, enclosed within the earth, they might "nourish" it; finally, the number of plowings would be increased to three per year. Likewise, La Blache would be "rigged out" during the first sunshine because, like the fields along the Claduègne, it held too much humidity, and "it is bleeding the earth to stir it out of season." The Couderc parcel would not be opened yet because, being very dry, it might freeze. As for the meadows, they would be amended, fertilized, and given over to the cultivation of grains, "for the earth rejoices in change." In an even more daring move, Olivier de Serres would become a master in pedology by choosing the most "valorous" field, plowing it over, bringing fresh manure to it in winter, carefully leveling it and sowing there a mixture of wild grasses so that, "tamed, reduced, preserved," and fertilized, it might turn into a meadow.

We can imagine our nobleman plowing. A countryman by residence, Olivier de Serres has never handled a hoe before. But he enjoys breathing the fresh air that comes down from the dark ridges at dawn, thus preceding him as he precedes the rising of the others, for "rising in the morning enriches." Blond and blue-eyed, he walks through the morning grass, short and sunburnt. The silence is absolute here; a truce has been called to battles. He seizes the ancient swing plow and plows the short and narrow lands between the Couderc and the Great Meadow. But when the time comes to work the plain or the Pradel, he uses the plow and the harrow that he introduced to the domain in 1564, a long time before he decided to live there. To plow such deep and regular furrows does the land as much good as a layer of manure.

The shed held several plowshares in hardwood armed with metal, colters, both simple and double moldboards, turning front-axle units and wooden pieces fixed on wheels supporting a horizontal bar pierced with five holes and connected to the plowshare with a pin and rope; rectangular or lozenge-shaped harrows, for the harrowing must corroborate the work of the plow. If Olivier de Serres invented only a few technical instruments, nonetheless he was the first to think of the mechanical seeder, a kind of harrow bearing a case with holes. He also invented a heavy rolling harrow composed of two tree trunks pricked with iron pins, ancestor of the roller, and a vast wooden rake of wood with curved branches of iron, drawn by animals, in order to gather the cut hay. Then, since "livestock is necessary in all places on earth," Olivier de Serres reconstituted a bouvine and paid good money for two mares and a stallion. He would eventually have an admirable livestock of bulls, mules, sheep, chickens, turkeys, geese, and ducks, which he described in the *Mesnage* at length, showing how to raise, instruct, nourish, tame, castrate, produce, and reproduce. His small livestock included the silkworm that he brought back in 1571 from a trip to Nîmes and cultivated with such success that thirty years later King Henry IV, having read his report on *The Gathering of Silk* (*La Cueillette de la soie*)—that "exquisite farming"—dispatched the superintendent of France's gardens, de Bordeaux, in order to obtain for his parks fifteen to twenty thousand white mulberry trees. After a course was given at the Orangerie of the Tuileries, Fontainebleau, and in the park of Madrid, in 1602 a royal decree ordered the creation of a mulberry nursery and a silkwork farm in each parish; instructions written by Laffemas accompanied copies of *The Gathering of Silk*; the purchasing of silk would be directed by the state while deals would be concluded by the tradesmen, Olivier de Serres and his friend Traucat. Dangon invented the loom for silkwork, and factories were set up in the

Cévennes and in Languedoc in order to "pull from the bowels of the earth the treasure of silk that is hidden there," as Olivier de Serres wrote about the "golden tree."

Meanwhile, the famines kept coming with crushing regularity: in 1580, 1585, and in 1586 the plague. Panic-stricken people, dying for lack of provisions, tore up vineyards, turned over ancient meadows, and attacked the forest. How were they to be fed? How could harvests be increased? How could the yield be doubled or tripled? How could the production of wheat and fodder be regulated "so that you will always be provided for"?

For his experiments Olivier de Serres chose a small, enclosed garden in the shape of a rectangle covering about four and a half ares near the house. He would later have the courage and daring to generalize its results over his entire domain, and even to imagine his domain as a model for agriculture in general.

Bernard Palissy, in his research into the secret of earthenware and enamels, studied earth powders and their "humors," such as their susceptibility to cold, heat, and humidity, but he was not a farmer. For the rest, *The Rustic House* and other so-called treatises were only scholastic ramblings and superstition, for example: "On the fourth day Abel was born: that day is good to start a work." But the most widespread idea was that the earth must "rest," that it gives only when it can give, and that to provide it with manure is not only a waste, but an offense against God. Just as Olivier had, like his father, rebelled against superstition, routine, and intellectual and moral laziness, so he desired to understand the earth: "Science, experience, diligence," he wrote, "form the summary description of agriculture." Or, humorously: "We ask for wheat from the granary, not in painting." The land's dependency on climate, which Bernard Palissy had demonstrated, was unquestionable: it was for this reason that Olivier de Serres, fearing the torrid summers of the Vivarais, established wide, parallel canals, paved at the bottom, in which clear water ran continuously, in imitation of the lord of Crapone's invention in the Crau, which Olivier had visited. But it was also necessary for water to "reach everywhere but stagnate nowhere." For this reason he had ditches dug to collect and drain the runoff; they were built in the shape of an underground aqueduct and meant to filter "bad humors." A channel branching off the Gazel supply canal brought water into a little garden containing cabbage, lettuce, carrots, onions, *sercifi*, red beets, peas, turnips, parsnips, and a shrub from America received by a botanist in Basel, the *cartoufle*, ancestor of the potato. There was even a square patch of "experimental" wheat with a yield of fourteen and a half to one. If a garden ardently tended, smoked, amended, hoed, plowed, irrigated, turned over, raked, and weeded can produce so well and so regularly, it must mean that the fertility of the earth, once understood, may be infinite and capable of providing for "man's living" in all seasons. Moreover, he writes, "the gardener is called the goldsmith of the earth because the gardener surpasses the simple plowman."

Nevertheless, Olivier de Serres's heart and spirit were those of a plowman, and he was able to enjoy himself in the fields as well as in his garden. After improving the fallowing of the "vain pastures" by practicing *déchaumage* (destubbling) and the ancient Macedonian method of burying the broad beans, peas, lupins, vetch, and other plants of more recent cultivation such as alfalfa and *esparcet*, or clover, Olivier de Serres, observing the variety of beds in his garden, decided to fertilize the "vain earth," that is to say the land lying fallow in the biennial rotation of crops, by spreading out the clover crops in time as well as space. Knowing nothing about chemical science or the live assimilable salts that Bernard Palissy called "vegetative salts"—"If I knew the properties of salts, I would think of wonderful things to do!"—knowing nothing about oxygen or nitrogen, Olivier de Serres calculated the way in which the production of wheat and fodder could be scientifically regulated; in other words, he discovered the artificial meadow and long-lasting rotation.

The application of his agricultural method was delayed, however, to the detriment of the land and of the French population, because of the resumption of the civil war after the July 1585 edict forcing the Protestants to convert. War, plague, and famine raged all around: two thirds of the population of Vivarais died. At the Pradel, where the harvests were fairly good, Olivier de Serres made no distinction between Catholics and Protestants, and, like his father, he kept "his granaries open at all times." It was during this painful period that he decided to write his *Theater of Agriculture* (*Théâtre d'agriculture*) and *Management of Fields* (*Mesnage des champs*).

On February 27, 1594, Henry IV, who had just abjured, was solemnly crowned at Chartres. And while the noblemen and bourgeois still distrusted the new king, the people crowded around and cried "Long live the king!" The ex-league of the duc de Guise continued its acts of savage vengeance. Jean de Serres was arrested, thrown in prison, stripped of an enormous sum he was supposed to transfer to the reformed churches, and ordered to pay a huge ransom. Olivier wrote the king to remind him of services rendered by his brother and, in 1596,

Jean was named historiographer of France with a very high monthly salary. Olivier, tired after the death of his mother Louise and the marriage of his son Daniel, traveled, visiting his friend Traucat who was a gardener in Nmes, Richier de Belleval who was a famous botanist in Montpellier, and his younger brother in Loriol. Then he went to Switzerland where he visited the botanist Baulin and to Germany where he visited the Orangeries of the elector palatine at Heidelberg. He had almost finished his book. After the Edict of Nantes, which finally pacified the unrest, and the signature of the peace of Vervins with Spain, by Jean, Olivier made contact with a printer in Lyons. But Jean and then his wife died suddenly, leaving a difficult and confused estate. The family council decided that Olivier, who was almost sixty years old, should go to Paris in order to attempt to get an audience with the king. His horse was harnessed with a leather chest containing the manuscript of the *Theater of Agriculture* and *Management of Fields*.

At the court, Olivier de Serres met the baron-duc de Sully, a Flemish Huguenot, himself a "good manager" of his domain, the Isle de France, who also advocated "a people of plowmen"; Laffemas, future inspector-general for commerce who had published a *Treatise of Treasures and Riches to Put the State in Splendor* (it was Laffemas who, speaking of Olivier de Serres's book to Henry IV, suggested that he look into founding a national industry of silk); and Claude Mollet, the king's gardener and author of the drawings in the *Theater of Agriculture*. Olivier met the king in the great gallery of the Louvre, and on July 1, 1600, the printing of the *Theater* was completed by Jamet Mettayer, the king's printer.

It is April, and the air is soft. Near the house, in the flower garden called a "garden of pleasure," are arranged the drawings of the parterres, showing their borders of myrtle, boxwood, thyme, basil, rue, lavender, mandrake, rosemary, and the squares filled with all kinds of carnations, violets, lilies, gladiolas, marguerites, hollyhocks, coxcombs, sunflowers, anemones, peonies, and tulips; and, beneath bushes in the shape of *tonnelles*, arches, small huts, bowers, and fences, many flowers are blossoming and releasing their fragrance: the red rosebushes of Provins, muscat roses, yellow roses, and the crimson roses of Provence; multicolored jasmines, herbs of the night, privets, cypresses, seringas, rhododendrons, lilacs, Spanish broom, laurels, Judas trees, hops "made to climb high," and white truffles.

In the garden of simples, now a "medicinal garden," blessed thistle, worm-killer, mallows, and hemps, or "warm plants"; to the east and west, angelica, mullein, mercury, valerian, periwinkle, absinthe, persicaria; to the north, the "cold plants," such as tormentil, goldenrod, and gentian.

After the vegetable garden and the lovely orchard full of peach, almond, cherry, pear, apple, plum, and fig trees, there is at the back of the enclosure a large and marvelous parcel of textile plants and plants used in dying: saffron, hemp, pastels, and madders that smell bitter, sweet, and wild.

We are in April, and as in any spring, the air, the earth, the mountains, and the forests are flowering again, like a great kingdom that was about to die but, having come under the double sign of peace and labor, is returned to prosperity and blossoming twice over.

Thus our man goes, bent over his plow, his feet sinking into the dusty trail and the beauty of the French fields, advancing against ruin and disaster, ingratitude and the woes of war, while his eyes take in the new grasses and all the other signs of renewal.

Parterres en broderies in front of the
Tuileries, by Claude Mollet. Photo
© Bibliothèque Nationale, Paris.

Allée Four

Places that give hearts so many lovable desires
Woods, fountains, canals . . .
MALHERBE

If Olivier de Serres is such an important figure in the history of the French garden, it is because he represents an attempt at a fragile equilibrium during the cruel watershed of the Wars of Religion, while also standing for a composite tradition that would subsequently follow one of several paths, either reemerging in the formal French garden in the seventeenth century or following a more subterranean route that would manifest itself later, or elsewhere.

Thus one can see in this attempt the result, or confluence, of two movements carried forward by different ethical systems and social forces. One movement, thoroughly practical, was aimed at the profitability of the agricultural patrimony based on an ethic that, if not "bourgeois," was at least solidly planted in the development of a landed elite suspicious of intellectual "fashions": a kind of continuo carried by a continually expanding social layer, intoning that "long time of history" described by Braudel. The other movement, livelier and more imaginative, reflected a learned culture with esthetic preoccupations that the agronomist from Ardèche did not condemn, but on the contrary thought legitimate since they celebrated a "wholesome" joy offering suitable pleasures to the aristocracy that had gathered under the banner of "good king Henry." In this will to bring together two apparently contrary registers one can also see a desire to effect a reasonable balance between art and economy according to a method close to that of Alberti's project.[1]

Similarly, it is possible to consider de Serres's work as the culmination of French horticultural mannerism. Basing itself upon the categories—by now firmly fixed—of art history, which see in the Italian Renaissance a kind of classicism soon followed by reinterpretations and transpositions of a recognized "manner," according to a spectrum of new and singular "manners," the history of the French garden in the sixteenth century can be interpreted according to this conceptual grid: via Du Cerceau, Philibert Delorme, or Palissy, the Italian heritage imported in France by Primaticcio, Serlio, and the *Dream of Poliphilo* was progressively adapted to French taste, climates, and landscapes, and then remodeled in contact with a continuous tradition that combined a specific horticultural savoir-faire with a boundless love of a formal universe that had peaked during medieval France. The graft was so successful that it explains Olivier de Serres's strangely patriotic formula: "There is no need to travel in Italy or elsewhere to see beautifully ordered gardens, since our France wins the prize over all nations." And it also explains the homage he paid to a master practician who was not an architect, and without whom such a brilliant victory could not have been won: the famous Claude Mollet.

Following these high points, one can also see the theoretical and practical work of the author of the *Theater of Agriculture* as the testimony of that short lull that, coinciding with the proclamation of the Edict of Nantes, occurred in the middle of a political and religious tempest. A preoccupation with agronomy and gardening is out of place when civil war is knocking at the door, full of furious passions, injustices, betrayals, assassinations, and repeated massacres. The earth requires care, calm, and patience, and nothing ruins it faster than anger, battles, and bloodshed. But, although de Serres took up arms to defend his faith and rights, although he fought courageously against intolerance, he was in fact never a real man of war, or as intransigent as that famous religionary, Agrippa d'Aubigné. He had no apocalyptic prophetism, no vindictive furor—only a total commitment to serve God and Calvinist Truth, regarding which he would never compromise, and an even stronger love of his neighbor, which caused him to look with horror upon the abyss into which France had fallen, and to hope with all his might for a moment of sunshine when human energy would not be exhausting itself in fanatic violence, but serving everyone's happiness. "My hand has remained pure in serving you, empty of your acts of kindness and free from the corruptions of you and your enemies." The passionate tone Agrippa used to address Henry IV after his "conversion" would not have suited de Serres. Peace was so valuable to him that he was willing to pay for it with a political compromise, which for him did not imply an inner compromise.

The fact remains that this lull would not last, nor would the unstable equilibrium of Henry IV's reign. The regency, a renewal of the Wars of Religion, and then the Fronde soon broke the short-lived consensus between classes and theologies, undoing the fragile alliance that mannerism had tied between novelty and tradition. A moral, religious, economic, and formal neoclassicism was potentially contained in Henry's famous declaration, *Paris vaut bien une messe* ("Paris is certainly worth a mass"), as in the peaceful creation of the Pradel. But the vertigo of the baroque would find its exalted space through Ravaillac's regicide.

Mannerism, baroque, classicism: Wölflin's categories are used in art history so frequently today and have been the object of such extensive inflation that—as a result of vague and simplistic readings—they constantly risk casting a smoke screen over the rich, contradictory tensions, asynchronous movements, and diversified influences[2] of a period as creatively diversified as the first half of the seventeenth century in France. When one tries too hard to clarify the matter by finding within it a conceptual thread capable of ordering such a sumptuous web, the idea of order itself falters, unless one's vision becomes selective, that is to say false.

Connections here, progressions there, supposed "delays" elsewhere; "precious" movements on the one hand, delectable "comic" reversals on the other: the mind boggles trying to qualify univocally a chaotic era the ambiguous charm of which resides in its mottled variety. How can a single unifying vision join together Sponde and Malherbe, Voiture, Corneille or Cyrano, Richelieu, Condé and Mazarin, Desargues and Descartes, Vouet and La Tour, François Mansart and Louis Le Vau? Surely, the object concerning us, given the fact that it cannot do without a large number of technicians who possess bodies of knowledge that cannot be improvised—and also because its creations are inscribed in a time whose rapid rate of destruction equals its slowness at shaping—is less susceptible to abrupt variations and singular fancies than poetry, music, or painting. Climates, seasons, reliefs, terrains, and species all resist within it.

However, the long garden dynasty of the Mollets, Du Pérac, or even Jacques Boyceau de La

Baraudière cannot be considered simply preparations for the garden à la française that would culminate in Le Nôtre's Versailles. They contained, as did other more obscure creators, a multiplicity of approaches that were sometimes inscribed (as in the case of Boyceau) in the general cultural debate and sometimes carried by a development more closely related to the profession—of which the Mollets were the most eminent representatives. All produced singular works, some of them as essential as the first Luxembourg or the older version of the Tuileries. And only a history fixated on isolating large currents can reduce this flowering to the minor status implied by the term "transition."[3]

In fact, once the two "classical" poles have been established—the Italian Renaissance model for the uphill slope, the formal French garden for the downhill, both sharing the ability to combine in a single movement what is strictly called architecture (villas, castles) and the ordering of gardens—nothing could be more unfair, or more false, than to make them the only possible measures of beauty. For that would come back to ignoring a wealth of apparently erratic detours, indirect paths, and shortcuts. These detours, favoring juxtaposition and "poorly joined marquetries"[4] over deliberately rational compositions, testify to a sensibility that is less intellectual than sensual, and more heterotopic than homotopic.[5] But, contrary to what we have for a long time been taught to think, the first is not less primitive or imperfect than the second, only different. As different as medieval Christianity was from Greco-Roman antiquity. That is to say equally constitutive of the substance of the West.

During the entire sixteenth century and the first half of the seventeenth, in fact, the art of French gardens, including its learned versions, persisted, like all other arts, in not definitely rejecting ancient forms, and was even less anxious to broach the problem of the tabula rasa. Painting, poetry, and music continued to combine the new forms with Gothic oddities, while architecture—to the displeasure of a certain critical school, best represented by Anthony Blunt[6]—continued to take advantage of previous layouts or already constructed buildings in order to expand and recompose them, instead of breaking radically with them.

Thus Philibert Delorme, while complaining about the difficulties entailed by the need to integrate into Anet an earlier "confusion" constraining his project, did not hesitate to recommend in his treatise *Architecture* that one should undertake nothing "in which one has to fight the nature of the site, which has so much force," and that one should not destroy anything in an inconsiderate fashion:

I have shown the way one can help oneself with uncomfortable, old, and poorly made houses in order to appropriate and make them agree with the new buildings, and to make comfortable, healthy, and habitable what was uncomfortable, unhealthy, and uninhabitable: without however tearing down, ruining, or demolishing the old buildings, *as has been too lightly done by those who do not understand the artifice of the geometrical line* (trait géometrique), *and in their ignorance order that everything should be made new forthwith.*

The remark is not only precise; it is savage. Coming from someone who had read Pérouse de Montclos,[7] it implies that those "ignorant" individuals who "do not understand the artifice of the geometrical line" are precisely those who wish to be servile[8] imitators of Italy: they do not know—and this is one of the results of their ignorance—that the art of the *trait*[9] was better developed in France than in Italy, because of the variety of stone there, and especially because of the more solid tradition of the cathedral builders.

Thus, regarding the century of creation that went in France from Francis I to Louis XIII, it may be more exact to speak of a pseudo-Renaissance and pseudo-mannerism, even of pseudo-baroque.[10] With this personal note (which situates our taste at the opposite end from the taste of Federico Zeri, who introduced this important nuance): just as we do not hide our preference for Uccello over Verrocchio, so we admit to preferring the proliferating variety of Blois or Chambord to the cold perfection of the works built upon the strict model of Florentine rationalism. Which is the same as saying that, in contemplating the surveys of the gardens of Gaillon, Fontainebleau, Blois, Ancy-le-Franc, or Anet as Androuet Du Cerceau drew them, or the plates of the first *parterres en broderies* (by Claude Mollet) reproduced in the work of Olivier de Serres, we do not deplore—far from it—a supposed absence of overall composition that should have subordinated the parts to the whole and the gardens to architecture. On the contrary. We are seized by the same joyous emotion that we felt upon hearing the songs of Janequin, Costeley, Sermisy, or Claude Lejeune,[11] where the voices sing each on its own, where the rhythms overlap, where comic inventions follow wild transports, and where everything is blended in a polyphony combining rustic greenery and the most refined acoustic science. Yes, we are moved. Overwhelmed and delighted by the evidence of a horticultural art lost forever, the singular magic of which resides in the marriage of the learned and the popular, of the picturesque and the sublime.

Let us consider, for example, since we have no effective evidence of his botanical art, Bernard Palissy's famous faience: the *Belle Jardinière*, or "Beautiful Gardener." The colors are bright, joyously suggestive of spring: green, blue, yellow and red ochres, as shining as those ceramic motifs in the shape of snakes, frogs, and tritons that he scattered in his grottoes and fountains. In the foreground, a buxom woman with breasts as round as apples, surrounded by gardening tools (a spade, a rake): not only is she brandishing bouquets triumphally, but leaves and flowers are woven into her hair, turning this comely gardener into an inverse, desirable Gorgon. In the background is the garden itself. Drawn in the perspective of a residence with a still medieval air, it remains enclosed between tall walls and is composed of two parts: the pleasure garden adjoining the castle without any other transition besides a large flight of stairs (neither a terrace nor a moat), and, separated from the stairs by a balustrade with a wide opening in the middle, the vegetable garden where a gardener is working. Of course this is only the decoration of a large plate of faience permitting neither details nor subtle patterns (thus the parterres, in a checkerboard layout, are only sketched, as are the fountain and the covered gallery on the longitudinal terrace to the right, next to the dovecote). In order to grasp something of the spirit of the gardens of this period, it is better to look at the atmosphere released by this virtuosic faience than to attempt an analysis of its contents: an almost flat terrain (the topography of the Ile-de-France and the Val-de-Loire being perceptibly less tormented than that of Italy),[12] the screens of greenery formed by vast stretches of foliage encasing the whole (unlike the Tuscan countryside where the trees are isolated), and, above all, a joyous ambiance, more rustic than intellectual (no antiquities, or very few). Freshness, then. Freshness *above all else*. A freshness that speaks to the senses rather than the spirit. One could easily attribute this charming naiveté to a somewhat crude vision, or to shaky systems of knowledge. For, by using a layout that was more topological than geometric, a patchwork in spots and seams, a selection of colors meant to create a delightful greenery, and a group of mineral or aquatic *joyeusetés* (merriments), the garden according to Palissy brings up out of the ground a sensual, cosmetic, and erogenous cartography that the sumptuous body of the *Belle Jardinière* allegorizes in a marvelous way, in a spirit close to the one celebrated by Michel Serres.[13]

And so it is no coincidence that the title of the treatise by André Mollet (the son of Claude), published in Stockholm in the middle of the seventeenth century—*Le Jardin de plaisir* (*The Garden of Pleasure*)—was faithful to the tradition begun by the *Romance of the Rose*, just as it recognized belatedly the necessity, where gardens are concerned, of separating *utilitas* from *voluptas* according to Vitruvius's categories. Charles V was already speaking of the Hostel Saint-Pol as a "place of great frolicking," and a poetic line, never broken, but revived instead by the reading of the *Poliphilo*,[14] designated the garden as a space specially devoted to amorous jousts in a fashion that was less and less allegorical. The insistence had entailed several semantic shifts: from Machaut to Deschamps, then from Chartier to Charles d'Orléans, the language of love had started to speak "flowers of rhetoric" and other garden metaphors. To such an extent that a collection of poetry gathered at the beginning of the sixteenth century—a *florilège* (the word comes from *flos* or flower) of a half-bawdy, half-courtly verse—bore the title *Le Jardin de plaisance* (*The Garden of Pleasure*). The work of an anonymous author who called himself the Unfortunate One, it was an anthology of songs without music gathered under the pretext that they had supposedly been composed by an assembly of ladies, young and old, and of lovers of both sexes, who were giving themselves over to pleasure in a charming garden.[15]

The convention was charming. But not without foundation. There were, in fact, many miniatures and engravings presenting singers and musicians holding a concert in a garden. And we know the joyous description that Rabelais inserted into the prologue of his *Quart Livre*: having evoked in a delightful fashion the assembly of musicians of Josquin des Prés's period singing "in a lovely flower bed" about an apparently delighted young bride's discovery of her husband's "large mallet," the creator of Gargantua and Pantagruel, that poet gigantic enough to have had the good taste to address himself only to those "most noble boozers" and other

"esteemed and poxy friends," goes on to cite his contemporaries—Clément Janequin's generation, then—who were assembled "in a private garden, beneath a lovely arbor, and behind a
rampart of bottles, hams, pasties, and dainty morsels in veils and skirts, singing most
charmingly:

If hatchets unhelved are quite useless,
And tools without hafts useless too,
Let us make the one fit in the other,
I've a helve. Let the hatchet be you.

We have come far, in this scene, from the *fin'amor* of the Middles Ages as well as the
Platonic ideal of the Italian Renaissance, and, on the contrary, moved closer to a popular
realism already transformed by Villon in *Regrets de la belle Heaulmière*, in which the garden
and the female genitalia are explicitly compared.[16] The image was repeatedly evoked in the
sixteenth century in a garland of ribald *Blasons* that equated celebrations of the garden with
celebrations of woman's body. "Wake up, sleeping hearts, the God of love is ringing for
you!" sung with elation, vigor, and sensuality those poets who, as erudite as they may have
been, seem to have had no interest in Marsilio Ficino's theories. For them, real paradise is
neither the original Eden, nor the Garden of olive trees, nor the celestial space of the *logos*;
it resides in silky skin, ample breasts, a smooth belly, fleshy thighs capable of "holding
amorous delights," and a channel lubricated like a fountain of youth. . . . And Priapus,
happy Priapus, who has no other desire than to taste these delights, has taken up residence
in the garden so that, his eyes shining through the boughs, he will never miss such a triumphant feast—a feast that Bernard Palissy's *Belle Jardinière* announces with her armfuls of
flowers, her joyous complexion, and the alluring silhouette beneath her dress.

This proud assurance, this faith in bodily happiness, and this confidence in the future could
not, however, survive the bloody massacre of Saint Bartholomew, and even less the assassi-
nation of the gallant king. The new century was disturbed by an agitation made first of
powdery snow, then of feverish shadows. The frisky god Priapus felt the marble within him
frittering, and his eyes were slowly covered by a veil of darkness. "Everything is swelling

against me, everything is assaulting me, tempting me," wrote Jean de Sponde as he abjured his Calvinist fervor, while the young Corneille, a few years later, would go into ecstasies over the "obscure light that falls from the stars." Is it possible that desire is not so simple, so tightly anchored to the great pleasure of living? Might it not somewhere be linked with death, with the smoking blood that flows abundantly from the open wounds of the flesh? And is nature—that bottomless *physis*[17] where clouds, waves, and aberrations float about—as warm and unsullied by error as it appeared to be in that vision of a time when everything seemed possible?

Less, undoubtedly, than all other arts, the art of gardens has been exposed to the fits and starts of history as well as the storms of conscience. Its works are collective and require much time and effort. Moreover, it would be absurd to try, under the pretext of unity and synchronism, to detect in its evolution a clearly circumscribed baroque phase.[18] This precaution is not meant to imply that one cannot see a change here. First because its most eminent practicians, who saw their status increasingly recognized, were forced to adapt themselves to the new taste of the day. Then because, continuing a social and cultural climb begun in the previous century, their profession would take its place increasingly at the heart of the artistic disciplines until it became, with Jacques Boyceau de La Baraudière, a full participant in the cultural life of the country.

Thus the parterres *en broderies* that became popular after Claude Mollet can be related to the taste for preciosity.

Box trees sculpted according to extremely complex geometric motifs, flowers grouped so as to create increasingly varied and controlled combinations of colors: there was a general taste for ostentation and ornament that passed from clothing to the garden, and from lace to the parterres. In fact, François Boucher wrote:

Between 1625 and 1670, a kind of correspondence was indisputably established between costume and baroque taste, the latter considered in the sense of a recourse to the imagination and to virtuosity. In fact, the essential characteristics of the baroque—a disdain of measure and a pronounced taste for freedom, a search for oppositions and movements, an abundance of details—are found again in clothing, which . . . is attracted by experiments, peculiarities, excesses attaining preciosity exemplified by the *canons* and *rhingraves*.[19]

The same can be said about the passion for water forming cascades and whirlpools—that *onde* or water present everywhere in the poetry of Théophile de Viau, Jean de Sponde, and Tristan L'Hermite; about the illusion-machines described in great detail by the physicist-landscapist Salomon de Caus in his study on *The Reasons of Moving Forces*; about the complicated routes that were strewn with labyrinths[20] and trials according to the literary model of the *Carte du Tendre*; and, finally, about that passion for the feast, which is above all a staging of *glory* (another major signifier of the period), and which consequently no longer requires an enclosure, nor even those "ramparts of bottles and hams" that delighted Rabelais, but a theater, a magnificent decor arranged like an outdoor stage, with foregrounds and backgrounds, artificial perspectives and trompe l'oeils, all cleverly laid out.

All these major components of the baroque period turned up in the garden, with an exuberant profusion increased by the fact that their sponsor was able to use them to astonish his guests.

The sponsors were, in fact, the readers of the famous *Treatise of Gardening According to the Reasons of Art and Nature* by Jacques Boyceau de La Baraudière, who sought to instruct them in an art that had become a sign of distinction: although published in 1638—a few years after its author's death, the precise date of which is as unknown to us as the date of his birth—this work constitutes the major theoretical reference book about the French garden in the seventeenth century, the basis of the thinking that Le Nôtre would value so much that he would see no point in producing a *Treatise* himself.

The figure of Jacques Boyceau, although still rather obscure,[21] was characteristic of the progressive shift undergone by his era. Everything, in the first part of his life, seems to have disposed him to receive without rupture the double heritage of Bernard Palissy and Olivier de Serres. Born into a Huguenot family, and a Huguenot himself, Boyceau, like the reinventor of ceramics, came from Saintonge and, like the master of the Pradel, was a man of war by necessity. However, having come from the gentry, he was not an autodidact and could rapidly profit from the friendship and protection of one of the greatest Huguenot lords—Biron, Henry IV's companion—a connection that gave him access to the most cultivated milieux of his time.

Victory came and, with it, the coronation of the Gascon king and the glorious entry into Paris. With much intelligence—and opportunism—Boyceau managed to stay out of the intrigues of his friend Biron who, convicted of treason, would be executed in 1602. It was a crazy and tragic period in which a young, elated duke thought it chivalrous to betray the man he had most loved, his companion in battle and pleasure whom he had carried to the throne, the king whom he forced, with death in his soul, to order his punishment. Boyceau, therefore, escaped disgrace. Better yet: chosen for his gifts and the breadth of his culture, he was made "ordinary gentleman of the King's chamber."

One can assume that Boyceau had by that time already participated in the development of the gardens of the castle of Brizambourg for Biron, as well as in a similar work ordered by the duc de La Force. That is to say that high-ranking nobles recognized him as a major talent. However, nothing about his horticultural training is known for sure. A gentleman, he might have received his education on location, like the Mollets, in the shadow of a father or relative who transmitted his knowledge to him; and as his entire youth was taken up with fighting in the Huguenot ranks, often bravely as in the siege of Luçon, it is hard to see how he could have had the time to expand his vision by numerous trips to Italy. There remains the hypothesis of the hobby, begun perhaps in childhood on the estate of his playmate Biron, pursued through military campaigns that also included long periods of feasting and idling, and reinforced by wide reading and a taste for botany that would not fail. Boyceau was more than a technician, consequently. He was an aristocratic intellectual, a man who, by virtue of his position and culture, frequented not the narrow circle of his "colleagues," but the entire learned and artistic society of his day. His special situation as a man of letters and a gentle-man undoubtedly explains the decisive turning point he impressed upon the French garden (the victory of "intelligence" over "sensibility," to sum it up), as well as the change of status of a profession the practitioners of which would, beginning with Le Nôtre, be on equal footing with other artists, including architects.

Thus, Boyceau was introduced to the *Cabinet* of de Thou and the *Académie putéane* of the brothers Pierre and Jacques Du Puy. Moreover, he became a good friend of Peyresc, president of the Parliament of Aix-en-Provence. Peyresc, one of the most brilliant intellectual figures of his time, was in touch with all that counted in Europe in the area of arts and sciences. In addition, he held our gentleman-gardener in such high esteem that he asked him to design the gardens of the archdiocese of Aix, and recommended him to his most famous friends—beginning with Rubens—as one of the best judges of the arts, including painting, in France.[22] Furthermore—proof that Boyceau satisfied the court completely—his position as "ordinary gentleman" was completed by that of "intendant general of the King's gardens," a very important position he would transmit to his nephew Jacques de Nemours.[23] His new position also gave him the notable privilege of living in the Tuileries, in an *hôtel* that Le Nôtre would occupy after him.

Thereafter, Boyceau's work would combine practice and theory. Everything suggests that he not only remodeled the Tuileries and defined Louis XIII's Versailles, but was the principle creator of the Luxembourg Garden, as Salomon de Bross was of the Palace. Hazelhurst has in fact remarked that the four other collaborators (Nicolas Descamps, Guillaume Boutin, Guy de La Brosse, and Louis de Limoges) were only "ordinary gardeners" placed under his direction; he has also demonstrated that, if Marie de Medici's explicit orders were to create in the Luxembourg a new Boboli—undoubtedly the most perfect example of a garden inspired by *The Dream of Poliphilo*—the arrangement of the Luxembourg Garden, "with its great simplicity" that "abandons the picturesque, the Boboli plan's quality of human scale, for a convincing sense of monumentality and grandeur," can only be attributed to a first-rate imagination. He thus concludes that "Boyceau de La Baraudière used an essentially Italian plan in order to transform it into something entirely French in form as well as spirit."

Which brings us back to the combination mentioned above: that of a virtually built work (even if the proofs of its attribution were destroyed in the fire that in 1690 devastated the

"Accounting bureau and offices of the buildings service of the King's House"),[24] following the expressible process of a theory exposed in a *Treatise* that announced its ambition in its title: to regulate gardening no longer according to rustic ways or the rites of the trade, but "according to the reasons of art and of nature."

Within the framework we have chosen for this book, which is more "romanesque" than historical, a close analysis of Boyceau's *Treatise* would be out of place. We will content ourselves instead with pointing out a few of its main themes.[25]

In the first place, the arrangement of the garden should proceed from a controlled process of reflection, not in order to obey any formal or routine a priori principle, but because the stakes involved are of a philosophical nature. The work should be entirely commanded by reason in that reason is the necessary path to a knowledge of the laws ruling nature, and thus to the art dependent upon it.

This fundamental postulate, which goes back to the new climate of thought impregnating the intellectual milieu Boyceau belonged to, was certainly never formulated in such an explicit fashion. However, as soon as he has to justify the originality of his *Treatise*, Boyceau reveals that his aim, in contrast with the "poor workers learning their trade from ignorant people," is to "penetrate to the reason of things, which is the guide of every good work, and very necessary in this one." And he goes on to distinguish, in matters of gardening, two classes of reasons: those commanding nature, upon which depend plants, soils, climates, the air, and waters, "which must all operate together"; and those of nature, which enable us to judge "the task before it is done, so that in getting down to the task we only work, reducing on a large scale the same things that we had designed on a small one."

This attitude would engender a change in the theory of mimesis:[26] if symmetry and variety are recommended, as in Alberti, because they are principles of nature translated into the growth of trees, leaves, and flowers, it is less out of a desire to represent the formal perfection of the *logos* than out of a conviction that natural laws can be understood, and therefore mastered. Whence the need, for the accomplished gardener, to be sufficiently acquainted with these laws. He must be a good practician—that goes without saying. But he must also be learned in a wide range of fields: botany, meteorology, geometry, arithmetic, etc. And if it is appropriate that he be versed in drawing and architecture, it is so that he can master the "science of proportions" without which he would be incapable of conceiving a harmonious parterre, or of correctly establishing the layout of paths, which must be ordered according to their dimensions. "In short," Boyceau concludes in the introduction to his third book,[27] "just as our first treatises depended on a knowledge of nature and the reasons of philosophy, it also depended upon the science of portraiture, the basis and foundation of all mechanics." The statement reveals a modern intellectual of his time, in whom the "enchanted naturalism" of the older humanism was erased to make way for a "philosophical mechanism" that was more pragmatic than metaphysical, that is to say closer to Gassendi than Descartes.[28]

In the second place, the space of the garden began, with Boyceau, to open up deliberately,[29] or rather to push its enclosure toward the horizon. Boyceau was undoubtedly not the first one to speak of perspective, to recommend the organization of elevated points of view permitting the discovery of vast expanses. But whereas Alberti saw in these proceedings an invitation to the eye to leave the garden and roam the countryside, the city, and even the sea, Boyceau's aim was completely other: to create, at the heart and within the space ordered by the gardener, the sensation of the infinite: "In them [the perfect square or the oblong] one finds straight lines, which make the paths long and beautiful and give them a pleasant perspective: for over their length the strength of vision, declining, makes the smallest things tend toward a point, which makes them more pleasant." This was, in our opinion, a crucial rupture, going back to nothing less than the epistemological break Koyré has convincingly explained in his book, the title of which seems to have been chosen to illustrate our argument: *From the Closed World to the Infinite Universe*. Indeed, if one considers the fact that, deliberately or not, the garden is a reduced representation of the perfect universe— divine or pagan paradise, what does it matter?—it goes without saying that it was enclosed in an era when cosmology, geocentric for the Greeks or anthropocentric during the Middle Ages, represented the world, following the Aristotelian model, like a sequence of envelopes forming a group of concentric bubbles. But while this vision was being attacked—and it certainly must have been at the *Académie putéane* and in Peyresc's entourage—it became logical that the idea of the limit of a microcosmic paradise underwent a crisis and that the new idea of the infinite entered in the garden.

One can call this a risky hypothesis. Or an intuition, founded upon no precise text, that is trying to turn a simple gardener into an actor in the history of thought and to present a "banal" change in sensibility as a shift of philosophical importance. Be that as it may, the case speaks for itself. Nothing permits us to think that Boyceau had a clear idea of what he was undoing and reconstructing according to another perspective; but the new spirit of the times spoke through him in spaces, unconsciously or not, but in an active fashion.

Thus it does not seem out of place to see in Boyceau a kind of gardening Malherbe, formed as he was in the Renaissance but already inclining toward classical reason. Especially when we consider that the poet celebrated by Boileau sang, in his famous sonnet inspired by Fontainebleau, the new spatial order that he saw already rising and that he greeted with his warmest wishes:

Beaux et grands bastiments d'éternelle structure
Superbes de matière et d'ouvrages divers,
Ou le plus digne Roy qui soit en l'Univers
Aux miracles de l'Art fait céder la Nature;

Beau parc, et beaux jardins, qui dans vostre closture
Avez toujours des fleurs et des ombrages vers,
Non sans quelque Démon qui deffend aux hyvers
D'en effacer jamais l'agréable peinture.

[Lovely and large buildings of eternal structure
Superb in matter and varied workmanship,
Where the most worthy King in the Universe
Makes Nature yield to the miracles of Art;

Lovely park, and lovely gardens, which in your enclosure
Always have flowers and green shade,
Not without some Demon who prevents winters
From ever erasing its pleasant painting.]

"Where the most worthy King in the Universe / Makes Nature yield to the miracles of Art." The vision of the age of Louis XIV is already present in this elegantly concise formula, concentrated according to a harmonious turn that fuses the poetic with the political. Space, form, inert or living matter, all must yield before the sovereign in order to be organized according to his will. Nature loses its enchantment in order to become an object-machine— an object commanded by the laws of a body of technician-artists whose mission is to form it in the image of the divine ideal of the monarchic order.[30] Boyceau describes precisely how this body of technician-artists should be formed:

Just as we choose for our garden young, well-developed trees from good stock with straight trunks and roots firmly planted on all sides: so let us take a young boy of good nature, good spirit, the son of a good worker, not delicate, thus appearing that he will have good strength of body with age, and, waiting for that strength, we will teach him to read and write, to portray and draw; for upon portraiture depend the knowledge and judgment of beautiful things, and the foundation of all mechanics; not that I mean he should go as far as painting, or sculpture, but that he should apply himself principally to the specifics concerning his art, such as compartments, foliages, moresques, and arabesques,[31] and others, of which parterres are ordinarily composed: once he begins to improve in portraiture, he will have to climb to Geometry for the plans, departments, measurements, and alignments, and, if he is a good boy, he will reach Architecture for a knowledge of the parts needed by structures in relief, and will learn Arithmetic to calculate the expenses that may pass through his hands, so that he makes no mistakes and so does not let himself be cheated when he needs purchases or supplies for planning, or other materials. All of these sciences must be learned in youth, if possible, so that when he is old enough to work in the gardens, he begins, with a spade, to plow with the other workers, learning how to lift soils, bend, straighten, and tie wood for works in relief; draw designs upon the ground, or those that will be ordered from him, plant and clip the parterres, and with a long-handled sickle the hedges, and several other specifics regarding the embellishments of pleasure gardens; there remains the utility garden producing edible fruits and plants, and requiring no less intelligence or work than the other: the knowledge of the nature of very different soils is even more necessary there, that of various manures, of the difference of climates and aspects, of the winds and the moon, so that one can use prognostication to foresee the weather; one must have a knowledge of plants, which is a great science; know their nature and the culture they require, the seasons when to sow their seeds, to advance them, transplant them to make them grow, delay and preserve, blanch and tenderize, and still an infinite number of other specifics, which the gardener must know in order to form and teach his people, for such and so many things are not done by a single man.

It is clear from the first sentence ("son of a good worker, not delicate") that this long list of recommendations concerns neither Boyceau himself, nor his nephew Jacques de Nemours, trained to succeed him, for in this case it is not a matter of fashioning a royal intendant, but an ordinary gardener—though he might be skilled and competent enough to become one day "ordinary gardener of the King." It concerns gardeners like the Mollets, for example, or like the Le Nôtres.

There has already been much discussion, in learned circles interested in exploring the genesis of the French formal garden, about the following question: who was André Le Nôtre's true spiritual father—Boyceau, Claude, or André Mollet? A discussion we deem it wise to stay out of, given that the essential, in our eyes, is that they worked together, Boyceau contributing a general learnedness that the Mollets evidently never mastered, while the Mollets (and a few other master gardeners such as the Descamps, or fountain-makers such as the Francines) implemented a slowly matured practical knowledge.

As for the Mollets, everything began—as far as we can tell—with a certain Jacques, gardener in the service of the duc d'Aumale. His son Claude—the one Olivier de Serres had such great respect for—learned his trade by his side and admired his learning enough to pay him tribute in his *Treatise of Plans and Gardening* published after his death.

Michel Conan tells us that, as first gardener of the king,

he was responsible for the royal gardens of Saint-Germain-en Laye, the Tuileries, Montceaux-en-Brie, and Fontainebleau. He then had the job of organizing the gardeners' work, and it was thus that he had Pierre Le Nôtre and his son Jean as collaborators in the Tuileries. His wife was moreover the godmother of one of Pierre's grandchildren, André Le Nôtre, born in 1613. André probably learned his trade as an apprentice under the direction of Claude Mollet, as his own sons, Claude, André, Jacques, and Noël Mollet had done. It was undoubtedly shortly after the death of Claude Mollet, in 1649, that André Le Nôtre, who had been named gardener of the Tuileries in 1637, became chief gardener there, thus assuring preeminence over Claude Mollet the Younger. The latter had three brothers, André, Noël, and Jacques, all three gardeners. In the years around 1615, when Claude, the father, was working on his *Theater of Plans and Gardening*, he had his children execute a group of drawings of parterres, *bosquets*, and labyrinths. . . . We know that Claude Mollet, the son, worked at Versailles, at the Louvre, and in the Tuileries, that Jacques was from 1612 on a gardener at Fontainebleau, where he died in 1622. We do not know what became of Noël. André, on the other hand, fared brilliantly. He occupied important positions in the court of England, in Holland, then in Sweden and, finally, at the end of his life, once again in England. The following generation seems to have been less well known. Claude's oldest son, Charles, was a gardener at the Louvre, and his brother Gabriel helped André in England, where he died around 1660; André's son, Jean, succeeded his father in Sweden and was widely employed there by the Swedish nobility. But it was perhaps *The Garden of Pleasure* by André, published in Swedish, in German, and in French in Stockholm, in 1651, then translated into English in 1670, that best assured the Mollet family's international circulation of the art of the garden in the French style.[32]

This biographical summary is striking. Everything, in this sequence of destinies woven together by family ties, some of them obvious, others more obscure, draws a line of artist-technicians adhering to a model typical of the period: that of musical dynasties, for example, which tends to be better known. The father, using a paddle if necessary, raised his son in his image, transmitting to him a heritage that would make him prosper or at least a trade that might enable him to find a job. The pattern was characteristic of the societies of the ancien régime: the Mollets and the Le Nôtres were for the garden what the Couperins, Scarlattis, and Bachs would soon be for music: the emerged part of a less brilliant network of instrumentalist-conceptualizers whose destiny would remain relatively hidden.

But if Claude Mollet the elder and his son André were creators with a broad vision, only André Le Nôtre had the good fortune and happiness to express genius. A genius that shone forth in his first great work: the gardens of Vaux-le-Vicomte for the superintendent Fouquet.

The fountain of Arethusa, colored
drawing from 1714.
Photo © Lauros-Giraudon.

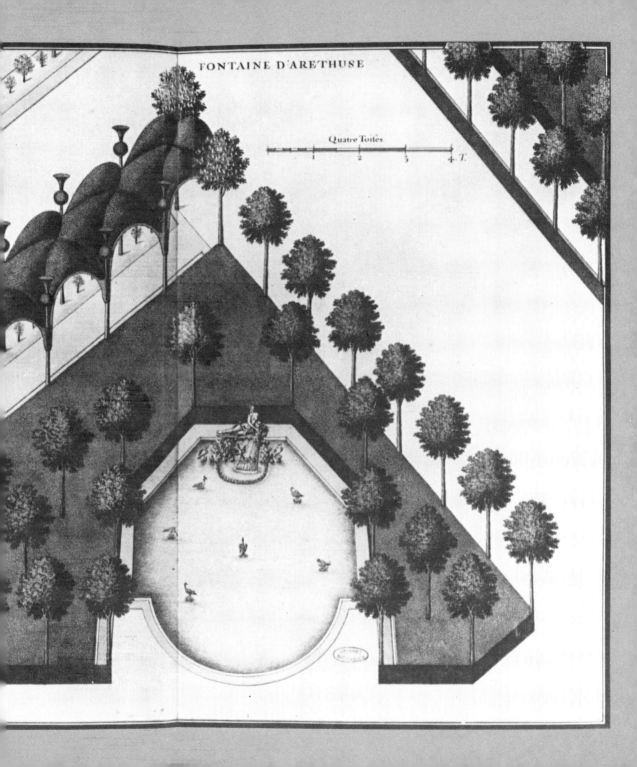

FONTAINE D'ARETHUSE

Quatre Toiſes.

1   2   3   4. T.

When Hyacinth's letter was brought to me, inviting me to the feast Oronte was having on his property at Vaux, I was in my apartment. I was in that state of light melancholy that often disturbs women while they are women. My heart, moreover, was pained by the sad rumbling over Oronte's head. I had always considered Hyacinth's friend and protector more than divine in the grace not only of his being but also of his spirit, and in all the qualities of beauty, wealth, intelligence, and genius that he demonstrated in the conduct of his affairs.

The complaint, come from above, was that Oronte was going too far in setting himself apart from the ordinary, and gossip was attacking the courteousness of his spirit as well as the magnificence of his estate, especially a certain work that he had just finished building in the beautiful region of Brie, paying homage to the Graces and insulting the imbeciles.

Meanwhile, as the heat of the season increased my weariness, I began to imagine that Hyacinth, brother of Pan and son of Orpheus, no longer loved me. So that, when the letter came into my hands through the devoted Madame de C., I found myself hating those gossipy tales more than I can describe and rushed to arrange my trip with Altée and Célimène, my very devoted friends. These two women asked a talented young couturier of the Court to come, and he, in the night, made a dress for me out of Siamese cloth the color of irises and green meadows, which he adorned with fine pearls, baubles, and a lace collar with *punto in aera*, while Madame Bailleul gave me a serpentine hairdo tied up with a silk ribbon. It was in this manner and attire that I left the city.

In accordance with etiquette, Hyacinth, whose comedy-ballet had been performed at the last Carnival and who was acquiring a reputation as a fable-teller, thereby exciting both gossip and envy, had climbed into another carriage. We followed the joyous course of the river, crossing quiet meadows and charming woods. Never had the wheat, which was being harvested here and there, been so golden, or the farmlands so alive with sound. "I'm coming, I'm coming," I cried, more joyously than usual, and I asked the carriage to stop so that I might compliment my beauty with one of those blue flowers that grow among the rye.

According to what Hyacinth had told me—he had spent good days there—the gardens and buildings belonging to Oronte were devoted to beauty; I had been transported by his description of them. So that, since my love attaches itself to what he loves, my only wish since then had been to visit that place in order to admire it in person to my heart's content. I had, however, not dared to say so. We had barely gone a few leagues out of the city when, without worrying about what people might think, I sat down beside my companion who was dozing like young Eros. And for the entire trip we had good weather, a good road, and beautiful countryside.

The heat was so intense, however, that Hyacinth woke up:

"Really," he said, "it's a lovely day. Let us pray that Vulcan does not come with his lightning. Monsieur de La Quintinie's new plants would be damaged, and the layout of Monsieur Le Nostre's paths, which he thought out so carefully, would be completely muddled. You should know that our host's guests include the king and his household."

"The king! Come on, you are teasing me! Surely Oronte is a sparkling fellow, but I have heard people say that the light he bestows upon all he owns has offended the king and his new minister. Remember that verse of Horace's that you have asked me to appreciate a hundred times: *Lightning strikes the top of mountains*."

" . . . *Feriunt que summos Fulgura montes*," Hyacinth murmured.

Shortly after this, I returned to my carriage, and Hyacinth stretched out comfortably in his. We entered by the great gate guarded by the giant Terms. We admired the brick façades reinforced with white stones and the high roofs of the commons. Then we entered the outer courtyard.

I'm here! Finally, I'm here! (I said to myself).

I adjusted my cape so that it covered my shoulders and adorned my hair with a small hat of blue taffeta in the English style, with a gold braid and a garland.

On the other side of the vast staircase that preceded it, Oronte's castle rose proudly in its beauty. I contemplated the large wings and the corner pavilions, the front with its three large arched doors topped by a pediment adorned with sculptures, and a large lantern reflected admirably in the water of the moats.

Describing a half-circle, the carriages stopped one by one in front of the steps where

Oronte and Cleanthia were standing. Cleanthia was wearing a dress of gold on gold, embroidered with pearls, and the corsage embroidered with a leafy design was brocaded with a scattering of rubies. Oronte, handsomer than Rinaldo in Tasso's *Jerusalem Delivered*, had a green doublet adorned with fine emeralds and shoulder caps of white silk, puffed-out chausses with gold aglets, and cavalier shoes. Standing on the last step, they greeted their guests. My carriage stopped right at the foot. Four valets wearing a tight costume in velvet brocade with silk threads and solid-colored stockings rushed forward to open the folding steps. I greeted Cleanthia, then looked about for Hyacinth, whom I saw shaking off the dust that the road had cast on his clothing. He stood in the brilliant light, looking distracted; the heat of the day had, however, diminished a bit. I went to join the crowd bustling about on the elegant *parterre de broderie* of the gardens on the façade side and along the double basin situated on the left side, which dominated a parterre adorned with an egret crown of spurting streams that rained down with much noise.

"That is the *Basin of the Crown*," someone said.

The garden, which was illuminated here by embroidered parterres and there by reflecting waters, had been composed in a valley softened by an extraordinary mind. In fact, it gave the effect of an enchanted clearing, in that it was located between two woods, the near and far edges of which could be seen in the distance.

"Isn't it the *luogo d'incanto* that I painted for you?" Hyacinth asked, smiling.

To which I answered: "The more my eyes remain on these gardens, the more I am charmed."

"Do not turn your amorous eyes away from them, unless it is to make me share their beauty."

We conversed in the shade of the linden trees bordering a path that seemed to be restraining the trees of the forest. Then we returned to the castle where the crowd had grown.

"The king!" someone cried. "The king!"

It was six o'clock in the evening. The shadows on the ground moved like the seven colors of Iris's scarf. The king's carriage, drawn by six white horses and containing the king, his brother, the duchess de Valentinois, and the countesses d'Armagnac and de Guiche, came through the great gate. It was followed by the carriage of the queen mother with her maids of honor, all dressed in heavy ceremonial dresses embroidered with silver, pearls, emeralds, sapphires, gold, and rubies. Madame was traveling in a litter. The suite included the Grand Condé and the duke d'Enghien, the dukes de Beaufort and de Guise, many lords and officers of the kingdom's high offices. The procession opened and closed with the *gardes-françaises* and armed musketeers.

"Doesn't it look like a military procession?" I asked.

"It is true that the king, like a second Mars, was made to win battles," answered Hyacinth, who seemed as amazed at the spectacle as I was.

"I have heard it said that the king has no affection for our friend," I continued.

"I have heard the same," Hyacinth answered, suddenly pensive, "but I am not a firm believer in all these rumors. The king is haughty who brings down his enemies with a slap; but our friend loves him and is endlessly devoted . . . Look at this lovely day, now that Apollo and Phoebus are calling us in unison to their pleasures."

Oronte went to open the door for the king, while many valets unfolded the carriage steps. Oronte also bowed. The king lowered his eyes, indicating he had seen him. They both climbed the stairs leading to the castle.

"Ah," I said to the poet, "don't you see that, although the king is great and well constituted and the majesty of his person is worthy of admiration, there is also some kind of marvelous light shining out of Oronte's eyes, for his spirit not only has the brilliance that nature has given him, having cultivated it with as much care as Mr. Le Nostre used in tracing his gardens."

"Undoubtedly," Hyacinth answered, keeping his eyes fixed on the two creatures who were at that moment standing together on the last step of the staircase. "*Quel idolo d'errori, idol d'inganno, quel che dal volgo insano onor poscia fu detto chi nostra natura 'l feo tiranno,*" he added.

These words did not belie the ambiguity of the situation. Moreover, I was beginning to feel tormented, sensing that, like many a lord and lady assembled there, in a century when too much wit leads to a fall, Oronte, who, it was said, was being worked by a strange fever, would have done better to control himself than to flirt so ardently with danger.

"May Heaven preserve him!" I thought. But Hyacinth, sensing that I was experiencing some sudden pain, said:

"Well, madame, although my heart knows not how to choose between the lily and the rose, do not try so hard to unravel the confusion, but admire instead the elegance of the Ionic order the architect used in this Arcadian spot. The three divinities tormenting you are monsters come from Vulcan's Empire. Allow me, I pray you, the privilege of placing your colors among those of these flowers."

Separating myself from the ranks of the envious, I set off into Laughter and Games, between the antiques of colored marble in the vestibule, the brocaded furniture, and the gilded chairs. My friend had accustomed me to the fact that Nature hides its treasures, to the abundant and sweet mercy of streams and forests, but I saw here such beautiful varieties that for a moment my mind was moved beyond all bothersome thought.

I admired the great caryatids of the oval Salon, the paintings, and tapestries. Many people were going there. On the one side I saw men doing nothing but trying to gain distinction among the women with their haughty words, titivating and affecting their sentences when, full of envy, they added gall instead of honey. There were also beautiful and lively ladies, whose brilliance contrasted with those whose beauty of ceruse, powder, and whiting was heightened only by art, affectation, and ornament, with their pearls and ribbons.

"My friend," I said, "I see there are great rarities in this place. Do me the favor of explaining them."

"Yes," Hyacinth answered, "the most exquisite things that can be found in the world are, so to speak, assembled here in abbreviated form. Recognize Mars representing *Valor*, Mercury *Vigilance*, Vertumnus *Abundance*, Jupiter *Power*; here, *Peace Restoring Abundance* . . ."

In the Hall of Muses, people were marveling over the ceiling where *Night Asleep* was painted. Hyacinth, in love with *The Chamber of Jupiter's Daughters*, had already described it to me a hundred times. He had even undertaken a composition on the subject in lyric and heroic verse, the structure of which—so he had told me—he had found in Indian tales and in the Dreams of the *Romance of the Rose*, of Colonna's *Poliphilo*, and Cicero's *Scipio*, under the pretense that reading the *Dreams* had caused Vaux to appear to him in a dream. I had the great fortune of hearing the verses from him right then:

"By calm vapors softly upheld / Her head on her arm, and her arm on the clouds / She lets flowers fall, and does not scatter them."

Upon which I smiled, and begged Hyacinth to take me to the gardens for a bit of fresh air.

The air had grown languid and heavy, and a low murmur of discord coming from the room Oronte had intended for the king, across from the painting of *Time Taking Truth from the Heavens*, had made me anxious. Oronte's heraldic squirrel and his *Quo non ascendam* seemed menacing, like the storm rumbling intermittently in the clouds above the chef d'oeuvre. And in my heart of hearts I mused: Ah! how can one serve the gods without exciting the envy of the petty!

We went down into the gardens laid out in long terraces up to the narrow valley of the Anqueil, where Le Nostre had dug the Canal de la Poêle and raised more than a hundred jets of water unequal in height but equal in beauty. Once the king and the queen mother had climbed into the barouches prepared for the occasion, we admired the three-tiered sequence of terraces, basins, statues, *broderies* of flowers and grass, against a background of red gravel, and the sequence of lawns between the paths and counterpaths. Near Hyacinth and me, there was a basin in the shape of a circle surrounded by four little cupids holding shells above their heads. It sparkled as its water poured forth and fell into small squares covered with turf. The music thus produced was so sweet that, like Oronte's guest, my spirit recovered its natural harmony for a moment.

But the king ceaselessly inquired about everything, and Oronte responded with the most charming courtesy. He seemed not to notice that the ire swelling the heart of his majestic host had not stopped growing since his arrival at Vaux. It now resembled the fury of the sky at sunset when its colors disappear under black spirals.

The courtiers were releasing a mounting flood of envious words.

"He has a gold mine in his house," one whispered. Or, from another: "He pays the queen mother, her confessor, ladies-in-waiting, and chambermaids, the Jesuits, the Parliament, the Academies, the ambassadors, the artists, lords, poets, mistresses, the king's doctors, and the king himself."

"He is the *Patron*," someone said.

"One is pensioned as soon as one wants to be," said another.

Hyacinth, in his dreamy naieveté, yawned at the marvels. As for myself, having ears only for the rumors being sown against Oronte, I wondered if it was possible that Oronte was being so liberal in order to acquire favor and to raise temples of caprice and frivolity upon the ruins of His Highness. By means of what monstrous confusion would he have bought the ephemeral eternity of gold at a price that any sensible man would have been ashamed to pay for peace? When only beauty was visible in all the things he took part in, the belief that Oronte was making projects contrary to the well-being and peace of our kingdom could only be the product of an extravagant imagination. I tried to discover the truth that might be found on certain points, in these opinions. I asked myself many questions, and considered many answers, interrupting my stroll only to unravel these confusions, in the spinning labyrinth of ladies and courtiers.

We reached the Grotto sheltering the Nymphs of Vaux, whose tear-filled eyes seemed fixed upon the king. I then had an appalling vision in which I glimpsed a gaping hell: the king, blinded by his minister, going up to Oronte and arresting him on the spot. I shared my fear with Hyacinth who, expressing complete astonishment, replied that I was quite mad to think in this fashion:

"Forgive me, madame," he said, "if I do not care to enter into such extravagances, even in your amiable company. Confine yourself to the conduct of our friend, who has never had any other goal but to honor our king, and never any other intention than that one, to which no one has brought more design or art."

"I quite understand," I answered, "but I beg you not to ignore the rumor spread about by the flatterers of the Palais-Royal. A merit as brilliant as his was needed until now in order not to be obscured, but history has taught us by example that the intelligence of extraordinary souls is not always strong enough to prevent the malice of the vulgar."

Hyacinth interrupted my discourse: "Your spirit is cluttered with too many stories. You know my position on the subject, and madame, you cannot make me express myself in your fashion. Take these rumors for the smoke they make, and, I beg you, do not let it blacken this sublime day."

These reflections, although wise and profound, did not convince me, because Oronte's conduct seemed, with each beauty he showed the king, to imply his fall with even greater precipitation. A flash of fire suddenly split the sky, in which I did not hesitate to read an ill omen, while the feast continued.

When we had reached the Spray of Water, which was making much noise, the king went and placed himself at the summit of the noble *vertugadin* closing the perspective. In that place one might have thought one could see the fire separating the mountains of Calpe and Abyla, while one could easily see that the king was the Son of a God, like the descendant of Perseus, the thief of the fruits of the gardens of the Hesperides, and ruling over a modern Argo.

The king looked at the gardens as though he were about to fall into a fit of rage, just as Hercules had done against the birds of Lake Stymphalus, against all that struck his eyes.

Friend and reader, I am afraid I will lose your good graces and you may resent me for showing people whose merit you so respect in such a cruel place, if, having only demonstrated my devotion to beauty, I do not warn you of the dreadful rigor of the denouement.

As far as I can tell, there is no man who, thinking that he is being scoffed at, instead of taking the time to persuade his mind that his reasoning stands on powerless foundations, does not on the contrary let himself boil, fixing his sight on what he lacks, rejecting the man when he would have done better to become attached to him. As for the one who owns, he cannot prevent himself from putting forward what he has, losing everything by his desire to show everything. This happens rather frequently.

But, in the story I am narrating, the spirit of the two people in this situation was, deep down, vast and elevated, given that one was a king and the other a very great man of the Kingdom. Forced to admire one man, I loved the other.

On the one hand, the glory of the State, on the other the glory of beauty. To which one might add one other thing: it was during the feast itself that horror plotted the darkness of its sons. And, even though Hell is a fable at the center of the earth, Hell was about to fall here, more horrifying and sad in light of the contrast developing between the continuing kindness and the horror that I must still describe.

We entered the castle for dinner. Their Majesties were served in vermeil crockery, while Lulli's beautiful music rose under the darkening shadows.

Pheasants, ortolans, quails, partridges, bisques, stews, pork pies, fruits, pastries, and all kinds of wines were served in five or six courses, directed by the sublime Vatel whose tragic fate would, about ten years later, accord with the terrible law about to swoop down in this very place.

Meanwhile, everyone ate and drank until they could no more. And the gravity of the situation seemed to increase as the pleasure mounted.

When supper was over, we went to the Gate of Water. It consisted of a triple terrace from which jets spurted in parallel columns: everyone exclaimed over the genius Monsieur Le Nostre had manifested here. We took our places around Their Majesties. The moon was making all the stars shine in the heavens, less however than the more than a hundred torches making each one glow. Less than the king who—painted in the color of gold and sitting on an armchair next to the queen mother, Monsieur, Madame, and the laughing Henriette—shined on the surrounding countryside with the fire of his gaze and of his clothing.

While waiting for the comedy that was to be performed for us, my eyes roamed over the new grace of the curved lines, accompanied by knots and arabesques of fine turf, where the elements of the design, devoid of symmetry and filled in by sand, black soil, brick dust, and iron filings, were of a ravishing delicacy. First parterres in compartments, constituted by box trees forming other arabesques, and colored soils reproduced an identical motif in their two halves; then came the parterres with motifs, with stars-of-Bethlehem, martagon lilies, aconites, peonies, snapdragons, damask roses, and cabbage roses; in the distance, near the castle, the magnificent embroidered parterre . . .

Certainly, the vows shining under the lights of the stars and lanterns were great. But I admired, even more than the harmoniously arranged parterres, the Canal, the Square of Water, the basins, and all the fountains projecting clouds of crystal droplets into the nocturnal air.

As I looked at the obedient grasses, box trees, yews, and beeches, this well-ordered nature, which Hyacinth had described to me so many times, seemed to be sighing from the effort of so much allegiance. The exercise of so many virtues exceeded what human reason is capable of imagining. And above all, weren't there in this place too many visible miracles destined to glorify the one who was not the guest?

As Hyacinth laughed over the machineries of Torelli, the great sorcerer whom Oronte and the Court had acquired at great expense from Italy, I let myself sink alone into the miserable suffering that preyed on my heart as well as my spirit. Molière, miming the fool and dressed in town clothes, appeared and asked His Majesty to order the performance before retiring—which the king did with a movement of his eyes.

I will not struggle to describe the comedy that gave Hyacinth so much pleasure.

Without being able to enjoy the least bit of rest, I felt that things were in such a way that the brewing storm was about to release its full rage. I thought about the happiness of those whose destinies were taking shape between the games and feasts. From all sides of the woods, satyrs and dryads made us laugh before they made us cry, so that as the fable mixed with reality, I thought I saw the Demons pursuing the daughters of the Alseids right into their obscure, singing grottoes. A shell rose and opened, and out of it stepped Mademoiselle Béjart, the actress, surrounded by twenty jets of water, open in a shower. She recited a prologue by Pellisson extolling the king: "In order to see on these lovely sites the greatest king of the world / Mortals, I have come to you from my deep grotto . . ." I cannot stop myself here: I have to describe the severe expression that the king wore throughout and the dark humor that marked his young forehead as he sat, as restive to the comic purpose as to the buffoon. The comedy did not uncrease his brow, for the tragedy was progressing, sinking Oronte further into hell with each step.

Gilded gondolas trimmed with white damask advanced on the Grand Canal where I thought I saw Charon passing in his fatal boat. A concert was given at the Orangerie where the gilded fruits of La Quintinie dotted the foliage. In the *bosquets* oboes and flutes offered a thousand different charms, brightening the scene harmoniously. At the edge of the Parterre of Water, there had been erected, in case of a storm, a tent of white damask containing ornamental buffets with terraces of mirrors laden with silver. And while Eraste exclaimed: "Under what star, good God, must I have been born / To be always assassinated by bores . . ." or "What? Bores again! Hold! Let these knaves here be taken away . . ." , I heard a thundering voice exclaim a verse by Scudéry: "I sing the conqueror of conquerors of the earth." The ballet was followed by the comedy and many other ballets and processions of pall-mall and bowl players, *Suisses*, Cobblers, and Shepherds. In short, I would say that everything had been put in place to enchant us, as though to give us a chance to taste a piece of Arcadia.

The Great Mademoiselle, in ecstasy under the artifice of a greenery-tapestry hung upon the greenery of the woods, said: "It is an enchanted place," while I caught Oronte taking his friend M. de Gourville aside: "Is it beautiful enough?" "Too much so, my friend, too much so."

Only beauty—I said to myself, following the Court from the Square of Water to the Grand Cascades, at the end of the gardens and at the beginning of the park, in order to witness the fireworks—can balance the vanity of everything. For everything is full of false lights. With how much fury did those lampoons composed some time ago about kind Oronte, a friend of Letters and Arts, try to make us believe that his own greatness was not compatible with the king's interests? Why did they take to attacking the little bit of order that appeared in affairs when the bloodshed of war was barely over?

The Court was laughing amid the display of lace, ribbons, breeches, trains three, nine, and twelve feet long, brilliants, gems, and diamonds of the Temple.

Four hundred girandoles, in the shape of fleurs-de-lys, indicating names and representing numbers, suddenly illuminated the castle, highlighting the lines of Le Vau's architecture, the sequence of gardens, and the brilliant patches of water. Statues of fire appeared on the balustrade of the Grotto, Roman candles furrowed the entire sky, Bengal lights illuminated the curtains of rocks and leaves, grenades fanned out, and fired wicks lit up the constructions of fire from above the constructions of stone. And on the Grand Canal a whale moved, releasing serpentine rockets and crackling bursts, while suns turning in opposite directions like immense flowers came out of Torelli's machines, which were raining down in a golden shower.

After the first display, in which we had seen water turn away from the earth and climb the sky, we were given one of fire. It was as though the figure of the Sun, which Oronte had had painted in the middle of his palace, appeared on its horses in apotheosis; the sculpted stone did not tremble under the burning breath, nor did the half-velvet cut grass of Genoa, the fine Persian or Turkish tapestries of the two great parterres open on either side of the central path: one might have said that all of Vesuvius's ardor had been turned into marvelous images in the sky that further demonstrated the glory of our host as it lit up the splendor below. Besides the place where we were standing, all of the castle and gardens could be seen by the subtle effects of the mathematics Le Nostre was said to have learned from Desargues and Mersenne as well as from René Descartes, whose work written in French had come to him from the entourage of the cardinal de Richelieu.

I tried to tear myself away from the incomparable beauty soaring out of this garden of fiery gems and silver crystals. I wished to reflect upon the cunning of an art that can produce so many sumptuous decors. It provides a sequence of forms and series that, in order to lead us back to the dazzling center, makes us escape it by decentering the points of view in the manner of those Italian gardens that open wide onto the countryside. Incapable of finding an answer, I considered two questions: the first being how truth chains itself to falsehood, and the second being the nature of that fantastic center the Jansenist Pascal had thought was everywhere and nowhere.

Although a woman and knowing that my mind was weak, having its seat in the heart and not in the pineal gland at the center of the brain, I felt sure, regarding the first point, that Oronte whose lips poured only sweet words, had a mind as crafty as the art he had put in his gardens, concerning which, past midnight as it was, no sensible person could have said where they began or where they ended. The main thing was to seduce through a display of wonders, but, in acting in this way, Oronte was rushing promptly to his ruin because the king had already understood through many inquiries the snare of these delightful displays. However, he was king and knew that it was the will of reason that He should be adored. As for the second point, it seemed to follow clearly from the first that I have just mentioned, that is to say that, in spite of all that Oronte had been able to show with supreme artifice, the center was in every place where the king was.

Once the dazzling spectacle of lights had ended, everyone followed the king in order to taste those many exquisite things, designated by the word *ambigu* and made of fruits, ices, and sweets, which soon brought my attention back to the situation, although twenty-four invisible violins had begun to play marvelously in an invisible loggia.

At that moment, Oronte proposed to the king that he go sleep in the room that he, Oronte, had prepared for him, having chosen the lamps of the walls, the porcelain sent by the Jesuit brothers of Japan, the lacquer come from China via Holland, the paintings discovered by Poussin in Italy, and the pieces of furniture covered with Genoa velvet, a taste he had acquired from his friends at the Hôtel de Rambouillet. But the king refused. At which point Oronte, in a supreme gesture, offered Vaux itself to the king: "Sire, all this is yours." "No," answered the king, "everything belongs to the Kingdom." It was then two in the morning. The entourage was silent and the atmosphere close.

The king gave the signal for departure.

A tremendous cracking sound was heard, which was answered by a thousand trumpets together as though for a last terrible battle. Invisible legions rushed from the dome, waking the castle from its massive sleep. A shower of serpents raised itself to a majestic height in the light of the lantern and made the night turn pale as it whistled by. Vibrating with a horrible shake of the tail against the white horizon, it stretched out along the tormented palace. I recognized the flat, treacherous head of the envious minister's arms.

The flame ran in the shape not of an azure snake writhing upon a stake but of a furious serpent, full of envy and hatred: hungry for everything, his blazing eyes set fire to the palace, which, suddenly lifted high, gave way piece by piece in a sinister crumbling of sparkling gold.

A violent spurt of blood splashed in a red panache against the stone of a jigsawed basin, while a dull roar and agonizing cries reached our ears.

At that moment, two of the queen's horses reared up and fell into the gaping moats.

Immobile in the center of this grandiose spectable, Oronte, who had already been wounded by the iron bite of humiliation, stood alone in the black smoke of a palace set on fire by rays more powerful than those of Phoebus, waiting for His Solemnity's iniquitous verdict.

Dear reader, as it was for Phaeton who, because he brought the magnificent Chariot of the Sun too close to the earth, almost consumed it, so it was for Oronte and the palace of Vaux.

The king, led by his minister, placed him in a dungeon for more than twenty years, until his death, taking everything that he had.

If you have not recognized the names in this story, learn that the king was the fourteenth, Louis his first name, Oronte was Nicolas Fouquet, superintendent of finances, and Hyacinth, Jean de La Fontaine. As for the serpent, or worse, the grass snake, which I mentioned before, recognize him as the infamous Colbert.

And moreover, if you have not recognized Molière, Corneille, Pellisson, and many literary figures and ladies, for propriety's sake, I will not reveal their names.

As for myself, only know that I am one of them and do not care, however, to glorify my name.

But if you happen to walk along the banks of the Anqueil, or if you happen to pass through the great gate of the castle, think of listening to the sad and beautiful voice of the man who was dear to us all, and who, by beauty, in less than a day enabled us to enjoy eternity. Listen to his sonorous voice proclaim:

"Stand back, Sun, I have uncrowned your Kingdom! And I do not fear the infinite darkness! Stand back! I have crossed into Erebus and jumped across the Acheron! I am not a groveling man and I have no taste for war, even if Mars has raised upon me his shining cemeteries in the dark dungeon where my spirit knocks! Back! For luxury and poetry, pleasure and light are not illuminated by infirm and false reason!"

Exit gate of the Parc des Plaisirs du
Prince, by J.-J. Lequeu.
Photo © Bibliothèque Nationale,
Paris.

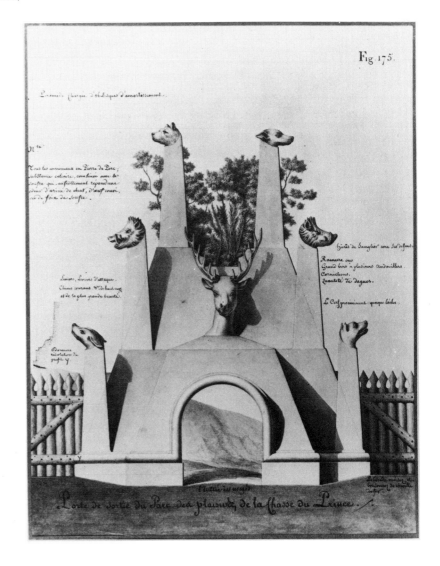

Allée Five

*All that is bizarre in man, and that is vagabond in
him, and wild, could undoubtedly be contained in
these two syllables: garden.*
ARAGON, Le Paysan de Paris

"The face of the theater is changing," Louis XIV declared, according to Brienne, when he announced to the Council on March 9, 1661, his decision to govern himself.

The entire drama of Vaux is contained in that formula.

One scene, two characters.

First, the court, the extravagant prop of a stage set planted in the middle of the plain of Brie. Resembling those rich trompe l'oeils or astounding machines that delighted the spectators of Cavalli and Corneille at the Palais-Royal, this court not yet trained in the ways of monarchy, a not yet completely courtesan court, covered itself indecently with powders, brocade, lace, and mythological luxuries without any awareness that it was itself only an ornament, mere human furniture parading shamelessly on a sea of poverty where each man's lot was to slave away in silence.

As for the characters, there was the superintendent at his peak: dripping gold, with a real taste for magnificence and the arts. A figure of the triumphant baroque, his eagerness to stake his glory upon an uncertain evaluation of the future was mitigated by the dizzying prospect of a fall that had haunted his soul like a night sun. Let us not forget that his love for the hieratic splendor of Le Brun's allegories was coupled with an equally strong passion for the tormented power of Puget, whose genius he alone, or almost, was capable of measuring.

And finally, there was the king, sure of his right to incarnate the world for the simple reason that he was king and that the troubled era in which he had spent his youth convinced him of the fact that the top rank was not meant to be shared, especially with regard to the mission that he, and he alone, had received from God, making him a god himself, and that charged him to organize the realm below upon the hierarchical model of the Most High.

"The face of the theater is changing." The King subdued the *Grands*, absolutism put the ministers back in their places, and classical order triumphed over baroque "excess," but it was all a theatrical production. "All the world's a stage / And all the men and women merely players." And if the drama continued far beyond that night at Vaux, if Louis XIV hesitated and multiplied his maneuvers, it was because he knew that he ought not to step out of his role or break up the setting where his fate was being played out. There was sure to be a rupture, one that, relegating Fouquet to darkness—and the baroque theatrical production with him—would open a new order of theater in the century. But this was no revolution. Classicism was only "the tautest rope of the baroque," as Henri Maldiney said in a formula quoted by Ponge.[1]

In choosing the feast at Vaux rather than the completion of the Louvre[2] as the theater of this fracture, we are avoiding the somewhat vain pleasure of breaking with an already well-established tradition. We are listening to Louis XIV and Colbert. For the lighting cast upon the problem changes radically depending upon whether one chooses Bernini's unfortunate expedition to Paris or Fouquet's defeat in his garden of Vaux as the principal scene: in the first case the conflict of the baroque with classicism is described as France's rejection of Italian taste, whereas in the second it is interpreted in purely French terms, becoming the singular issue of a crisis that had affected the heart of Europe for almost a century and had created a network of tensions within French culture.

The center of the baroque was clearly Roman. It is also clear that the second half of the French seventeenth century saw the development of an anti-Italian discourse, which had been a popular one during the Fronde and a monarchic one with Louis XIV's Gallican enterprise. But it was not, at least originally, a matter of an antibaroque reaction, since at that time the forefront of the adversaries of ultramontanism included the cohort of the *Grands* opposed to Mazarin, who, paradoxically, supported an anticentralizing baroque politics as well as a hyperbolic esthetics and ethics very close to those Jean-François Maillard has described as characteristics of baroque heroism.[3] This suggests that the indisputable xenophobic stiffening of the "century of Louis XIV" was not the first cause of the rupture, but rather an effect of it—in other words, that it was in fact at Vaux that the principal scene was enacted, the episode of the Louvre being the necessary consequence, as inexorable as the *y* that came to replace the *i* in the excessively "exotic" name of Lulli.

Thus the victory, in France, of classicism was the political conclusion of an already old—and not essentially exogenous—cultural conflict. A surgical denouement operated "from above" upon the "icy summits of the political," according to a national tradition that has more than once been celebrated by Marxist theoreticians of the coup d'etat.

In France, it was with forceps that the West was born twice: once as a premature democracy, at the junction of the serene *Lumières* and anguished romanticism; but also, earlier, in a cesarean cutting right into the long disequilibrium of the baroque, which expressed the immense anxiety of a world watching itself change, torn between the heterotopic but unbroken space of tradition and the space of distancing and representation opened by the *Cogito*.

Let us then return to Vaux where the drama was played out.

Le Nôtre was forty-three when he was summoned by Fouquet; Le Vau was forty-four, Le Brun forty-one, and La Fontaine was not much younger, since he had just turned thirty-five. Which is to say that it was a generation getting down to work. A generation mature enough to deal a decisive blow by astounding the world with a full display of its art. For if its formation was already assured and its reputation founded upon already famous works, the program offered by Fouquet—a man who, at forty-one, also belonged to this generation— took its place alongside their maddest artistic ambitions. Nothing less than to construct a *Dream*, as La Fontaine would say. The dream of a total work where each, without any other limits besides those of his own genius, would finally be able to show his worth—his entire worth. Unlimited credit, a site that could be infinitely remodeled (at least three villages would be razed!), first-rate collaborators,[4] an army of masons, decorators, fountain builders, gardeners, workers of all kinds: ideal conditions for creators sure of their art, demiurges who, like Faust, would have willingly sold their souls to the devil eight days earlier for such superb conditions, without any concern for the horrendous misery that made them possible.

Then the work began. Magnificent. Sublime. Sketches were drawn up (and we know that Le Nôtre did many, correcting himself constantly, even on the site), a forest of pickets was planted in the fields without regard for crops, in front of the despairing peasants: the marking out served as a reference for the designs, as the major layout was established. Then foundations were dug, terraces made, backfill transported, and machines installed; immense pipes made of wood, pottery, or lead were buried, a thousand precautions were taken as already tall trees were transplanted, and box trees were brought in for hedges. In the temporary buildings, built of bricks or boards, surrounded with mud in the winter and chalky dust in the summer, the masters of the construction site engaged in endless discussion over materials, equipment, stucco, the exact slope of the *vertugadins*, the precise adaptations of the planted specimens, the exact colors of the parterres, according to each season, and the eventual size of the banks. Each decision was accompanied by quarrels or arguments over who was in charge. But as soon as the superintendent appeared, the team came back together again with the common goal of integrating a new requirement into the project or demanding further financing.

For Fouquet was not absent from the site.[5] On the contrary, he was eager to visit it whenever he had the opportunity because it was his money that was being spent—or rather that he was skillfully manipulating—and also because his advice usually proved invaluable. A widely cultivated man with clearly defined tastes, he was able to gather around him an artistic academy that brought together the best writers, painters, musicians, architects, and landscape gardeners of the time and to become friends with them. His library was sizable, and his greatest pleasure was to study there. Among the books on gardens, which included the *Treatises* of Serlio, Boyceau, and Mollet, there was one he cherished above all: the *Dream of Poliphilo*. He warmly recommended the *Hypnerotomachia*, two centuries old at this point, to La Fontaine, as though to indicate the spirit of his project. And, in fact, the atmosphere of this masterpiece attributed to Colonna was what actually inspired Vaux. Not only because the future author of the *Fables* would himself undertake a *Dream of Vaux* to celebrate the project under way—going as far as to sign some of his works with the name of Poliphilo, thereby playing a game of vowels that seems altogether bawdy coming from an avowed womanizer—but because everything at Vaux, the castle, its decoration, gardens, grottoes, and basins, points to an allegorical passion stemming from the *Hypnerotomachia*, which took shape and substance in a science of space that leaves one confounded.

Franklin Hamilton Hazelhurst has, in a detailed study, analyzed the optical devices implemented at Vaux-le-Vicomte by Le Nôtre and Le Vau,[6] and the landscape architect Michel Corajoud has tried to illuminate the geometry implicit in their layout by recording the parterres of Versailles in their present state.[7] Without entering into these analyses, which are a matter for specialists and require plans and sections, let us simply note that the sum of dazzling impressions one gets at Vaux or Versailles—the long perspectives that, as one approaches, reveal hidden basins, parterres with constantly new motifs, and points of view commanded by other axes, while the whole is surrounded by a screen of foliage leading to the lawns through refined transitions (pruned trees, box trees, copings, etc.)—is the result of a dynamic use of space that only Le Nôtre could have orchestrated with such perfect mastery.

Everything can be summed up in the refutation directed in advance at Baudelaire's famous phrase: "I hate movement that displaces lines." For, unlike Jules Hardouin-Mansart who seems enclosed in a static geometrism, Le Nôtre knew how to articulate movement and linear layout, avoiding in this way both rigidity and pretentious posing. The distinction is so clear in his work that we think it wise to oppose the architect and the landscape gardener:[8] the first being, as Gaston Bardet has remarked, the inventor of the violent piercings with "target-monuments" of later urbanism,[9] while the subtle lesson of the second has been for the most part lost. These two voluntary geometrizations of space confront each other by their intervention. One proceeds from a uniform crisscross pattern applied like a grid against the white page of the plan; and the other organizes the tensions produced by a precise marking out of the terrain into a network of predetermined figures, in such a way as to multiply the sensations and pleasure of the eye. Whence a gap—let us try out this comparison as hypothesis—comparable to the one separating, on the level of the representation of space, Descartes and Desargues, and analytic geometry from projective geometry.

We know that the first half of the French seventeenth century saw the elaboration of two different problems in geometry. The first, the evolution of which had long been hegemonic, proposed a decisive innovation with Descartes: the location of each point according to coordinates related to an abstract framework permitting calculation. The second, following in the path of the treatises on perspective, attempted to discover, without any resort to algebra, the invariants between a figure and its projection. A method that was radically developed by the engineer-architect Girard Desargues, who was most admired by Pascal and had with Descartes a relationship based on mutual esteem: it is to him, for example, that we owe the invention of a properly geometric infinity (point at infinity of a line, line at infinity of a plane, plane at infinity of space) permitting generalizations of previously inconceivable theorems. Everything leads one to think that Le Nôtre's geometric formation was marked by Desargues's problematics. We know, in fact, that in his youth he studied many treatises on "curious perspective" (especially the one by François Niceron, dating from 1638), and that, in addition, he probably benefited from Girard Desargues's direct teaching.

Although Desargues had a strong penchant for demonstrations formulated so strangely that they often became obscure, he was aiming for a practical science destined for workers and technicians of civic and military genius, to whom he graciously dispensed lessons. Moreover, during the period when Jean Le Nôtre, father of André, was called upon by Richelieu (1626) to assist his architect Lemercier in the capacity of master gardener, it so happened (according to Baillet, Descartes's biographer) that Girard Desargues was employed as an engineer in the Cardinal's service. We have no hard evidence that the young André acquired his geometric formation from a scholar moving in the same circle as his father, thereby constituting for himself a theoretical baggage conforming to Boyceau's recommendations—since we know that he studied drawing with Simon Vouet and architecture with Lemercier or François Mansart. But the hypothesis is not absurd, and the idea of such an exceptional meeting strikes us as entertaining. All the more so given that the dynamic spirt of Le Nôtre's compositions (and Le Nôtre remained one of Bernini's most faithful friends in France) seems more related to the baroque genius of one who called his treatises *Brouillon project d'une attente aux événements des rencontres du cone avec un plan*, or, better yet, *Leçons de ténèbres*[10] than to the rigorous classicism of the *Geometry* or *Dioptrics* of Descartes, with whom he has often been compared.

We are, in short, of the opinion that Le Nôtre was never classical in the sense that the term is understood in the schools.[11] A creator who avoided dogma, he was the indisputable master of the formal French garden. But, like Le Corbusier later on vis-à-vis his epigones, Le Nôtre remained foreign to univocal interpretations.[12] In him, something of the movement and living sensibility of the era that had formed his taste remained linked to a desire to celebrate plastically the greatness of a reign and the intelligence of a century in quest of reason.

This ambiguity, consubstantial with true genius, appears at the right time to remind us that, if the opposition baroque/classicism provides a grid for reading that is convenient today,[13] the protagonists did not experience the crisis in these terms, which resulted from an a posteriori historical conceptualization and not from a debate in which they confronted each other. With perfect unity, Le Vau, Le Brun, Le Nôtre, Corneille, Molière, the Italians Lulli and Torelli, and La Fontaine himself, crossed a limit that they did not distinguish without any fundamental denial, called upon as they were by their sovereign, that is to say by a master whose orders were not to be questioned. And if they had to bend their art, and if they undoubtedly had the regret of a friend, there is no doubt that the *Pleasures of the Enchanted Island*, for which they were soon required, struck them as the royal sequel to a feast that began at Vaux, under the aegis of a master who was freer and more fantastic than a few years before.

Le Nôtre died before the end of the century and would thus never know the rigid dogmatism that seized Versailles during the last fifteen years of a reign increasingly overshadowed by wars and poverty. An order formed by rule, etiquette, and convention became frozen in an austerity that was especially glacial given that the real France, the France outside the walls of Versailles, only wanted to throw off the shroud of mourning and suffering that a bigoted monarch, at this point detested, was trying to impose. Centrifugal forces appeared, which would liberate their energy under the Regent, while the aristocratic-intellectual scene entered into the now explicit quarrel between "Ancients and Moderns." The period, characterized by somewhat Byzantine arguments and more interested in theoretical clarification than creation, nonetheless saw the growth of superbly constructed architecture and garden art—that of the Parisian *hôtels*, in particular—while numerous *Treatises* appeared, one of which was of capital importance for gardens: that of Antoine-Joseph Dézallier d'Argenville.

A typical figure of the first half of the eighteenth century, A.-J. Dézallier d'Argenville, was a man of quality and a scholar, a lover of the fine arts.[14] His family, having fled Savoy when civil war broke out there, established itself in Paris where the father, although a gentleman, found himself forced to "take the part of commerce." So it was that on July 4, 1680, Antoine-Joseph was born into an aristocratic but déclassé milieu. He was a brilliant student at the Collège du Plessis, but as soon as he graduated he began devoting most of his time to drawing (with Bernard Picart), to painting (with Piles), to architecture and the art of gardens, which he studied with Alexandre Le Blond, who was a student of Le Nôtre.[15] Did he then conceive—or participate in the conception—of "a few well-ordered pleasure gardens"? It is possible. The fact is that he took pride in it since, detailing his rights to discuss this matter, he mentioned "the care he had taken to have several beautiful gardens planted." But, besides the fact that he cites no precise example, no well-known work could until now be attributed to him; so that it is reasonable to think that his personal contribution to this art would have sunk into oblivion without that treatise entitled *The Theory and Practice of Gardening*, which appeared in a first version in 1709. The work was the result of his close collaboration with Le Blond, who drew the plates for it.

The book's success was big and lasting enough to call for three new editions, each time revised and enlarged, until the one of 1747, and to entail the English and German translations that turned it into a "Bible of the French garden." His were "well-ordered pleasure gardens" as he called them, unlike those "resembling a full countryside covered with apple and cherry trees, or swamps full of vegetables"—that is to say pleasure gardens in the classical spirit that had become, at least among the aristocracy, the model and reference point in Europe: those "one takes care," consequently, "to maintain properly, and in which one mainly seeks regularity, arrangement, and whatever flatters the eye most, such as parterres, *bosquets*, lawns adorned with porticoes, with cabinets of lattice work, with figures, stairs, fountains, and cascades."

In many ways, Dézallier d'Argenville's treatise constitutes an a posteriori theorization of Le Nôtre's work, if only because nearly all the examples it was founded upon (he cites in particular Chantilly, Sceaux, and Saint-Cloud) were creations of the master of Vaux. But, besides the fact that it was a subtle and learned theorization quite different from the exercise of an epigone, his text also resonates—especially in its final version—with the insistent echo of the intellectual mutations that marked the first half of the eighteenth century. That is to say, first and foremost, those that the Moderns introduced; then those resulting from an evolution toward an increasingly technical and encyclopedic attitude characterized, in the final version of the work, by a deepening of botanical categories and especially by the addition of a treatise on hydraulics.

Dézallier d'Argenville is a Modern because of three striking traits.

In the first place, his criticism of the Ancients. He writes: "The Latin and Italian writers[16] who have treated this subject are full of excellent maxims that concern architecture more than gardening, and we have among our French ones only two or three authors[17] who have spoken of beautiful gardens. These authors have only broached and, so to speak, grazed this subject; the very drawings that accompany their books are in very common taste and no longer in use at present."[18]

Secondly, Dézallier d'Argenville presents himself as a scholar,[19] an intellectual equipped with that "spirit of geometry" animating those followers of Descartes led by Malebranche and Fontenelle. He also reproaches La Quintinie for his point of view as a practitioner incapable of leaving the confined space of "orchards" and "vegetable gardens."[20] He did not, however, shut himself into abstraction:

The manner of drawing on the terrain consists more in great practice than in a deep science; one only needs to know a few rules of practical geometry to become very skillful at it in little time. . . . However, if one fails to learn these rules, and works first on the terrain before drawing on paper, or at least before knowing the manner of reporting the figures from paper onto the terrain, one will run the risk of frequently being wrong.

Thirdly, Dézallier d'Argenville made himself the apostle of the "natural" as opposed to the "extravagances" still in use in some places:[21]

One must, in planting a garden, consider that it must take after Nature more than Art, from which it must only borrow whatever may help show it off to advantage. There are gardens where you only see extraordinary, awkward, unnatural things, and which are made at great expense, as are the walls of very elevated terraces, great staircases of stone that are real quarries, overdecorated fountains, and many bowers, *cabinets*, porticoes of treillage adorned with figures and vases, suggesting the hand of man rather than of Nature. This affectation is overshadowed by the noble simplicity of the staircases, embankments, and ramps of turf, the natural bowers and simple palissades without treillage, upheld and raised in certain places by a few figures and other ornaments of sculpture. Regarding the parts of a garden, they must be so well placed that one would think them made and planted where they are by the Author, so to speak, of Nature: a wood, for example, to cover the heights, or to fill the depths, situated on the wings of a house: a canal, in a low place, resembling the sewer of some nearby height, in such a way that the embellishment and art subsequently given to it are overshadowed by this naturalness.

We should not, however, let ourselves be deceived by this "naturalness" in the shape of a credo. It was advocated by the Moderns, in the continuation of a classical spirit opposed to baroque *déraison* or folly, as they tailored it, most often, to the standards set by *L'Astrée*; it was then taken up again by Madame de Sévigné and adapted by the shepherdesses of Trianon. Moreover, during his long stay in Italy,[22] Dézallier d'Argenville faithfully visited the Academy of Arcades, which pretended to live in the fashion of Greek shepherds.

This said, the praise of modern "naturalness" also implied a rupture with the dogma stated by

Malherbe[23] at a time when, in spite of naturalist or libertine tendencies, "nature" was for the most part being repudiated as vile, marked by the inerasable stain of the fall, or reduced to the insensible state of a machine waiting to be mastered, according to strict Cartesian metaphysics. For, if Michel Corajoud's study on Versailles has demonstrated that Le Nôtre never gave in to a certain classical vulgate according to which art could only develop from a tabula rasa, that is to say an artificial space denying history as well as the *genius loci*, Dézallier d'Argenville, on the other hand, made his own position clear: "The disposition and distribution of a general plan, in order to be perfect, must follow the disposition of the terrain: the greatest art of arranging a garden well is to know and examine the natural advantages and defects of the site, in order to profit from the former and correct the latter." Similarly, he condemned perfect symmetry in the name of variety.

There must be variety, not only in the general design of the garden, but also in each separate piece. If two *bosquets*, for example, are next to a parterre, although their exterior form and size are equal, one should not repeat for that reason the same design in both of them, but vary the inside. It would be unpleasant to find the same design on both sides, and one can say that a garden thus repeated can only pass for a half-design: this mistake, which used to be made (the Tuileries, similar on both sides, more or less), is presently avoided, as people are persuaded that variety is the greatest beauty of gardens.[24]

While holding fast to rules he thought immutable, Dézallier d'Argenville announced with these words a change in sensibility: one that would soon make the straight lines of the classical garden seem unnatural, because Nature would change status. It would no longer be the Nature of ancient *mimesis*, nor even that of the "naturalness" dear to the classics, then to the moderns; it would become the Nature of the bourgeois-philosophers,[25] essentially good because it was the essence of an industrious, simple, and positive ethic, that is to say opposed to the conventional splendor of a now disqualified aristocracy.

Regarding this mutation, this slow shift from "naturalness" to an apparent apology for Nature, we can only indicate a few scholarly works that have formed our thinking on the subject.[26] We will content ourselves with insisting upon a few characteristics that have been less clarified than others.

An impressive collection of works has sought to highlight, as essential factors of change, the discovery of English and then Chinese gardens. And these influences were indeed of capital importance, as the vocabulary indicates: the new landscape gardens that spread in France in the second half of the eighteenth century were in fact designated as "English" or "Chinese" by the general public as well as the scholarly *Treatises*. In the Parnassus of those who created earthly paradises, Kent and "Capability" Brown tried to knock Le Nôtre off his supreme pedestal. It was no longer France that was exporting gardeners, but Scotland that was supplying Ermenonville with battalions of technicians (two hundred?) and the Folies-Mousseaux or Bagatelle with a designer—Blaykie. Temple, Pope, Walpole, and Wately were being translated, devoured. As for the sinomania sparked by Father Attiret's famous letter of 1745, it was immediately translated into a mad passion for "irregularity" and "aberrant" taxonomy (according to the model of the *Sharawagdi*, which became the object of much rambling) by filling Chanteloup, Saverne, the Folie-Saint-James, the Isle-Adam, Châtillon, Bagatelle, and Kerlevenan with pagodas and pavilions.

It may not be known, however, that a century earlier a whimsical creator, as spendthrift as he was talented, had dreamed of thwarting Le Nôtre's plans by presenting two of his own projects for Versailles, with "mottled and hilly drawings." The anecdote is told in the note accompanying the posthumous edition of his *Works* (1731):

Louis XIV, having resolved to make at Versailles gardens grander and more magnificent than everything seen and even imagined before then, asked him for drawings. Dufresny did two different ones; the prince examined them and compared them with the ones that had been presented to him; he seemed content with them, and only rejected them because of the excessive expense that the execution would have entailed. This monarch who loved the Arts, and had carried them to their highest degree of perfection by giving rewards to those who distinguished themselves, awarded Dufresny a title of Inspector of his Gardens.

Charles-Rivière Dufresny . . . an eccentric lost right in the middle of classical order, an "accursed poet," who inspired Voltaire:

Dufresny, wiser and less extravagant,
Did not die of hunger, death worthy of an author.

He was born in Paris in 1648, and his very birth created a legend. And wasn't his grandfather—Louis XIII's wardrobe valet, as he himself was for Louis XIV—the son of the "Beautiful Gardener" of Anet, one of Henry IV's many mistresses? The descendant of a royal bastard in consequence, or reputed such, he was thus a cousin of the king via the "horticultural" branch, which may explain the almost tender concern the monarch had for him: "I am not powerful enough to enrich Dufresny," Louis XIV is supposed to have declared, though he has not gone down in history as a sovereign with a great sense of humor.

The fact is that Dufresny, always short of money because of his love of good times and gambling, did not hesitate to resell all the offices that his royal cousin had generously granted him. This went on until one day he found himself so crushed by debts that he married his laundress in order to clear himself of what he owed her![27] It was an alarming "advance" for the times—or perhaps an equally astounding archaism.[28]

A man of the theater like his friend Régnard, Dufresny had a great number of his comedies performed at the Théâtre des Italiens and at the Théâtre Français. Some of them were extravagant (*Les Chinois, La Baguette de Vulcain, Les Momies d'Égypte*), others satirical (*Le Double veuvage, La Réconciliation normande, Le Dédit, L'Esprit de contradiction, La Coquette du village*), and all offended classical rules: "This variegation," he explained, "seems rather natural to me: if one examines well the actions and speeches of man, one will find that in them the serious and the comic are very close."[29]

A skillful musician although he could not read music, he composed songs from memory, several of which would be successful.

An ingenious plastic artist, he invented collage.[30]

But it was his original art of gardening that made the strongest impression upon his contemporaries:

He had for this Art a singular genius, but one that can only be compared with that of the great men we have had, and that we still have in this genre. Dufresny worked with pleasure and, so to speak, with ease only on an irregular and unequal terrain. He needed obstacles to conquer, and when nature did not provide him with some, he found them for himself; that is to say that out of a regular site and a flat terrain, he would make a hilly one; in order, he said, to vary the objects by multiplying them, and to guarantee nearby views by opposing them with mounds of earth that also served as belvederes. Such were the gardens of Mignaux near Poissy; and such were also those he made in the faubourg Saint-Antoine during the last ten years of his life, one of which is known by the name of *Moulin* or Mill, and another he called the *Chemin Creux* or Hollow Path. Everyone also knew the house and gardens of Abbot Pajot near Vincennes, according to which one can judge the taste and genius of Dufresny in this genre.

The Mill, the Hollow Path, collages. . . . It is clear. Even if, for lack of a visual document confirming the "horticultural" genius of our "heterodox" figure, we only have this undoubtedly partisan evidence.[31] Dufresny's imaginary opened onto a world foreign to classical space: the world of landscape, of the picturesque and the unexpected, of the tender (or perhaps ironic) look at the countryside. His sensibility would become the dominant one only about ten years after his death (at the age of seventy-five, on October 6, 1724). Thus it is only fitting that Morel, Thouin, and the school of Barillet should have claimed his heritage, although the way they tried to make Dufresny the true ancestor of the "English garden" was certainly curious: applied to a cousin (even a bastard one!) of Louis XIV, the assertion reveals a somewhat surprising patriotic impulse.

In truth, the position of our "eccentric" was undoubtedly not as singular as it may seem today. Too many manuals, in trying to establish a univocal version of the cultural history of the French seventeenth century, have taught us to read in it only the "classical" works by erasing the traces of creators who were much less marginal than we have been told. Thus have we just rediscovered a musician as important as Marin Marais,[32] who, alongside operas of a Lullist cast, left a body of work for the viola da gamba characterized by a descriptive picturesque, a taste for frenzied contrast, and a sonorous exaltation that is alternately spectacular and interiorly elated. Moreover, it is only recently that scholars have begun to question the strange titles François Couperin gave his pieces for harpsichord[33]—or the fabulous success of Lesage,[34] whose neo-Spanish picaresque was a furious denial of classical conventions.

Usage dictates that we speak of "rococo" at this point. This somewhat ridiculous term suggests a kind of exhaustion that affected the "grand style," a degeneration into a mannerism for which ornamentation was the goal and affectation the principal register. La Pompadour's mannered charms would thus have followed upon La Montespan's haughty nobility. The theory is surely practical, but disobliging, as much for Louis XV as for a collection of works remarkable in all ways, beginning with those of some exceptional painters who can take credit for having brought landscape into the space of sensibility.

With the eighteenth century the painter undoubtedly installed himself as master at the heart of gardens, displacing the architect from his ruling position. Poussin and Lorrain had already excelled in landscape composition to such a degree that their models remained central. But with Watteau, Oudry, Lancret, Boucher, Fragonard, Vernet, and especially Hubert Robert, the art of gardens tended to blend with the art of the landscape painter. Not that it was a matter of reproducing *in situ* models already elaborated on canvas (even though all echoes were allowed). The interest lay instead in composing sites that deserved to be painted—in creating something like real paintings, adorned with elements capable of awakening sensibility and meditation, and offering in addition the ineffable happiness of movement, touch, sounds, and smells. This sensualist aim was in harmony with the climate of an era that did not intend to submit itself to the sole dictatorship of the eye, but wished to open itself up to the complete lyre of the body, out of which comes the intoxicating emotion of the soul. The painter became the motor of this mechanism not in order to limit the garden to the surface of his canvas, but in order to transgress it: to enter into the dream of a total art leading to a complete communion of the sensible and the inert, of thought and effusive emotion, of being with *there is*.

Whence the capital role that Hubert Robert played in the development of gardens in the eighteenth century.[35] During his long stay in Italy he had acquired a taste for ruins and rocks covered with moss and ivy. In this he resembled Kent, whose vocation had been shaped by his trip to Rome (completed in 1719), rather than by his English countryside. But it was at Versailles, at some point during the year 1775, that Robert made the decisive leap. Under the influence of Marie-Antoinette, gigantic works were undertaken on the castle and park, the vegetation of which had aged considerably, in order to make them conform to the taste of the day. "All the woods of forests, of line and of decoration and of copses in massifs of the gardens of Versailles and Trianon" were put up for sale on November 20, 1774, by order of the Count d'Angivillier, general manager of the royal buildings.

It was a searing defeat, after barely a century, for Le Nôtre's *Dream*. A court whose dream had changed blithely sacrificed a framework it now considered boring, without realizing that by destroying geometry it was breaking the ground it stood on—the hierarchical order that supported absolutism.

Here, parterres were overturned and trees chopped down; there, box trees, now considered too rigorously architectural, were razed. Everywhere, the harrow and felling axe. Everywhere, empty steles and displaced basins. Children dressed in silk and lace made seesaws out of mutilated tree trunks while the king and queen conversed with their people in the allées.

Hubert Robert noted the details of these scenes. He painted two pictures that were ordered from him for a price of 5,000 livres. And there is no reason to think that he did not enjoy the spectacle as much as everyone else, for he took great pleasure in fixing the cruel effects of time on canvas. That "slow magic" acting on the heart.[36] That strange turmoil created by the furtive idea of death. That vertigo of flight leading to infinity.

Yes, it was with voluptuous pleasure that Hubert Robert painted this scene of destruction suggesting the end of a world. He painted it almost lovingly. And in painting it with the greatest precision possible, and suffusing it with all the autumnal light he could capture, he constructed new landscapes from the heart. Places of emotion where time would, so to speak, contract, where the rushes of the soul would chase away calculation, and where, in seeming harmony with the adventurous beauty of the sites, the completely new invention of freedom would find both its form and its container.

For the world and the era called for a transformation. A re-form, in the total sense of the word. The paradise that had been thought lost, or that had supposedly been cut to fit the geometrical norms of despotism—straight allées, ball and cone trees, rigid treillages—was within the heart's grasp. For Eden to become possible once again, one only had to abandon one's soul to "naiveté," to nourish one's mind with history and philosophy, to orient one's fate according to the common good as the Physiocrats demanded: the "beautiful nature" at work in the new gardens was its prophetic image, as well as the proof of its likeliness.

Hubert Robert then began to expand. Associated with his friend Watelet who wrote the theory,[37] he drew sketches for the new Trianon, perhaps for Bagatelle and Les Folies-Mousseaux,[38] and surely for Betz, the many *fabriques* of which he designed. It was with even more passion—for it was undoubtedly one of the most beautiful gardens of the period—that he made designs for Méréville.[39] A work commissioned by an enlightened financier, Jean-Joseph de Laborde, this marvel is today almost destroyed, because of revolutionary violence and the unfortunate negligence of its subsequent owners. But we know, from the pictures Robert painted for the decoration of the castle as well as descriptions of the period, that this immense park composed in the Beauce, in the narrow valley of the Juinne, was much more complex and magnificent than anything else made at the time.[40] Conceived on a gigantic area in the years preceding the Revolution (Laborde bought the terrain in 1784), its landscapes included ruins (for which Vernet contributed his advice), a dairy, a round temple encircled by a colonnade, a rustic bridge cast across a rocky site, another one of Chinese make, a large lake surrounded by a "prairie," an impressive cascade topped by a Trajan column dominating the entire park and, lastly, the famous "grave of Cook," a majestic dome held up by four columns truncated according to the order of Paestum, which recalled, paradoxically, not so much the memory of the famous English navigator, but the memory of the owner's two sons who disappeared with La Pérouse during his voyage around the world.

It was the dream of a world recomposed by art and philosophy, whose cruel destiny was at bottom a symbol. But, though one may regret the irreparable destruction of Méréville, it would have been contrary to its genius to travel through time without being tried by it and to continue—embalmed in the bandages of "conservation"—to present itself in a perennial splendor: the garden has the distinctive ability of effacing itself to a rhythm where its visions blur, thus multiplying our daydreams, which may be scholarly for some and are nostalgic for all.

At this point in our walk through the parks and gardens of preromanticism, we must clear up one misunderstanding.

In order to describe the eighteenth century's rediscovery of nature, the terms "naiveté" and "simplicity" are often used. The fact is that the major voices of the period, beginning with Rousseau, continued to sing the virtues of these two qualities. But nothing would be more untrue than to deduce from this a rejection of artifice, illusion, and deliberate complexity, to the benefit of a return to the original without any preparation involving human intelligence. On the contrary. If it is true—as Mornet has shown, for example, and more recently Keith Thomas regarding the English case[41]—that wild mountains, untouched forests, seas beating furiously against abrupt cliffs began to become objects of admiration although they had previously been considered loathsome, nothing could be further from the spirit of Méréville, Bagatelle, or Ermenonville than to relate their "Follies" to a desire to let brute nature spread out freely as though art had suddenly been disqualified.[42]

While repudiating Malherbe, Girardin revered Rousseau but also Montaigne, a quotation from whom he placed as an epigraph to his annotated copy of the *Essais*.

It is not reasonable that art should win the place of honor over our great and powerful mother Nature. We have so overloaded the beauty and richness of her works by our inventions that we have quite smothered her. Yet wherever her purity shines forth, she wonderfully puts to shame our vain and frivolous attempts. (I,31)

But this reference designates more a climate of thought than an effective *praxis*. For this nature, beautiful and good in its principle, is most often occulted. Such is the explanation given by the Rousseauists who want to find it again. So that, rather than exposing it in its brute form, we should raise the veil that hides it, in order to discover it in the depth of its generosity. This we do in order to show that we are capable of knowing it and describing it so that we can better be inspired by it. This program, a naturalist and encyclopedic one almost in spite of itself, implies and designates the precise place where the alliance between the progressive *Lumières* and the Jean-Jacques of *La Nouvelle Héloïse* was concluded: in a common rejection, in spite of d'Alembert, of geometrism to the benefit of natural history, in other words in the rejection of a reductive kind of abstraction in favor of a cumulative and descriptive approach of a reality both protean and inexhaustible.[43]

Which, in our opinion, explains the *furor hortensis* that Gusdorf has isolated as one of the major traits of the culture of the second half of the eighteenth century.[44] A *furor* that was not only a passion for gardens themselves, or the commentaries relative to them, but also a determination to gather the world in a kind of puzzle (English? Chinese?) uniting sensations, emotions, philosophical initiation, social or esthetic didacticism, botany, lithology, citations from great men, "fabricated" historical and geographical testimony, and the humblest with the greatest. Did Carmontelle not pretend, at the Folies-Mousseaux, that he was not only introducing opera, but reuniting "all times and all places" in a single garden?

Standing before these landscaped microcosms where, right in the middle of arcadian meadows full of flocks, stand pyramids, pagodas, and temples dedicated to science and philosophy, we are a hundred miles from "simplicity." On the contrary, we are in the middle of a serious fantasy, or even, as Jurgis Baltrušaitis has said, in the "land of illusion."[45]

We have thus passed from Vaux or Versailles to Méréville or the Desert of Retz. First we followed the straight allées with their axes established according to a staging based on "greatness" and "reasonability," then we sank, along a path that has become sinuous, into an increasingly composite sequence of landscapes. Behind us, the "gardens of intelligence."[46] In front, those of feeling.

It is morning when we leave the castle. To the right, a softly undulating park rolls toward a stretch of meadows bordering a forest; there is a pond, with an island, a few pseudo-Chinese *fabriques*, a fake temple, fake ruins. To the left, on the other side of the grottoes, rocks, cascades, and arbors, smoke rises in the sky, signaling a cottage where, disguised as shepherdesses, beautiful and distinguished ladies are busy milking cows or playing the part of wool-spinners. The weather is mild. The air palpitates like the leaves on the trees. Between the fluffy clouds of spring, groups of swifts and swallows draw their arabesques. This is happiness—walking along through this peaceful setting, collecting plants here, resting there, in the shade of a tall oak, one's head among the lilies of the valley and primroses. Filling one's heart with the singing of birds. Meditating while the light dies down, next to some tomb dedicated to Montaigne, or Pope, or Petrarch. Returning to the castle as evening falls, with a bag full of grasses and a notebook scribbled over with free thoughts, humming the musette of the *Devin de village*, or walking to the rhythm of abbé Delille's *Chant des jardins*:

Be a painter. The fields, the nuances without shade
The jets of light and the masses of shade,
The hours, the seasons, varying one by one,
And the enameled meadows, the rich broderies,
And the laughing hills, the green draperies,
The trees, the rocks, the waters, and the flowers,
There are your brushes, canvases, and colors,
Nature is yours; and your fertile hand
Has, for creation, the elements of the world.

But, for the time being, the sun has barely risen and we have to quicken our pace. We have a rendezvous with the garden's creator at the edge of the park, where the allées end and the road leading to Paris begins. With a man not only of great wealth, but of great intelligence, experienced in philosophy as well as the composition of landscapes, economical with his wealth when necessary, but ready to ruin himself when the work undertaken imposes sacrifices. He is waiting for us next to the fence, very English in appearance, thin, with greying temples, dressed in leather trousers and a cloth outfit. As we approach, the dog sleeping at his feet gets up and greets us with gleeful yaps.

"We will begin with the Desert," announces the marquis de Girardin. A wood, a pond, rocks, which reminded *him* of Bienne. A cabin, too, where *he* used to rest. "What does one enjoy in such a situation? Nothing outside oneself, nothing if not oneself and one's own existence, as long as that state lasts one is as self-sufficient as God."

Then, parting the ferns that threaten to cover the path where, for the last time, Jean Jacques dreamed: "Be so good as to wait. I will show you my letters this evening."

The Temple of Love at Malmaison, lithograph by Langlumé after Guérard. Photo © Bibliothèque Nationale, Paris.

Ermenonville, February 10 [1778].

I was just coming back from rue Pâltrière, where our famous friend and his companion have lived for more than two years—a modest place that I again encouraged him to leave because of the material difficulties of his household and the illness keeping Thérèse in bed—when I found your letter.

He has had to hire a servant, which, as you can imagine, is not to his taste, but, forced to give up transcription because of his own weak condition, he can only dedicate his energies to the writing of what he sometimes calls *Walks* and other times calls *Reveries*. He is writing in a duodecimo notebook of around two hundred pages where he gathers with great difficulty the course his thoughts follow during the walks he takes whenever the weather permits. I have also noticed two small octavo notebooks, one of which is bound in parchment and—astonishing!— a few playing cards written with ink or pencil, or with a pencil then gone over with ink.

In spite of the poverty afflicting him and even though he no longer has any hope among men, he shared with me his *Art of Enjoyment*, which consists in the idea that writing, by fixing the memory of happiness, recalls it and makes one enjoy it again. In this he disagrees with Condillac, who says that reminiscence does not let us experience the concrete presence of past sensation.

He has thus evoked with much delicacy the raptures he experienced during his long walks by the village of Charonne, or along the Bièvre on the side of Gentilli, remembering the shores of Lake Bienne and the shores of the Isle de Saint-Pierre where he was fifteen years ago, and how his solitary soul enters a sweet revery when freed of the tumultuous passions engendered by life in society.

He has made me appreciate that this kind of reverie is most likely to occur in places where there is nothing to remind one of the rest of the world and where society, while being engaging, is not too demanding. The site, he told me, ought to be *romantic*, and the spirit ought to be equipped with a laughing imagination. Whereupon he begged me to share with him the distinctions I am currently making in my work on the *picturesque*, the *poetic*, and the *romantic*. You know how much this interests me since, having found them in the good work of Watelet, all of whose opinions I do not share, however, I am attempting to define them further. The *picturesque situation*, I answered him, enchants the eyes, while the *poetic situation* interests the memory and spirit and draws Arcadian scenes again within us. The *romantic*, taken from the English word, is the situation that only nature can offer us and the touching impression we receive from it, uniting the effects of picturesque perspective and the sweet, tranquil effects of the poetic scene . . . Together we recalled the description that Letourneur gives of the romantic in a note of the *Discourse* preceding his translation of Shakespeare: a tender and melancholic sensation that the two words *romanesque* and *picturesque* are incapable of conveying. "Such was my affection while I remained on the shores of Lake Bienne!" cried out the man I have always considered my beloved master, while pale Thérèse, stretched out on her bed, repeated: "Jean-Jacques, Ah! my dear Jean-Jacques!"

I described to him the banks of the Nonette, which goes from Ver to Ermenonville, shaded by willows, and how, from a bench near the water, one can enjoy a view of the wide expanse of the Arcadian Prairie; then how one can, from that spot, reach my favorite part of the Boscage, which, as you know, I have made Virgilian and poetic—with its limpid streams and grassy grottoes forming charming refuges from the violent sounds of the waterfalls or the regular noise of the cascades one can hear there—with the dedication *Otio et Musis* that I inscribed on a building at the entrance. I described to him how the shade of the alders barely lets the sun cast its rays, and how only the *romantic* can describe it, for nothing there is picturesque, and everything is enchanting.

The old man listened with pleasure to my account until he exchanged a look with his companion, at which point he interrupted me: "I will come, sir, I will come . . .," he murmured. His eyes filled with tears and he hugged me to him.

Soon after, I asked my eldest son, Stanislas—who often accompanies me on these visits and whom you saw when he was only eight years old and work on my garden was beginning—to sit down at the spinet in order to decipher some scores that Jean-Jacques Rousseau had written himself. In a weak but passionate voice, my friend began to sing: I heard him, dearest, I heard him! I heard his voice. The recollection of this scene still awakes in me the grave, heartfelt rapture that I experienced but cannot describe. All this happened less than three hours ago so that I am still overwhelmed by it. Believe me, dear friend, I long for the man and his good companion to agree to stay here. In its situation as in its manners, Ermenonville was made to please him. Goodbye. Although it has been a cold winter, the coming spring may soon see him in this place.

February 14 [1778].
After a calm and tranquil morning *à l'anglaise*, during which I set in order some of my drawings of the Garden while my wife, who had entered my study with the delicate grace that is the privilege of feminine beings, embroidered next to the window, and the pouring rain struck my ear without respite, making me softly regret that I could not take a walk in the direction of my Boscage, I have decided to answer your letter and satisfy you with a description of my feelings and ideas, since you have asked how I am. The pleasant freshness brought by the water upon the dark shade of the entrance fills my senses and my spirit with a vivacity enabling me to turn toward my past, although I consider the events of my life very common, with the exception of the great passion that I continue to experience and that, although moderated by respect and admiration, still marks what I do. You know its famous name.

I belong to an ancient Florentine family by the name of Gherardini. My father, the Marquis of Vauvray, was lay-counselor at the Parliament of Paris and old master of requests of the Hôtel du Roy. My mother was the daughter of the fermier-général, René Hatte, who left me a considerable fortune including, to my great happiness, when I was thirty-one, the Ermenonville estate.

I was born in 1735 and, after some schooling, I was at the age of nineteen made an officer in the armies of Louis XV. I left before the end of the terrible Seven Years' War in order to settle at Lunéville, at the court of the king of Poland, Stanislas Leszczynski. There I married the daughter of the marshal of the camps and armies of Lorraine, and we had four sons and two daughters named Cécile, Angèle, Stanislas-Xavier, godson of King Stanislas and future viscount of Ermenonville, Louis, Alexandre, and Amable-Ours-Séraphin who, although he is timid and has met him rarely, seems to have already won Jean-Jacques's affection. I was very friendly with King Stanislas who, as you know, died in an accident in the summer of 1766.

Nonetheless, I quarreled violently with him about the *Discourse on the Origin of Inequality*, when it appeared ten years before. Since that time, my admiration for Jean-Jacques Rousseau has been complete. I consequently defended him when Stanislas, not content with the refutation of the *Discourse* that he himself had written, arranged the performance of a play by an author of his court named Palissot and entitled *The Philosophers*, in which our master was ridiculed for having advocated a return to nature. Some time later, reading and annotating Theocritus and the good Latin authors, Virgil, Horace, and Longus, not to mention Petrarch and Milton, Montaigne, Descartes, Newton, Voltaire, and our beloved William Penn—thus leading what in France is called the life of a "philosopher"—I decided to go visit Germany, then Italy, and above all England where I met you, dear friend, in your lovely garden.

This was shortly after my visit to the Park of Stowe, that estate belonging to Lord Cobham where, I was told, *Capability* Brown learned his trade under Kent's direction. But I was as disappointed as Rousseau had been in the company of Hume and Luze. Undoubtedly you will remember what Rousseau has Saint-Preux say: "It is a combination of very beautiful and picturesque places . . . all of which seems natural except the assembly . . . and the times as well as the places are gathered there with more than human magnificence. This is precisely what I am complaining about." The master explains quite rightly that in admiring this form of beauty the imagination gets *tired* of representing the works as well as the expense that they have cost. Your compatriots want at all cost to make landscapes that resemble paintings, and their gardens are in the style of Claude Lorrain, whom I myself admire greatly, having conceived to the south of my castle a landscape that may, in a few places, make one think of Claude's light. But, for me, the art of landscape should owe nothing to anyone except itself and nature, and it is their beauty that should in turn inspire paintings. For, in the end, the art of the garden is to *make pleasure*, as well as virtue, out of *necessity*.

We need, in fact, to lead a peaceful, family life among our friends and fellow men, the peasants. And this estate of Ermenonville where I am writing you breathes order, peace, and innocence, in all things concerning man's true destination. Such are the truths I have developed in my life, following Jean-Jacques Rousseau and supported by him during the time I have known him. But I needed a project that would complete my knowledge by applying it, and, with the conception and construction of the gardens of Ermenonville, I seem to have reached my goal, without hesitation.

While I have been writing you, the rain that was coming down in torrents has stopped, and I feel that my throne awaits me under the nascent cradles of foliage. After the sweet melancholy of quivering water, the light has reached the summit of its beauty in all these rural places where I have been for more than ten years, working at writing and drawing every morning, walking and meditating in the afternoon, and, in the evening, making music with my musicians and my family. It is for that reason that I ask you now to excuse me while I break off this account of the events of my life in order to go to my delights.

February 20 [1778].

Yesterday I met my friend, the famous painter Hubert Robert, whom I spoke to you about when I was still in England. I like this man, who is about my age. He was educated in Italy over a period of almost ten years. With Nicolas Poussin, Peter Paul Rubens, Claude Lorrain, Fragonard, Salvatore Rosa, Antoine Watteau, and Joseph Vernet, he is one of the great painters of our time, and I have requested his services for the colored engravings of the Ermenonville site before it was composed upon the terrain. He was supported by the director of the Academy of France in Rome, a certain Natoire whom I know by name only, and claims that Pannini has been the greatest influence upon him. Fragonard is so close to him that certain amateurs confuse their works. In our country, he is known by the nickname his works have earned him, that is to say *Robert of the ruins*.

Hubert Robert appreciates reading the works of that philosopher who, as you know, was a friend of our friend Jean-Jacques and then his enemy. In spite of this misfortune, I agree with what Denis Diderot has written in his *Salons* about the need for *few figures* in landscapes, on the condition that they be *exquisite* so that the silence is not broken and the site may promote reverie. The eye should rest upon some skillfully and tastefully arranged detail in order to offer what I have designated in my *Treatise upon the Composition of Landscapes* as a "landscape made interesting" through the effect of that happy intelligence that satisfies the eye and spirit at the same time. In this way, Hubert Robert arranges in his compositions *fabriques* in ruins that are not so vague or confused that they disorient our vision, but make us associate melancholy with the obscure depth of time instead of with displays of magnificence or the monotony of perspective *de more geometrico*. The contemplator dreams upon the ruin of Hubert Robert as he dreams about the *dead tree* of the Orchard of Clarens, and if the tomb is a refuge where the weary walker may rest, the ruin is the place of regret and of *noble melancholy*.

Nonetheless, if I love the man and admire the painter, I do not appreciate it, as some do, when the landscape is ruined by too many *bizarreries*. And here I completely agree with our Jean-Marie Morel. The ruin in its variety of forms, with the greenery that may adorn it and its *tone of color*, enriches the site and pleases only insofar as it is composed in a *picturesque* manner; its place is not alongside dwellings, but in the wider, less worked-upon *country*. The abbey of Chaalis is interesting not only because it is venerable, but because its outline intensifies the view toward the horizon, which it retains in some fashion. But it is possible to arrange ruins so as to provide shelter, as I have done in transforming the grotto on the edge of the large lake into *Jean-Jacques's House*, where I have covered the rock with thatch and let the moss, grass, and ivy grow, so that, with its sharp angles and brilliant color, it would not stand out too harshly against nature, which agrees better with it in this fashion. But to this picturesque effect of the ruins, which I call an "emblematic air" in my *Treatise* and is apt to exercise with pleasure the imagination or memory, one may add the inscriptions dedicated to friendship by great men. It is another misuse of most English gardens—with all due respect—quite similar to the *chinoiseries* and *folies* that are ridiculous out of place. The *Pleasure of Mystery* by Bernardin is the *Pleasure of Ignorance*. I like a ruin when, like the old pruned oaks of Julie's Garden from which garlands of woody nightshade escape, it works with nature, showing tufts of wild rosebushes through the debris, and becomes its own work again, while remaining in part the work of man . . . on condition that it not be seen . . .

It has been sweet to interrupt this letter for a moment so as to enjoy rereading the description of Julie's *Élisée* imagined by our great friend. I have found again the passage on ruins I wanted to share with you. Taking as his example the famous park of Lord Cobham at Stowe, our friend wrote:

The master and creator of this superb solitude has even had ruins constructed there, temples, and ancient buildings, and times as well as places are gathered there with a more than human magnificence. This is exactly what I am complaining about. I would like men's amusements always to have an easy air that does not remind one of their weakness . . .

In his paintings, our host knows how to please us, for the composition of his ruins, far from causing pain, throws us into the infinite time and space of nature; there is no longer either a victor or a vanquished, but an alternation that moves human pride back to its correct level and lowers our pretensions. The effect of one of Robert's paintings is to plunge you into a reverie that consoles you for loss, since it stages grandeur by the continuous passage it forces us to make between the object and the group that, so to speak, receives it. Faced with this infinity that repeats itself, we feel a kind of vacillation in our spirit and in our senses. Forgive me for having taken the path of Denis Diderot to tell you about my "poetics of ruins," as he called it in his *Salon* of 1767, talking about Robert's tableau: *Ruin of a Triumphal Arch, and Other Monuments*. Do not, however, believe that I get excited over ruins the way he does. After welcoming my friend the painter Hubert Robert yesterday, I tried to tell you that, for me, the ruin is an extremely interesting element when it is placed in a painting, but when it comes to the art of landscape composition, I will always prefer over a ruin the view of a rock for the way in which it opposes the peace of the natural order to the agitation of men and the disorder of passions. Good-bye. Tomorrow I am supposed to go to Paris on foot in order to meet our venerable friend.

March 3 [1778].

This time I would like to paint for you one of my favorite spots in the garden to which, along with my happy family, I have happily dedicated the most sacred part of my life. You are aware that my dearest wish is that men should abandon the sad vanity of cities and build where they can draw upon the resources that gentle nature and the genius loci offer them. In this way they can return to true happiness. I wrote on the terrace this inscription, inspired by your good poet William Shenstone, whose *adorned farm* of Leasowes we visited together during that unforget-table summer day. There I truly thought myself in the Arcadia of that painting by Poussin we both love, where it is written: *Et in Arcadia ego*. Let me give you the beginning of the poem:

We, Fairies and gentle naiads
Have decided here to stay:
We delight in the sound of the cascades,
But no mortal has seen us in full day. . .

I would have you walk there as though I were with you, since there lies the landscape of *old loves* that I have entirely dedicated to Rousseau.

From the terrace, one must follow the shaded path along the river and go to the Grotto called *Jean-Jacques's House*, carpeted with creeping plants that contribute to an appearance of age, which you have seen develop; from this spot, between different vaults of rocks, one sees the brilliant cascade, then, following a staircase built between the vaults and rocks, one has the pleasant surprise of finding oneself on the edges of a lake that seems to have no other limits besides those of the valley. From the terrace of the castle, one only sees the infinity of natural space, as if the two arms of water did not meet, so that the sky seems to mix with water. The pond is not visible, so that the distances are in no way shortened, and the view is such that, through the effect of colors, it enables one to imagine the planes, nature giving itself over like a theater with its first wings, successive planes, background and elements . . .

Excuse my digressions, but when you came to Ermenonville the road was being built, and you saw everything in a state of incompletion. Remembering our gentle evenings when you recited verses from Thomson's *Seasons* for us, and I verses from our Saint-Lambert for you, I remembered the following lines: "impatient to see, impatient to give myself over / To the pleasure of feeling, living, and admiring . . ." Ah! it is here, my good friend, that I feel myself born again: the winds murmuring in the poplars bring me the perfumes of the surrounding countryside, enchanting my senses and delighting my soul. I understand the *law of nature*, in which human reason, especially if it is enlightened, listens to the precepts of divine reason and heeds the Creator's dictates and advice, and I compare myself to its noble energy, which sows its good deeds and enables its sensitive and fertile luxury to escape the shackles of art. I return, dazzled by the laughter and beauty of nature, along the path where alders grow and wild rosebushes too, marking the road, and, turning back toward the lovely landscape, I admire, under the tranquil and pure sky that the light reddens with fresh enamel, the charming contrast between the green of the lawns and the darker green of the woods.

You see oh how much pleasure I take in confiding in you these moments of pensive and solitary ecstasy; I learned the secret of its manner from our famous philosopher. Like him, I honor that *law of nature* that resides in the form and matter of places, and that speaks to man *in foro interno*, since it is as though "engraved" in his heart. As for me, nature has dictated all I have done, the work on my gardens as well as the education of my children. It is a law that commands without tyranny and harbors in its commandments a kind of charter of morality that brings members of the human community together, whether they are masters or valets. It is thus that I imagined a Bench for mothers on which I had these four verses engraved:

> *He restored the tenderness of mother for child,*
> *He restored the caresses of child for mother;*
> *Of man, at his birth, he was the benefactor,*
> *And made him freer, so that he would be better.*

On the road, traced in the English manner, not far from the Hermitage and the Temple built to glorify modern philosophy and Montaigne, one comes upon a majestic beech tree. A rural orchestra has been built in its shade: on Sundays the peasants of the village gather there and hold rustic dances to the music of the fiddlers; should a storm occur, the villagers can take refuge in a big building covered with planks located at the entry of the square. Tennis, ball games, and archery take place around this big beech that seems, because of its prodigious height, to be the sacred tree of the entire forest. In this fashion my family and I lead a simple, cheerful life that astonishes our visitors. As for myself, I am barely able to confess the name of the visitor whom my heart awaits. I would like him to do me the honor, and I sense that in spite of his cautiousness a glimmer of the same hope burns in him. But the day is advancing. Farewell. I am leaving on horseback to go ahead of my eldest son who is supposed to arrive this evening.

May 19 [*1778*], *in great haste.*

You know my point of view regarding the passions: if I admit that it is necessary to measure their use, that does not mean one should cherish them any less. Thus I will not circumvent the issue. My dear friend is coming, yes, he is coming. I was about to say farewell when he stepped toward me, his hands trembling, and tapped my shoulder gently: "It's decided, my good friend, we'll come." Should I confess to you that the pleasure made me feel faint? Then, gathering my wits, I sent for two men to put their things away and bring what remained. Luckily I had my horse. And it was at a rapid gallop that I covered the fifty odd kilometers separating us from Paris: here I am. I wanted you to know the news before anyone else. He will come to Ermenonville with his physician, Le Bègue de Presle. Thérèse will join him later.

P.S.: Rousseau told me that he was not able to finish his *Tenth Walk* and that he delivered various manuscripts, including a copy of his *Dialogues* and a copy of his *Confessions*, to his old friend from Geneva Paul Moultou, in the presence of this one's son, Pierre.

May 25 [*1778*].

He finally came—the great, the famous, the dear man. Thérèse has joined him. Since his arrival the gardens have seemed even more beautiful to me. It is as though all the Graces have come to rest here. His presence reflects upon all of nature and makes all beings more beautiful. Even the sun in its glory casts webs of gold over the landscape inspired by this sublime soul. Like the birds flying two by two in the boscages, they go, one of them a pensive and gentle old man, and the other an innocent and beloved child, my young son. One morning they visit the *Prairie*, the next the *Desert*: they collect plants together, and their fruitful hands gather fragrant grasses and heaps of flowers that they inspect with a magnifying glass, then clean with a brush until no soil remains; they secure the plants with lead weights or farthings on quires of gray paper and on thick, well-pasted white paper of the same size; they place samples in a press and change the paper underneath every day. They are promising us a lovely herbarium, for which I have bought a few vignettes in alphabetical order, but Rousseau likes to write what he jokingly calls his "scribblings," for he is perfectly acquainted with Linnaeus's *Hortus Cliffortianus*. One of my daughters, who has become his student, helps him in the evening with the writing. "One must not," he tells us, however, "give botany an importance it does not have; it is an occuption that has no other usefulness than what a thinking and sensitive person can draw from observing nature and the marvels of the universe . . ."

He cries out over the mutilation that man uselessly inflicts upon nature, rejects double flowers, and goes to look for the pear and apple in the forest. He walked around for more than four hours today in the *Desert* and asked me to accompany him, which I agreed to do with pleasure. We left the castle some time after nine in the morning and hardly spoke as we walked. Having reached the wide, sandy path that separates the *Desert* from the enclosure around the forest, we stopped at the *Shack* made of old, piled-up tree stumps; I had this inscription posted on the door: "The Coalman is the master in his own home," after I won my lawsuit against the prince of Condé who, during the shooting parties he led in the plains of Ermenonville and Nanteuil, overstepped the privileges of his captainry [the office of the superintendent of hunting] and jostled and destroyed my fences without shame. I have had the fence rebuilt since, and I hear from my eldest son, Stanislas, that, having come to the castle very early with his family and visited the gardens in my absence, the prince read my inscription and said: "It is at most what someone who is not in the captainry might be allowed to say to himself," which gave me as well as my son cause to hate captainries. I told this story to our old friend, and we spoke until a late hour of the plenitude of liberty, and the rights of the individual, to which he has dedicated a large part of his works.

But let us return to my *Desert*, so vast and magnificent in its savage splendor under the cloudless light that expanded it as far as the abbey of Chaalis, which was visible in the distance. The colors of the heather on the hills were animated by the light haze rising at dawn; the stretches of sand were turning gold; like torches of heaven burning in the heat, the rocks crowned with pines excited in us a sweet feeling of melancholy. The smell of sap, the pleasure of emotion. A mist rising from a great stretch of water; mountains and forests on the horizon, solitary powers banishing deceitful dogmas, feeble laws, and vain prejudices. The scent of junipers hung heavy in the air, and Rousseau stopped to tell me how very disgusted he is with medicine that poisons; but then he went on to quote Linnaeus for me, the famous Swede fought by our Buffon: "Nature never betrays," he said to me, quoting his master, raising his arms to point to the landscape. Then he spoke to me about the grasses he was sorting, the drugs he was pounding, and the stills he was managing at the *Charmettes*, at Madame de Warens's, his *Dear Mommy*, alongside Claude Anet, who is for him a kind of schoolmaster. He recalled his meeting, arranged by Monsieur Gros de Bose, with the great Réaumur, and the garden of Mongenan d'Antoine de Gascq where he said he had worked like a peasant, turning an orchard enclosed by walls, half a hectare in size, into a garden . . .

We then went down a dirt path made by nature herself; we passed that tree I have called the *happy Elm* whose branches caress the earth, and we crossed a small wood of pines: Jean-Jacques, who was then walking in front of me, said his mind was spinning with delight and that he wished to continue wandering endlessly among these trees and rocks so suited to the infinite revery of his heart, which always feels too confined when he is with other beings. We passed *Joseph II's Rock* (he visited me in my gardens last year), and we avoided, because of the fatigue it would have caused us, the *Painters' Path* where one can find all of nature's wild productions and where Rousseau often goes to gather plants. We climbed down the mountain and, back at the Boscage, we arrived at *Jean-Jacques's House*, which is covered with thatch and made entirely of rocks on the inside: "Jean-Jacques is immortal" is written on one of the rocks. You have seen with your own eyes the cottage that I dedicated to Rousseau at the beginning of my enterprise. You yourself, you sat on one of the mossy benches, enjoying the view of the lake and the Gabrielle Tower, and the vista of the river. Since your visit, other rocks have been inscribed with your friend's writings. The water laps up against the rocks covered with honeysuckle, wild roses, and firs. Rousseau often sits down here after gathering plants. Sometimes, in the evening, if a small boat stops on the shore, he takes charge of a few of us and leads us to the island of poplars so that we have called him our "fresh water admiral," and, like Julie and Saint-Preux at Meillerie, we find that *Chi no sa come dolce ella sospira, E come dolce parla, e dolce ride?* . . .

We went along the lake and crossed the roadway that separates it from a smaller body of water. From the *Fisherman's House*, we contemplated the two views, the one of the lake in its greater expanse where the first rays of the setting sun were shining, and the one that makes the front of the landscape in which, as I have written in my *Treatise*, one's eyes rest with *strokes of day* on the groups of trees going toward the abbey of Chaalis. Turning toward me, I saw that our friend had his eyes filled with tears: "*The monument of old loves*," he murmured, "you thought of them . . ." Upon which I recited to him passages from Letter XXVII of *La Nouvelle Héloïse*, and he told me he could feel his heart reliving the delights he had experienced in his land and the happiness of his youth. I helped him rise from the bench where he was sitting, telling him:

"Let us go, my friend, the air of this place is not good for me." He gave me a gentle smile, and we returned slowly along a sandy path where we met a young farmer carrying a plowshare and singing, then a shepherd bringing back his bleating sheep: "Yes, this really is a scene from the *Happy Countryside* and everything here is well linked with the land." Ah! Sir, judge the emotions I experienced when, about to reach the terrace, and walking, near the Gabrielle Tower, on the lovely Prairie, the man, whose every thought was first emotion, leaned tenderly upon my arm. Nature, friendship, the supreme happiness of two souls forming one single soul—I taste your delights. Farewell. I have passed over a thousand details that are more easily felt than expressed. Art is powerless when it comes to giving us a *landscape* if the Artist does not seek his pictures in those places where the soul can give itself over entirely to the sweetness of the *Romantic*.

June 15 [1778], Ermenonville

I have just given Jean-Jacques Rousseau the news: Voltaire has died. Can you believe that Jean-Jacques, far from deriving any pleasure from this, was instead moved to the bottom of his heart: "He did not endure persecution as I did, but he demonstrated courage on different occasions in his life, and his thinking had hints of boldness. But he did not understand what meditation was . . ." And the other day, while we were strolling together, not far from the grotto I have dedicated to your good Thomson, Rousseau wrote with his own hand: "To reverie" upon an altar where four verses of Voltaire were written, on the value of thought and love. Thus, to my guest's pleasure, I had Voltaire's text erased, and I decided that the monument would henceforth be called *The Altar of Reverie* . . . Upon which, Jean-Jacques, the most famous writer and philosopher of Europe, went off to the Swiss chalet around which I have tried to reconstitute the *Orchard of Clarens*, and which he loves very much. Following which, undoubtedly recalling the "thousand birds" of his *Nouvelle Héloïse*, he went to throw seed to my birds in the park. During your illustrious visit, you made me notice how many species of birds live in my *Élisée*: turtledoves, robins, chaffinches, linnets, blackbirds, goldfinches, warblers, nightingales, and waterfowl, just as I have filled my *Arcadia* with rabbits, squirrels, and also donkeys, sheep, goats, horses, cows, bulls, and oxen. Whenever Rousseau leaves the two parks here, the *Arcadia* and the *Desert*, in order to visit the neighboring forest where he likes to collect plants at his leisure, he takes bread in his pockets to give to the fish in the lakes.

It is lovely out today, and, back from his usual walk, my young son Amable who accompanied him told me that he stopped to rest in the hut bored into the rock, having classified the plants of the herbarium he is composing. Amable also told me that he separated out a bouquet of his favorite flowers, periwinkles, and asked the servant of his "good friend" to gather them in an opaline vase in the room of the pavilion he is occupying with the woman he calls his "dear wife," that is to say Thérèse Levasseur whom he met in Paris twenty-five years ago and for whom I admit I have no affection. Did Jean-Jacques wish, perhaps, to render homage with that bouquet to the man who had been his "worst enemy"? For this is how good his heart is. I wanted you to know what had happened. Farewell. This evening my musicians are playing *The Village Soothsayer*, and Jean-Jacques has promised my children that he will sing a few parts of it with them.

P.S.: Rousseau has shared with one of my guests his project to write a complement to *Émile* as well as another opera whose title is borrowed from Longus, *Daphnis and Chloe*. But since his arrival here Rousseau has written nothing at all, for every day he takes walks and gives lessons to my children.

July 12 [*1778*].

You know the unhappy news from my message. Jean-Jacques, our beloved Jean-Jacques Rousseau, is no longer. On the second of this month, after a gentle walk in the park whence he returned carrying roses, wild hyacinths, garlands of honeysuckle, branches from wild apple and pear trees, white bryony, morning glories, and especially white saxifrages, speedwells, buttercups, and butter daisies in the meadows where the tall daisies, blue bellflowers, and gentle scabious all grow . . . He is no more, our good, marvelous friend. My young son dried the grasses and milfoil, and my daughter picked the bouquets of black clover and pink soapwort . . . "It costs me no expense or pain to wander nonchalantly from grass to grass, from plant to plant," he liked to tell us smiling. Then he breakfasted, as he likes to do, with Thérèse and his servant toward half past the tenth hour of the morning. But he was immediately taken with violent pains in his head and my servants carried him to his bed. He died at eleven o'clock. We treated him as though he were one of the family and, in truth, he was. The next day, after our women sat up with him the entire night, Houdon, the famous sculptor, came, as I had sent for him, and brought his death mask. He then performed an autopsy. On July 4, at eleven o'clock in the evening, accompanied by my family and a few village people who knew our friend for having met him when he was collecting plants, Rousseau, the sweet Jean-Jacques, was buried by my orders on the Island of Poplars that he cherished so. We climbed down the bridge to the right of the castle terrace and left the enclosure in order to reach one of the front pavilions that our friend occupied; the island separates from the shore a few meters from there, after the *suave cascade* with the greenish, mossy bottom matching the grotto of your Shenstone, the melancholic music of which can be heard on the rocks, at the end of the lake where various plants grow. Above the grotto, I had this verse of Virgil engraved: *Speluncoe, vivique lacus, hic frigida Tempe*; the waters escaping to supply the cascade are *rapid waters* which, however, do not boil. In this spot is our most dear and illustrious friend. May he rest in peace. Farewell.

I pass my mornings rereading the pages of my *Treatise on the Composition of Landscapes*, a part of which was printed a few years ago but prevented from circulating. The days are beautiful and, after lunch, instead of going toward the *Prairie*, I take a walk in the *Desert* where I enjoy moral and solitary reverie as the landscape engages me. Upon returning, when the cool evening spreads its vaporous hue in the distance, my eyes fix my soul upon the gentle distant green of the *Prairie* and glimpse the sixteen poplars whose tranquil shade invites sweet rest.

P.S. I have decided to have a little philosophical monument built, dedicated to the memory of the man who was alone and persecuted during his life for having put himself above vain grandeur, and whose genius has not ceased to illuminate the world.

"Jardins, parcs ou carrières, projet pour le domaine de Versailles," in *Plans raisonnés de toutes les espèces de jardins* (pl. XXV), by Thouin, 1820. Photo © École Nationale supérieure des Beaux-Arts.

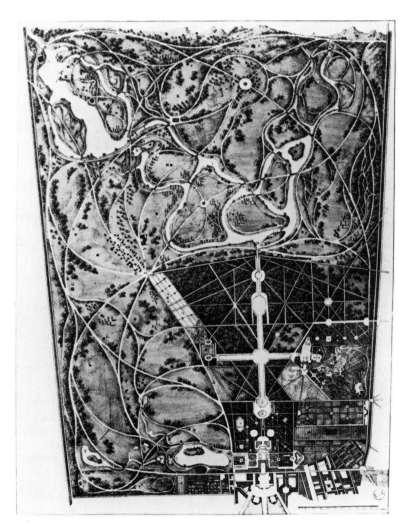

Allée Six

*Pécuchet made several diagrams, using his
mathematics box. Bouvard gave him advice. They
came up with nothing satisfying. Fortunately they
found in their library the work by Boitard, entitled*
The Architecture of Gardens.

FLAUBERT

In fact, the man who had, since his early childhood, placed his life, ideas, and the Ermenonville—that is to say his work—under the aegis of his illustrious contemporary, Jean-Jacques
Rousseau, and who received the old man after waiting for him so long, did not know that his
own tragedy would begin about ten years after the philosopher's death, forcing him, who
would be stubborn until his last days, to leave the estate he had conceived and built.

René-Louis de Giradin was thirty-one when he arrived in Ermenonville in 1766. Unoccupied
since the death of the king of Poland, Stanislas Leszczynski,[1] he had just inherited from his
mother an estate of 850 hectares that the landscapist Morel,[2] whom the marquis employed
for transformations and improvements, described as "a vast stretch of impracticable marshes,
with miry soil, exhaling unhealthy vapors in all seasons . . . hills varied with secondary
valleys, a beautiful forest nearby," which had been "ignored" and "sacrificed to a marshy
parterre." The marquis de Girardin had some parts of the castle—part of which dated from
the Middle Ages and part from the seventeenth century—demolished and remodeled in order
to turn it into a more livable residence; but he would direct most of his attention toward the
remodeling of the rest of the estate. He wished to create a park, a meadow, an "arcadia," a
"desert," and landscapes filled with *fabriques* in which one might, following the example of
Jean-Jacques, both "philosophize" and pay homage to Nature.[3]

His work fell halfway between the "jubilant baroque" Starobinski speaks of in connection
with Watteau and Fragonard[4] and the "neoclassical" tendencies that would soon predominate

in the return to antiquity undertaken by David, Boullée, and Ledoux. Once it was completed, the marquis settled into a life that he wished to be perfect, in all ways resembling his philosophical ideal.

He passed his days reading or writing in the morning; in the afternoon he took walks by himself or in the company of his children whose education he was overseeing personally, trying to implement the precepts described in *Émile* and going as far, it is said, as forcing them to climb a pole to gather their own food. In the evening, Monsieur de Girardin had concerts performed; in the summer they took place between the sky and the water, on the Island of Poplars where he had a pulpit of stone built. On Sunday he often walked toward the Rond-Point of Dance and Archery, accompanied by his guests, Sedaine, the Alsatian watercolorist Frédéric Mayer, Franklin, the abbé Delille, perhaps Fragonard, and a few "philosophers" who were passing through, Frenchmen or foreigners: these distractions, the personal inventions of the marquis, were meant for his "dear" peasants, for it is "in these rustic dances that the loves of the villagers are born, loves that begin with pleasure in order to end in marriage."

Thus the marquis de Girardin spent his days, in a happiness not so different from the happiness Jean-Jacques Rousseau described for us through the character of Monsieur de Wolmar: he was an industrious, caring, and just man, and his wealth made an "honest man" of him, a lover of comfort but virtuous and concerned about the lower classes. His happiness was deserved and serious.[5]

This philanthropic landowner and aristocratic philosopher might have enjoyed this happiness for many more years. But as the irony of fate would have it, it was broken by two events. Two miracles that the creator of Ermenonville had always been waiting for, both of which would turn to catastrophe: the arrival of Jean-Jacques, and the revolutionary upheaval dictated by his political philosophy.

The philosopher's brutal death, in fact, caused a horde of elated pilgrims to come to the estate, and their emotional transports, extreme and almost fetishistic at times, troubled the peaceful life that had been the object of his retreat. Thus, an entry dated July 22, 1783, in the journal of the young Anacharsis Cloots, the future Hebertist leader, contains this astonishing confession:

Jean-Jacques Rousseau's snuffbox, given by his widow to Antoine Maurice resident of Ermenonville: my fingers touched this box, my heart trembled, my soul become purer. Signed: the baron de Cloots du Val-de-Grâce, defender of J.-J.R. in my book: *On the Certitude of Mathematical Proofs*.

And, further on, in the account of a pilgrimage to Ermenonville undertaken by someone who, at the Convention, called himself the "orator of humankind," we get this description of the "expiatory sacrifice" he performed "on the tomb of the great man" on the Island of Poplars, on July 25, 1783:

We throw a few flowers on this tomb, rose mallows that seem to be growing there on purpose, then we prepare ourselves for the great sacrifice. My friend and I, we fight over the honor of burning Diderot's lampoon. We have brought everything that is needed: we draw out the lampoon, we tear out the guilty pages, and both of us on our knees, each holding one side of the infernal lampoon, we pronounce out loud the words: "To the manes of Jean-Jacques Rousseau. May the memory of the cowardly enemies of the man of nature and truth be forgotten. We, J. de Cloots, baron du Val-de-Grâce, and Gabriel Brizard, archivist-abbot of the order of the Holy Spirit, make an expiatory sacrifice on the tomb of the great man by delivering to the flames a lampoon that falsehood claims and truth disavows: the *Essay on Seneca* by the living Diderot against the dead Jean-Jacques Rousseau.[6]

One can only hope that, in a century when the grandiloquent exteriorization of emotions was rather common, the Girardins' tranquil way of life was not disturbed too often by such visits of their attendant holocausts and fanatical ceremonies.

But this was minor, compared to what followed.

Acquainted with Mirabeau, Vergniaud, and Sieyès, Renée-Louis de Girardin had watched the Revolution approach without fear. He applauded the reforms it proposed, for in them he saw the realization of his philosophical ideas. But, as early as 1791, in response to this thought of

Rousseau's in *The Social Contract*: "Let us never lose sight of the important maxim not to change anything without necessity, neither to take away, nor to add," de Girardin noted bitterly: "We are experiencing the truth of that maxim thoroughly now; if our representatives had been imbued with it, they would not have suddenly surrounded us with ruins."

He nonetheless continued—until 1792, when he was named commander of the national guard and gave a banquet for the volunteers in his castle—to entertain hopes about this Revolution that would, in the end, force many "miseries and horrors" upon him. In Paris, he attended club meetings regularly and even addressed the Jacobins, in 1790, a motion in which he recommended that one should never attack, but that a free and armed France should be erected against the invader. This speech, which was most inspired, was printed along with two others: in one, given on May 29, 1791, he condemned the caste system of the army of the ancien régime and complained about those old soldiers who were left to "rot in the captivity of the garrisons;" in another, given on June 7 of the same year and entitled *On the Necessity of Ratification of Law by the General Will*, he defended Jean-Jacques Rousseau's theses and demanded that all the laws voted by the assemblies should be subjected to a referendum, an operation that, according to him, would be made possible when couriers and stagecoaches were perfected. The true sovereignty of the people and the ratification of all laws by the suffrage of all citizens, this is what the Marquis de Girardin recommended in a rush of fervor for direct democracy against the excesses of the Convention. But the representatives of the people did not want to hear him, and he retired to his estate at Ermenonville in the company of the family of his friend, the knight Tautest du Plain.

It was then that his dark hours began. His civism—that is to say his support for the principles of the French Revolution—was questioned on the grounds that, as an aristocrat, he was of dubious origins and that he had had friends who dealt in the occult sciences—proof that he was plotting against the Republic. This provided the pretext for a search of the castle, and on August 31, 1793, the mayor and prosecutor of Ermenonville, equipped with a warrant, arrived once more at the estate to demand from "Renée Girardin, proprietor and cultivator at Ermenonville" a declaration of civism. René-Louis de Girardin declared that "the old and faithful friend, to the grave, of the author of *The Social Contract* and of his principles could in a free country only be considered suspect by bad citizens." But his sons had already been arrested in Paris and in Sézanne, and the Committee for Public Safety (Comité de Sûreté générale) judged him insufficiently pure. His daughter was locked up at Chantilly, then at the abbey of Chaalis, while he and his wife were placed under police surveillance in their home, where seals were put on the doors. As for the gardens, they were devastated, and the pyramid of the bucolic poets, Virgil and Theocritus who seemed foreigners, and Shenstone, Thomson, and Gessner, the "henchmen of the foreign tyrants," was overturned. The marquis de Girardin and his wife were only released on Thermidor 22 of the Year II, thanks to the intercession of their daughter and of Marie Joly, the actress who had come to place a crown of roses on Jean-Jacques Rousseau's tomb. Shortly thereafter, the men of Thermidor decided to transfer Rousseau's ashes to the Pantheon. The Marquis de Girardin let them do so and retired to Vernouillet, to one of his properties, where there was a castle belonging to his friend Tautest du Plain. He lived there for more than ten years in total retreat. He sometimes went to Ermenonville or to his estate of Puiseux. In his quarters at the castle, he read and drew a few designs for the estate's park as well as a *fabrique* in the shape of a small temple with twelve columns. On March 21, 1808, he wrote his last will and testament, in which he left the Ermenonville estate, to which he "had dedicated forty years of care and expense," undivided to his three sons who were supposed to have "a common steward, share revenues, and each live in a part of the buildings."

Renée-Louis de Girardin died at Vernouillet on September 20, 1808, and was, according to his wishes, buried alongside the friend of his dark days, Tautest du Plain, in the small village cemetery where his tombstone can still be found. Thus ended the existence of a just man, whose vocation lay in one of the most beautiful gardens of the world, a garden in which one can read the destiny—tragic given the hope that lay behind it—of an entire century.

The great Revolution had wanted to force the conservative course of history, to impose an abstract liberty by pretending to mold the soul according to a universal model and thus to unify civil society. According to Jacobinic radicalism, there could be no contract without an ideal body of reconciled citizens; nor could there be, as a consequence, any complete break with despotism. The central importance of the king, residing in his body—symbolic undoubtedly, but also material—was the exclusive principle of a tyrannical order that needed to be replaced by a contrary unity in the shape of an oath, of passionate fusion: the Nation. An imaginary institution that could only be incarnated through allegories and was open to the threat of the enemy (interior and/or exterior). But its fictional character made it all the more constraining. The sequence of slogans, "Long live the King / Long live the King—Long live the Nation / Long live the Nation," which describes this shift, only demonstrates this aporia: not how to dissolve the sovereignty of the State, but on the contrary to affirm it as unique, while the body of the king, who had incarnated it thus far, not only had to be repudiated as a delusion, but destroyed, cut into two parts to show everyone that the false, tyrannical unity that he had sustained was forever broken, divided into the head and torso of a designated Capet. The Convention stumbled over a terrible dilemma here, for contrary to the task that had faced the American Federalists, it was not a matter of *beginning* history with the help of the Republic, but of *beginning it again*.

We know what resulted: the Terror, Thermidor, the great Napoleonic dream of unifying Europe annihilated in the mass graves of Eylau, Madrid, and Moscow. But also a decisive impulse, a democratic energy that would swell throughout Europe. That is to say an extremely unstable situation made of reactionary exaltation nourished by the nostalgia for a lost social order, of revolutionary impulses animated by the dying ideal of 1793, and, finally, of nationalist furor, all against a background of a technical and industrial revolution entailing new antagonisms and pushing back the horizons of conflict.

Nostalgia for the past, on the one hand, and on the other, a frenetic appetite for the future: the romantic neurosis resides in this gap. Europe discovered Milton[7] and reinvented its Middle Ages, while getting excited about Watt and the progressive history invented by Hegel. And this schizophrenia was not satisfied with a univocal break. It sought complex divisions and cut all the great ideological currents in contrary fashion, pulverizing the visions of the past as well as those of the future: the "lost paradise" of the ultraroyalist conflicted with that of the liberal and that of the revolutionary, which also came into conflict with each other.[8] And as for the proletarian messianism soon theorized by Marx and Proudhon, it was only superficially related to the industrial religion of the Saint-Simonian entrepreneurs, to say nothing of the *rentier* ideal of the landowners.

Conflict became the rule and equilibrium the exception, demonstrating that Europe had irremediably entered an era of possibility as well as danger. For a century later it would seem proven that modernity is nothing other than democratic risk. And, since without God, the risk came without any safeguard besides the opinion of the "greatest number."

Whence two major tendencies, contradictory but complementary, concerning our object. The first was a return to the private garden on the one hand, in which the individual displayed his hopes and nostalgias.[9] The second was the opening of the public *promenades*, in which one can see several things: the return, after a period of revolutionary austerity, of a desire for urban pleasure; the social and hygienist concerns of a society beginning to recognize the emergence of the masses and the urban explosion; and the necessity to master its potential violence through edification, that is to say the presentation—exhibition—of a new ideal capable of policing it, in this case the continual progress of knowledge and the possibility of acquiring it, which form the two sides of the modern democratic myth par excellence.[10]

Before the middle of the century, Stendhal's "mirror" began reflecting this duality, central to the history of gardens in the nineteenth century. If *The Red and the Black* in fact, at least in its first part, is concerned above all with the conflict of its subjects, making the garden to the Rênal family the scene of its drama, the famous description of Verrières that opens this "chronicle of the nineteenth century" insists with irony upon the creation, by an ultra mayor, however (that is to say, someone unlikely to worry about the common good), of a large "public promenade that goes along the hill a hundred feet above the Doubs." A work of genuine merit, the author of which would only deserve praise, if it had not been due to a

very petty taste for walls,[11] and, even worse, if the cutting and clipping "to the core"—
which, moreover, took place twice a year—of the "vigorous plane trees" bordering it were
not signs of the despotism ruining Rênal's conservative spirit.

This dual development of the pleasure garden, which the Restoration could only witness,
more or less symbolizes the new social relationship that democratic principles wanted to set
up. Before it, in fact, there was no sharp and stable distinction between the public and
private. Thus there were the "commons" in the parishes, and it has been established that
many domains connected with royal power were open almost permanently: the Tuileries
gardens,[12] for example, where Restif de la Bretonne daydreamed, or the gardens of the
Palais-Royal, which Rameau's nephew adored and Camille Desmoulins often visited in order
to exhort the crowd to take the Bastille. But these were only franchises,[13] more or less
arbitrary and selective customary favors, since, in the case of the Tuileries, the "people in
rags" and those "in livery"—the great majority of people, that is—were excluded. So that it is
no surprise to read, in 1798, this triumphal cry written by the chronicler Louis-Sébastien
Mercier: "For a crown, one buys the privilege of thronging with the multitude these magnificent gardens that one could not enter. . . . This was no small pleasure for an enemy of the
Ancien Régime."

Customs, franchises, and favors, even if widely dispensed, were in fact not rights, those
rights that only a State of rights could found, by clearly separating the public sphere from
private spheres.

This is the essential explanation of much of the phenomenal blossoming of collective urban
life in France of the nineteenth century: if Paris imposed itself as the intellectual capital of the
West at this time, it was of course because of its already acquired position and the growth of
its population (much less than that of London, however), but also because of this first breath
of air given by the Revolution and the First Empire—before the Second Empire gave it real
lungs—which prepared it for all kinds of encounters, discussions, and combinations. When,
intoxicated by the news of the July 1830 Revolution, Heinrich Heine rushed to Paris from
Heligoland, it was the giraffe of the Jardin des Plantes, the allées of the Tuileries, and the

open-air balls on the left bank that he visited first—which suggests that to the arcades (which Heine visited often, especially the ones of the Panoramas) Walter Benjamin, another German Jew in love with Paris, could have added the "promenades" that formed gigantic outdoor "salons" in the summer months.[14]

In fact, beginning with the First Empire, the exceptional favor these public promenades enjoyed would increase until the Second Empire, when Haussmann undertook the project of opening new ones. All of society arranged to meet there. Lovely ladies paraded to the west, in the Tuileries or at Longchamp, before dazzled gentlemen. Young people danced into the night and remade the world at the Palais-Royal, offering a "spectacle of absolute voluptuousness unequaled in Europe."[15] The bourgeois gallivanted at Tivoli[16] or at the Champs-Élysées, delighted by the modern cafes and entertainments that could be found there. Daydreamers strolled in the Luxembourg or meditated near the dilapidated *fabriques* of the Bagatelle or the Folie-Monceau. And the people, that motley crowd of grisettes, street urchins, gossiping housewives, workers proudly wearing caps and broad belts of red fabric, would spread out on sunny Sundays toward the villages of the east and north, where the Bois de Vincennes and the Buttes-Chaumont would soon be constructed according to Hausmann and Alphand.

But the supreme attraction, the magical place that all Parisians gravitated to without distinction, was the Jardin des Plantes, where the old menagerie of Versailles had been transported after the Revolution. A baroque and solemn cortege that the Convention had, in an ironic twist of fate, scheduled for the 9 Thermidor!

Feast of Liberty, and triumphal entry of the objects of the sciences and arts. On Thermidor 9, at 9 o'clock in the morning, all citizens invited to compose the cortege will gather on the left bank of the Seine, near the Museum of Natural History. The first division of the cortege is dedicated to natural history. The chariots streaming by between two rows of professors and students carry minerals, grains, and foreign plants. The fifth, an African lion, the sixth, a lioness, the eighth, a bear from Bern. Then there will be two camels and two dromedaries. . . .[17]

The inventory, to use Prévert's word, is a little short, especially for an institution that was supposed to compete with the zoos of London or Loo.[18] So they began to improvise—to

improvise and decree. The fairground menageries of Paris and the provinces were national-
ized, and, for better or worse, the young Geoffroy Saint-Hilaire found himself the head of a
zoo that was heterogeneous but worthy of the young Republic's ambitions.

For all that, the history of the Museum is the stuff of a novel. An accumulation of characters
and adventures as varied and strange as the collections displayed in its galleries.[19] A dizzying
mixture of botany and zoology, of scholarly manias and classificatory passions, of infatua-
tions, intrigues, superb improvisation and absurd conservatism, of personal ambition and
obscure devotion, opinionated works, dreams, idleness, rapid decisions, and long-term
labor.

The story began at the beginning of the seventeenth century—Paris was somewhat behind
Padua, Montpellier, London, and Amsterdam, which had already launched into the adventure. Around 1626, the botanist and gardener Guy de La Brosse—who had been Boyceau's
assistant in the Luxembourg—tried, against the will of the Faculté's many lobbies, to convince Louis XIII of the need of organizing a royal garden destined to "cultivate medicinal
plants, which your people might turn to in its infirmities, where the disciples of medicine
might learn, and where those who teach it might address their needs."

The king let himself be convinced, and, as early as the middle of the century, the famous
English traveler, John Evelyn, a great lover of gardens to whom we owe several descriptions
of marvels that have since disappeared, could exclaim over what he called "the King's
famous garden":

It is a large enclosure with all the varieties of terrain needed for the cultivation of medicinal
plants. Its placement was well chosen, for it contains mounds, valleys, meadows, woods,
and it is richly supplied with exotic plants. In the middle of the parterre, there is a beautiful
fountain. Adjoining this garden there is a beautiful house, a chapel, a laboratory, an orange-
ry, and everything needed by its director, who is always one of the King's first physicians.

Thus began the first era of the garden, which one might call prescientific. It was a cumulative and descriptive stage, when observations piled up but thinking remained scholastic:

although Isidore of Seville's astonishing taxonomies had been left behind, Aristotle and Hippocrates continued to impose their *logia*. And alongside such skillful practitioners and truly original minds as Fagon, Rouelle the Elder, Duferney, and Tournefort, one also finds a few of Molière's doctors, including a certain Chirac, a despotic and incompetent individual who diverted "public" funds into his own pocket and used his position of intendant to bully two remarkable botanists, Antoine Laurent and Bernard de Jessieu.

It was these two men, however, who, working along the lines of Tournefort's tentative classifications, brought about an epistemological turning point in the Jardin du Roi. A new scientific approach to the world resulting from the emergence of natural history came to the fore alongside the geometric system. From being obscure research categories—obscure because unmathematical—botany and zoology became the ruling sciences of the period, for they seemed to incarnate the infinite richness of the concrete as opposed to the dryness of the abstract. Newton was overshadowed by Linnaeus, while the "curiosity cabinets" progressively fell in line with the rules governing scientific collections, which were in turn founded on the theoretical constructions of Buffon and Linnaeus.

This regulatory process, in which Foucault has perceived an almost perfect "disciplinary operation"—emblematic of those institutional procedures uncovered by the first part of his work[20]—has, once again, never been better incarnated by anyone than Antoine-Joseph Dézallier d'Argenville. At the beginning, he was an art lover who turned himself into a theoretician of the classical garden. But also a collector whose cabinet—one of the most remarkable in Paris—gathered pictures, art objects, stones, and shells, all of which he collected with passion. Moreover, as a researcher, Dézallier d'Argenville was interested in doing more than expanding subsequent editions of his *Traitée de jardinage*. Following a pattern of evolution that was characteristic of his century—one that led from Fontenelle to the Encyclopedists—he gradually moved the center of gravity of his work, and published, between 1742 and 1757, a *Lithologie*, a *Conchyliologie*, an *Oryctologie*, and a *Zoomorphose*, all provided with superb color engravings and conceived as "clarifications" of essential areas of natural history.[21] The considerable success of this didactic and classificatory enterprise would only be eclipsed by the concurrent appearance of the much more complete volumes of Buffon and Daubenton's *Histoire Naturelle*. It was also an enterprise—and in this it differed from the scientific spirit of the Museum directors—in which the scientific dimension remained subordinate to the passion for art. Not only because, in 1747, Dézallier d'Argenville followed his first two treatises on stones and shells with an *Abrégé de la vie des plus fameux peintres* (*Summary of the Lives of the Most Famous Painters*), which, in an encyclopedic fashion, makes an inventory of one hundred and eighty eminent artists, but because for him knowledge remained a category of the fine arts. "The aim of the fine arts is to imitate nature: but, to imitate nature, one must know it," explained his biographer, who adds: "The decided taste for natural history had been spreading in Paris for several years: a large number of people gathering, at least for their amusement, shells, insects, stones, minerals. Monsieur d'Argenville taught them to put, as he did, choice, and elegance in these kinds of collections."[22]

With Dézallier d'Argenville, in short, we are very far from any kind of *disciplinary operation* attempting, by neutralizing nuances and amplifying identity, to reduce live alterity in favor of a unity that was impoverished but scientific because connected to immobilization, ordering, and quantified classification. Although recognized as a scientist by his peers[23]—a scientist, his biographer tells us, who had the advantage over Tournefort of being able to do his own drawing—d'Argenville was first and foremost a man of taste and quality addressing men of taste and quality who were less informed than he was. The classical spirit, in short, remained essential for him, with elegance taking precedence over formlessness, and embellishment over spontaneous naturalness; the desire for knowledge came out of personal pleasure.

Elegance, pleasure: these qualities were also present in Buffon. If only at the level of his writing. But the collector-artist and the enlightened amateur have been replaced by the specialist for whom the beauty of collections is of secondary importance. It was his way of assuring his position in the world and attracting endowments for his research. Thus, explained Guy Barthélemy, Daubenton's first concern was "to complete collections, that is to say not to run after rare or curious pieces, but to establish series and to compare analogous objects." He then goes on to quote Cuvier:

The study and arrangement of these treasures had become for him [Daubenton] a true passion, the only one perhaps that has ever been noticed in him. He enclosed himself for entire days in the cabinet, he turned over the objects he had gathered there in a thousand ways; he examined all their parts scrupulously; he tried all possible orders, until he reached one that shocked neither the eye nor natural relationships.

Does it make sense, then, to say that, in the "tableaux" commanded by scientific order, the "disciplinary" was taking power over the poetic? This hypothesis, which we used to find convincing, no longer seems so obvious. So true is it that the great conceptual and linguistic constructions of Linnaeus or Buffon, each in their concurrent directions, were and continued to be fabulous poetic machines; and so true is it, also, that the gardens, greenhouses, and collections gathered at the Museum have not ceased to nourish an imaginary that was both troubling and wonderful. And—under these bluish windows where, like fossil dreams, the patiently assembled, powerful bones dream side by side; before those windows where, labeled with both their Latin and common names, in the old fashion, thousands of graceful skeletons in dizzyingly long lines expose the secret texture of the universe; in the jabbering aviaries, the parterres, the staggered rows of trees, the garden of the School of Botany where studious young girls walk about; and, finally, in the hothouses where, in a tropical triumph, the poisonous flower of flesh painted by the Douanier Rousseau is forever enclosed—in all these places it is the magic of the world that is gradually revealed to us. Something like an entrance to those "strange domains" designated by Apollinaire "where the mystery in flower offers itself to whoever wishes to pick it." It is the reverse side of discipline, the secret side that also evokes the poetic space of modernity.

The famous episode of the giraffe, insofar as it marked one of the strong moments of the collective imaginary of the nineteenth century, is unambigious on this point. Offered to Charles X by the pasha of Egypt in 1827, this elegant young creature from Abyssinia landed at Marseilles in March, flanked by three cows that would supply it with twenty liters of milk a day. In spite of the amulet around her neck, containing verses from the Koran, the threat of plague forced the new arrival into quarantine. Then came the departure for Paris, carefully prepared by Geoffroy Saint-Hilaire. A raincoat of rubberized cloth was cut out for the animal, with a hood and emblazoned decoration—one side for the king of France, the other for the pasha of Egypt—and they set off on an odyssey of 880 kilometers broken down into stages of 20 each. The *Croix de Paris* reported:

In front, and at a certain distance, a squad of policemen on horseback, their sabers out, clearing a passageway, instructing all the conductors to draw their horses to the side; then came the nursing cows whose familiar presence served to reassure and conduct the giraffe; behind, the Princess advanced slowly; she carried a leather collar with six tethers held solidly by her Sudanese guardians and some employees of the prefecture, like dignitaries encircling a catafalque; to the sides in the rear, the policemen on foot restrained the curious crowd. What joy for the people! From the entire region they came to enjoy the spectacle!

By the end of May, she was in Lyons; on June 30, at Villeneuve-Saint-Georges. Finally, at the beginning of July, the star, who had been lapping up all the attention, made her triumphal entry into Paris amid hundreds of thousands of curious onlookers who had come to see her do splits while drinking milk. Never, since Napoleon's return from the island of Elba, had such enthusiasm been seen in France. People wore "giraffe" clothes, had "giraffe" hairdos, filled their homes with "giraffe" bronzes and housewares, and in the streets and newspapers, there were "giraffe" debates. Charles X, who paid the animal the uncommon honor of letting it eat rose petals from his hand—on July 9, 1827, at the castle of Saint-Cloud—must have recalled on this occasion the far more menacing triumphal march of March 1815, and considered himself lucky to benefit from the popularity of a giraffe when his brother had been forced to duck before the approach of an "eagle," also from Egypt, who "flew from belltower to belltower" on a similar itinerary.

The destiny of a star is cruel, however. Your audience forgets you as soon as you cease to interest it. If the "giraffe fashion" survived the Restoration, as Heine's impatience to see the Museum suggests, the actual giraffe only died in 1845, and Flaubert did not mention her when he had Bouvard and Pécuchet visit the Jardin des Plantes.

In the galleries of the museum, they passed the stuffed quadrupeds with astonishment, the butterflies with pleasure, the metals with indifference; the fossils made them dream, the seashells bored them. They examined the hothouses through the windows, and shuddered to think that all those leaves were exuding poisons. What they found remarkable about the cedar was the fact that it had been brought back in someone's hat.

Is the omission due to a lack of documentation (the scene is supposed to have taken place around 1839) or does it prove that the animal was no longer considered a novelty? The second hypothesis seems more likely, especially since this visit, although summarized in a few lines, turns out to be essential to the action of the novel. For it concentrates the future destiny of the two assistants (one of whom was returning from the Jardin des Plantes, we should note, at the time of their first meeting on Boulevard Bourdon), and it indicates the strategic importance—in the astonishing didactic system set up in the nineteenth century by (and for) the neobourgeoisie—of the public promenades, which had found its scientific expression in the Jardin des Plantes.

The nobility's past was a web of great events and genealogies. The new ruling class built itself a past—a patrimony—that was to take the credit for its industrious present. As though its entire legitimacy was being played out in this relationship. As though its survival hung upon the multiplication of characters such as Homais (representing self-satisfied imbecility) and Bouvard and Pécuchet (representing a good will that was touching, albeit without hope).[24]

Whence the didactic vertigo that seized town councillors and found one of its main expressions in the construction of the "public promenades" that would soon appear on a smaller scale in the world's fairs.

At the end of the eighteenth century, Alexandre Lenoir began gathering in a garden on the Quai des Célestins all the evidence pertaining to French history that he could save from the iconoclastic furor of the revolutionaries and, even more dangerous, the speculators in national property. In the middle of the lawns or in the shade of trees, in an atmosphere of "sweet melancholy that speaks to the sensitive soul," one could visit a concentrated tableau of national genius, composed from fragments of monuments, sepultures of great figures from the past, and statues. It was a kind of outdoor historical museum where the designer's devouring passion and furious desire to edify the people sometimes led to the false getting mixed in with the true, as in the case of the alleged tomb of Heloïse and Abelard. But the enterprise was essentially fertile, since it created the matrix of the actual Musée des Monuments Français, which can be visited today at the Palais de Chaillot.

In a spirit close to Lenoir's, Antonin Cailloit suggested that the Père-Lachaise should no longer be considered an ordinary cemetery, but a museum-promenade, a "profane garden" destined to bring together the funerary monuments of the modern era.

Even more extraordinary, because crazier, was the project of the count Léon de Laborde, a man belonging to the cultural and administrative establishment, who dreamed of a great project for a "Union of the arts and industry"[25] and proposed in 1856 that six large didactic promenades should be opened in Paris; these would become "an auxiliary, a place for experimentation, and a spillway for the Museum of Natural History and the Louvre Museum."[26] "In less than ten years from now," he said enthusiastically, "we will have in our promenades an outdoor Museum, made lovelier with all of nature's charms. Everything that is restricted in a museum will be welcome in our promenades, framed with ivy and covered with bramble."

This project, the aim of which was to place in exceptional garden-museums a few important relics, such as blocks detached from Mount Sinai, Mount Calvary, and the rock of Sainte-Hélène, was judged to be excessive. But, as the historian Michel Vernes has remarked, it foreshadowed the world's fair project in which gardens played an essential role.

Elaborated very quickly each time by the new masters of the French landscape garden,[27] the world's fair gardens constituted a technical wonder, an autonomous marvel destined to inspire astonishment and admiration in the public, and a capital piece in the vulgarizing and apologetic equipment displayed by these events. Kaempfen exclaimed over the 1867 fair in the following manner:

Formerly, from the wooded heights of the Trocadéro, today metamorphosed into an immense grassy amphitheater sloping gently down to the Seine, and cut by a gigantic staircase, the eye, crossing the river, first stopped on an arid and naked plain of sand.

This Parisian desert was called the Champ de Mars.

The Champ de Mars is now but a name and a memory. The desert has become the most visited spot of the world; better yet, the entire world itself, Europe, Asia, Africa, America, Oceania, with their human types, their animals, plants, minerals, natural products, industry, sciences, fine arts, are contained in these forty hectares.

A prodigious number of buildings of all kinds, of all styles, of all times, surging in the middle of the trees and arbors; domes, bell towers, the chimneys of smelting furnaces, towers, lighthouses, cupolas, minarets, outlined against the sky; great green masses crowned by the dazzling glass windows of the winter gardens; in the center of this confusion, the arc of an enormous ellipse; this is what one sees from afar and from a bird's-eye point of view in the spot where the Champ de Mars used to be.

Carmontelle, who wanted to unite "all times and all places" in a single garden, thus saw his dream realized; and, in this taxonomic space, this odd collection of gardens, a garden-museum exhibiting, among other marvels, gardens following a general plan, in a perspective close to Gustave Thouin's. Around 1820 Gustave, the son of the Museum's gardener, drew "reasoned plans of all the kinds of gardens." One of these—number 25—sought to gather the "parks of Versailles, the big and little Trianon, a garden that was sylvan, pastoral, country, Chinese-romantic, and French-romantic."

This shift in didactic desires toward megalomaniacal, almost delirious enterprises could have been frightening. But it was, on the contrary, reassuring. Just as the "disciplinary operation" of natural history had its reverse side, the history of public promenades opened in the nineteenth century cannot be reduced to the single aspect of social edification, destined to cast a new elite in the mediocre mold of an Homais. Because there is an evident heroism here, both democratic and Saint-Simonian, commanding the direction of these enterprises. Heroism because these works, which were artful in a way that was neither fortuitous nor foreign to their premises, enriched our cities with spaces that still exist, that we can enjoy every day, and that our technological modernity seems incapable of equaling.

In fact, if we consider Paris only—but the example could also be repeated in the provinces—the triumphant springing up of the Bois de Boulogne and the Bois de Vincennes, the multiplication of neighborhood squares, and the creation of three interior parks,[28] including an exceptional masterpiece, the Buttes-Chaumont, are to the credit of an era that was surely less worthless and grotesque than the one described by Flaubert, Offenbach, and Labiche. Joseph Prudhomme was certainly sententious and timid, the "synthesis of bourgeois stupidity,"[29] and Perrichon's empty moral vanity was nauseating. But this society was, however, worked by an ambition that went beyond Bouvard and Pécuchet's ridiculous projects. An essentially democratic ambition[30] that, on the other side of the Atlantic, in an even more shrunken cultural universe, would end up by giving birth to the United States of America. Proof enough that the nonromantic side of the French nineteenth century deserves a new reading, without the blinkers we have inherited from the antibourgeois alliance of an intelligentsia—which was itself divided between the party of the Commune and the party of the Action Française—with the varieties of antiparliamentary radicalism (anarchic-unionist or "patriotic") flooding the public.

There remains the fact that we owe the horticultural flowering of the second half of the nineteenth century to the work of five men. Five representatives of a milieu that preferred the lukewarm but stubborn genius of the engineer Eiffel—whom Huysmans loathed, calling him the builder "of the new church in which the divine service of the high bank is celebrated"— to the feverish genius of Baudelaire or Gustave Moreau.

Five men: Napoleon III, who, as a result of his exile in London and his old Saint-Simonian passions, had become something of an entrepreneur gardener; the prefect Haussmann, who in this matter proved he had more judgment than he did in a strictly urban domain; Adolphe Alphand, the chief engineer Haussmann put in charge of the promenades; and the two who actually created the masterpieces, Davioud for architecture and Barillet-Deschamps for horticulture and landscape art.

It is hard to be enthusiastic about Haussmann's evisceration of the capital, which was dictated by the "logic of an artilleryman,"[31] the promotion of real estate speculation, a disdain for the suburbs, and a naive vision that saw modernity as the penetration of the railway into the urban fabric.[32] His work destroyed the Ile de la Cité, curetted the square in front of

Notre-Dame, cut back the Luxembourg and the Parc Monceau, and "rectified" subtle layouts only to create theatrical vistas for the pleasure of the parvenu. In short, it cut, in the heart of a complex fabric, straight boulevards and avenues that were without grace, since they lacked diversity. The idea of applying such surgery, which prefigured the urban catastrophe of the twentieth century, to Rome or Venice—and Paris was at the time comparable to Rome or Venice—is enough to make one shudder.

The fact remains that this evisceration, even in its detestable violence, was inseparable from a project conceived as a condition of industrial modernity, itself impossible without the appropriate hygiene. Whence Haussmann's interest in creating public promenades—"those verdant spaces that dispense health, defending the human life that their beneficial influence prolongs" and that "in addition offer workers and their families places for rest and pleasure."[33]

The promenades of the Second Empire, consequently, ran the risk of taking as brutal and pretentious a shape as the ravaging brutalism into which they were to be integrated. And, if they escaped such a fate, it was not because of the prefect's many interventions. In an astonishing passage of his *Mémoires*, Haussmann tells how, having gone to visit Constantinople in 1873 upon his friend Ismail Pasha's invitation, he suddenly recognized a "familiar land" in a park of the Bosporus as he was "coming up from the shore to the dirt road from Constantinople to Thérapia, then to Buyuck-Déré." Here was the style of his ex-gardener Barillet, who had offered his services to the Porte from 1869 to 1871 shortly before his death. And although Haussmann praised the "great qualities" of this Ottoman park—"a perfect understanding of the distribution of the ground between undulating lawns, clumps of trees or rare bushes, baskets of plants and flowers"—he could not restrain his usual criticisms: "A certain abuse of details and too few allées." "I wanted," he added with renewed furor, "in embracing all of the park, to beat several of the paths with a stick, as in the past on the plans of that skillful landscapist, to give more breadth to the parts unfortunately cut by useless paths."

"An abuse of details." "Useless paths." Fortunately there remains, at the Buttes-Chaumont, at

Vincennes, and Montsouris, some of those "defects" that the baron, who loved "breadth," could not "beat" according to the plans of his landscapist. But the anecdote is significant. First, because of what it tells us about the esthetic conflicts between the prefect and artist whom, however, he had been smart enough to distinguish in Bordeaux, when he was only the subprefect of Blaye, and the modest, very obscure and self-taught horticulturist with an independent business in the region. Second, because of what it reveals about the historical injustice that credits Alphand—whom Hausmann also noticed in Bordeaux—for a project in which he was, in fact, only the organizer and intellectual commentator. The magnificent promenades of the Second Empire were executed under Alphand's direction, and the theory behind them was described in a superb work, recently reprinted,[34] in which he took care to erase, if only by implication, all traces of the one who was their true creator and recognized by his peers: Jean Pierre Barillet, called Barillet-Deschamps.

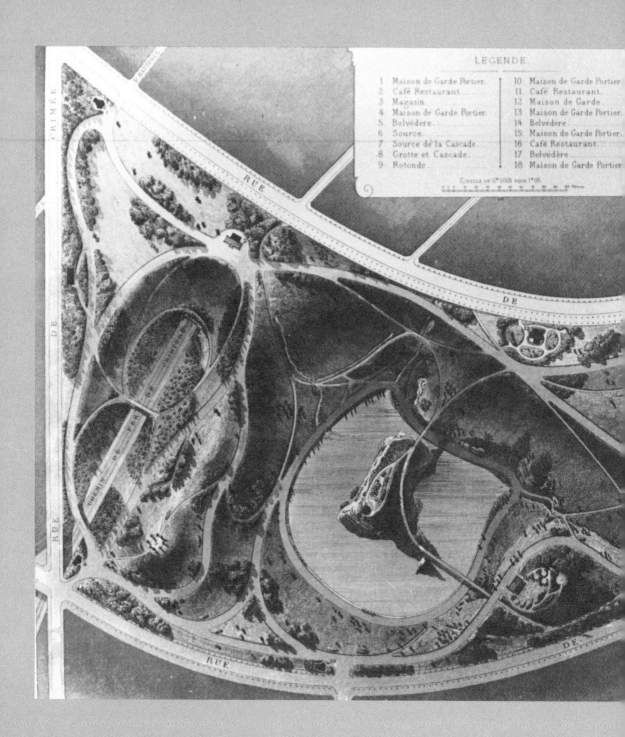

LEGENDE

1.	Maison de Garde Portier.	10.	Maison de Garde Portier.
2.	Café Restaurant.	11.	Café Restaurant.
3.	Magasin.	12.	Maison de Garde.
4.	Maison de Garde Portier.	13.	Maison de Garde Portier.
5.	Belvédère.	14.	Belvédère.
6.	Source.	15.	Maison de Garde Portier.
7.	Source de la Cascade.	16.	Café Restaurant.
8.	Grotte et Cascade.	17.	Belvédère.
9.	Rotonde.	18.	Maison de Garde Portier.

Echelle de 0ᵐ,008 pour 1ᵐ,00.

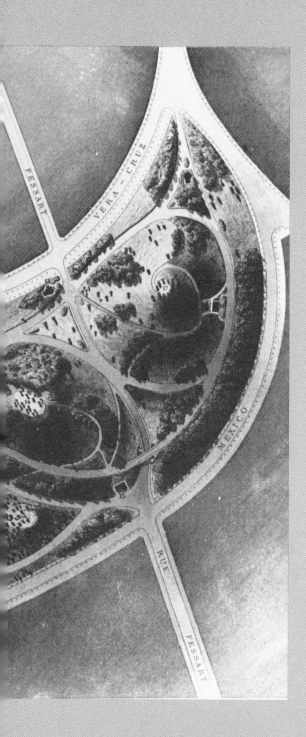

The park of Buttes-Chaumont in *Les promenades de Paris*, by Alphand, 1867–73. Photo © École d'architecture Paris/La Villette.

I had decided that morning to go by way of the Père-Lachaise Cemetery. I don't know why. Maybe because it was cold. Or because of the atmosphere at the office, which was as cutting as the knives of ice hanging from the gutters and divided into two irreconcilable clans the "old ones" of the imperial administration from the "new ones" appointed by the young Republic.

One morning in December, shortly before ten o'clock, I was briskly walking down the central allée of the cemetery that leads from the northern gate to the main entrance on the boulevard. The marble monuments looked like giant pastries frozen in a crystal crust. Stiffened by the cold, the cypresses and yews creaked like poorly greased gallows. No one in the allées. Not even a soldier in search of servant girls.

"Good heavens," I said to myself, reaching the circle where about twenty men in formal dress were standing. "What a funny idea, to bury someone on a day when the gravediggers are going to have a hard time cracking open the earth!"

I was about to continue on my way, when suddenly:

"Hey, Brizeux, what a surprise!"

"Ernest!" I exclaimed as a thin silhouette detached itself from the silent gathering. "Ernest André! . . . It's been at least ten years, I think!"

"Ten years exactly," the young man answered, embracing me. "Ten years since the Pension Labadens!"

Ernest seemed delighted about our meeting.

"So you too came for the ceremony? I didn't know you had a taste for horticulture, and you carefully hid it from me that you knew Barillet!"

"You are mistaken, my friend. It's a coincidence that I'm passing through. My office—"

"It can wait. Two civil servants at the beginning of their careers can only profit from hearing people sing the praises of a man as talented as Barillet."

Ernest looked scornfully at my outfit, which was not as elegant as I would have liked:

"For you're a civil servant, too . . ."

"Exactly. The Office of Weights and Measures."

"And I'm in the Administration of Parks and Gardens. My father became the director a short time ago."

I wanted to go to the office about as much as I wanted to be hung. The cold, after all, would provide an excuse. I would only have to cough very loudly the next day.

"Good for you!" Ernest cried out on seeing that I had decided to stay. "This twenty-second of December, 1875, will remain engraved upon the annals of the Collège Labadens!"

This exchange had made us lag behind the cortege, so that the ceremony had already begun by the time we joined up with it again.

"This isn't a funeral," Ernest said. "But the celebration of an anniversary."

The circle of men in formal dress had grown somewhat. Enough so that one could deduce that the deceased had a certain reputation, but not enough to justify the obsequious respect paid to the monument that had just been uncovered. It was a simple bust, the effigy of a man who could not have been more than fifty, whose gravestone bore only these words: "To Barillet, his friends." I was about to ask Ernest who this Barillet was, when a tall man, looking very dignified in his tails and top hat, approached us.

"Vilmorin," Ernest whispered. "Henry Vilmorin."

The name was not unknown to me. It evoked strange sensations: the smell of humus, a vision of greenhouses, a sparkling of colors, tastes, and bizarreries, all of which seemed out of place on this glacial morning.

"Come on, Gustave . . . Vilmorin . . . The nurseryman!"

My friend sounded scandalized. I reassured him with a smile. I had recently read, in *L'Illustration* or *Le Globe*, an article dedicated to the fellow. It described his property at Verrières-le-Buisson, built by Louis XIV for Mademoiselle La Vallière, which his family had acquired at the time of the Revolution. It spoke of a garden in a state of confusion, with flower beds taken over by seedlings instead of parterres and incongruous groupings in which, for example, a strange plant from the Himalayas might turn out to be the cousin of our potato. It narrated the life of a researcher, shopkeeper, and industrialist, a man respected by his colleagues, who was always ready to scour the countryside and had been honored around the world.

"Sirs," Vilmorin began in a declamatory tone. "In uncovering this monument, we are performing our first duty toward the man whose loss we are grieving today: allow me now to pay him the tribute of our memories and our regrets. All of us knew, admired, and loved Monsieur Barillet; all of us have lost in him a true and devoted friend; all of us also deplore, in his loss, the loss of one of those men of valor and initiative whose work shall be remembered as epoch-making and who bring honor upon themselves in honoring their country. Barillet was, in fact, the sole maker of his fortune: as such, his career can provide encouragement and set an example for those who might wish to walk in his footsteps."

The orator paused, disturbed by the wind ruffling the pages of his speech. I glanced furiously toward my companion, who seemed indifferent to the cold sawing at my own legs, if not his. Vilmorin went on:

"Born in Saint-Antoine-du-Rocher near Tours, Barillet demonstrated early on a decided taste for gardening, a common enough thing in a province where the humblest houses are hidden under roses and climbing plants, where the love and cultivation of flowers are so widespread that the entire region deserves to be called the Garden of France. As for this love of flowers, Barillet was destined to propagate it far and wide and to make it penetrate right to the center of our crowded cities. But, near Saint-Antoine-du-Rocher, there was the agricultural and penitentiary colony of Mettray, a masterpiece of charity and wisdom, which every year transforms hundreds of children apparently destined for poverty and vice into honest and industrious workers. You all know Monsieur Demetz, its illustrious founder, who was still its director at the time. Well, this great educator noticed the young Barillet, who had been placed by his parents, poor but wise farmers, as a supervisor and instructor of gardening in the penitential colony. In fact, Demetz was so impressed with him that first he sent him to Paris in order to take courses in horticulture at the Jardin des Plantes, and then he asked him to organize a school of gardening in Mettray. Barillet's success exceeded all expectations. Soon the colony was no longer a match for him, and, with the support of his old teacher, he set himself up in Bordeaux under the sign of Barillet-Deschamps. There he proved himself to be an outstanding landscape architect, and attracted the attention of the two men who would be the future transformers of the city of Paris but worked in Bordeaux at that time. Barillet would become more than an ordinary collaborator for them. After these men were brought to Paris, they called him in turn to the banks of the

Seine, and Barillet became the artist charged with translating their grandiose ideas into marvelous realities."

Thus far the nurseryman's voice had been controlled, but strong with the sure passion carrying it. Suddenly I heard it tremble, as though he were approaching a dreaded passage that had undoubtedly been carefully weighed, but remained perilous nonetheless.

"If Barillet owed to his supervisors many magnificent occasions to display his talent," he continued, clearing his throat, "he repaid them by executing their plans the way no one else could have done in his place. Moreover, he more than earned his share of honor and glory in the history of the embellishment of Paris, although one may seek traces of his efforts vainly in the many works, some quite detailed and remarkable, that treat this subject. Remember, sirs. The Bois de Boulogne and Vincennes, the Parc Monceau, Montsouris and the Buttes-Chaumont—would these marvels be envied by the entire world if Barillet's expert hand had not commanded their learned execution? And need I remind you of the gardens of the 1867 world's fair, which sprang up from the earth in a few weeks through a miracle of daring and activity, and then disappeared, but not without having been admired by visitors from the entire planet? At the time when Barillet accomplished this miracle, his name was already known throughout Europe and his work had crossed frontiers. He was beginning works on the park of Laeken and sketching out the parks of Prater in Vienna . . . Soon seduced, like many artists of his caliber, by the marvelous sky and incomparable light of the Orient, he left Paris to dedicate himself to gigantic works in Egypt, but death left him barely enough time to sketch out a rough plan for them. The ceaseless activity of his last years, the constant traveling, the sleepless nights, worries, and rivalries had all exhausted him, and he died two years ago, not yet fifty, in a spa in Vichy, where the beneficial waters had not, alas, been able to cure him."

"That's right on target," Ernest whispered. "And ought to set tongues wagging in my department!"

I did not understand why he was getting so excited. True, I had admired the garden at the world's fair, and I enjoyed nothing more than dawdling about on Sundays, in search of a sister soul, near the waterfall of the Buttes where my father, before the works had begun, used to forbid me to go play for fear of pestilence. But I had never thought to ask myself about their creator . . . That would have been as incongrous as asking myself who had built the building where I was born, on the rue de Ménilmontant.

The next part of the speech escaped me. It concerned technique, the selection of plants, the creation of flowers. Barillet—the orator loudly proclaimed—was a true poet, an artist gardener, versed in the cultivation of those flowers called pansies, a species he had diversified by transporting pollen from one to another with a brush. And so he obtained original colors, inverting the color of the heart and that of the petals, marrying red, garnet, yellow, indigo . . . The artifice interested me. Enough to make me regret that those of us who worked in Weights and Measures did not have such clear-cut opportunities to demonstrate our talents.

But the orator had finished. There was the patter of clapping hands. Taking advantage of the pause, a beanpole of a man with a tanned face, looking uncomfortable in an oversized suit, came up to Ernest and greeted him warmly:

"Quite nice, sir, quite nice. It takes a certain amount of nerve to be here, when your father chose to decline our invitation."

My friend was about to answer him, but the other had taken the place that Henry Vilmorin had occupied thus far.

"Ermens," Ernest told me. "People were saying beforehand that he would conclude. He was Barillet's right hand and succeeded him in the position of principal gardener of the city of Paris."

Ermens may have been a brilliant gardener, but he was certainly a paltry orator. He stammered out a distressing chain of anecdotes about Cairo and Constantinople where he had gone with his master, got tangled up in a joke about the waist measurements of the pasha's wives, and ended with some doggerel verse his father had composed in memory of the deceased:

> In the parks and gardens throughout our city
> The pleasant and the useful are joined in harmony.
> Travel and work shortened his days;
> Death with its scythe interrupted his course.
> His works will survive, and with horticulture
> Barillet was ready to tame nature.

In payment for your works, take this crown:
Regrets have woven it, friendship gives it to you.

The affair was turning to farce. The crown was late because of the ice, and the principal gardener of the city of Paris did not know what to do. For a moment he hesitated between making a piteous retreat and renewing his eulogy. There was a silence punctuated by shrugs and embarrassed looks when suddenly, as though incapable of containing his anger any longer, a ruddy man sprung out from the group.

"But go ahead and say it! Say it finally! . . . Make the scandal public! Let them know about our astonishment! . . . Two years ago we parted without there having been any official gesture of recognition for Barillet's grave! . . . It was the least, however, that certain gentlemen could have done—to bow before the man who had served them so well! . . . Who would these folks be, without Barillet-Deschamps? . . . Upon what works would their fame rest? . . . But look who's here today. Those gentlemen are absent again. They even forgot to pay their offering! Forgotten . . ."

The little man in the frock coat, his face red either from the cold or with indignation, turned toward the tomb and cried out, choking: "You will have missed nothing, dear Barillet-Deschamps. Neither brilliant services, nor admirable creations, nor the ingratitude of those who are obligated toward you and owe you the most!"

Had the dead risen from their tombs, the ensuing tumult would not have been greater. There was whistling, insults, clapping, in short a hubbub of the kind the Père-Lachaise had not seen since the executions against the Federates' wall. The beanpole was waving his long arms to restore order, Ernest was insulting one of the protesters, the little ruddy man seemed about to fight it out with a beanpole who seemed completely enraged, while Vilmorin ran from one group to another screaming: "Sirs! . . . Sirs . . . !"

I would have liked it if the scene had continued thus and if, after beginning in the contemplative atmosphere of a cemetery, it had ended in a meadow. I rarely go to the theater, but the farce that was performed there, *gratis pro deo*, equaled the best play by Messrs. Meilhac and Halévy. Unfortunately, the delivery man had the stupid idea to arrive at that precise moment, carrying a monstrous wreath in which roses, begonias, primroses, pansies, petunias, and carnations, asters, and marguerites formed a dazzling rainbow where one could read, in gothic golden letters stitched in silk: *Your memory lives on in us, Barillet, and it will survive you.*

It was over. I walked down the path leading to the boulevard with Ernest. It began to snow and, given how heavily it was coming down, I told myself that the wreath everyone had waited for so impatiently would be a real disaster before nightfall. Flowers, leaves, and ribbons, the whole thing would be eaten by the cold and snow, and would form a grayish pulp that the guards would undoubtedly throw on the manure heap. "Such is the fate of poets' dreams," I mused with an odd pleasure. "In school they are praised, and penniless teachers make us shed tears over their delirious rantings. Nonsense . . . rubbish . . . nothing positive about it. Just smoke . . . Is he further along, this Barillet-Deschamps, for having had a few original minds support him? . . . Are his fortune and family any better off?"

As for Ernest, he was walking briskly. He told me he knew a fabulous cafe on the place Voltaire where they served the kind of food you could find before the Siege.

"And in this filthy weather, Gustave, old-fashioned tripe!"

I approved the idea while promising myself that I would enjoy several bottles of old Cahors wine at his expense. But we had barely crossed the Roquette when the beanpole gardener stopped us.

"I wanted to say again, sir . . . well, thank you . . . You made a beautiful gesture there. A truly beautiful gesture . . ."

Then, seeing that we were eying the menu exhibited in a glass box outside the restaurant, he added: "But you are going in to eat, undoubtedly . . . May I treat you?"

When you earn a hundred sous a week, you don't turn down an opportunity to save ten. Especially when you were getting ready to eat tripe, after having noticed that the menu vaunts foie gras, stuffed quail, potatoes *à la sarladaise*, preserves, and other sweets you cannot afford.

The warmth of the cafe was most welcome. As for the food served there, it was truly scrumptious. So scrumptious in fact that, diverted by the sauces, sauternes, and Saint-Émilion, I hardly followed the conversation, which struck me as trivial. Over the liqueurs, however, I dared the following remark:

"Tell me, Monsieur Ermens—and let's be honest about it—that Barillet-Deschamps, he made a mess of his life!"

"A mess, young man! Think about what you're saying . . . He left a body of work—"

"Which others take credit for, as far as I can understand."

"Haussmann and Alphand? . . . Whatever you do, don't believe the ravings of someone like Lepère. One can be a distinguished arboriculturist and know nothing about politics."

"All the same," Ernest interrupted, excited, as I was, by the Bordeaux wine, "you aren't going to pretend that their absences were accidental. Nor that Alphand's omission of Barillet in his work was not calculated! Do you know what my father spouts today? That his works are collective and that—I quote from memory a passage from the book he is currently writing— 'the ideas, the experiments combined by the various departmental heads of the Promenades and Gardens of Paris gave rise to a new genre that has since been attributed to a single artist who perfected it, but by no means invented it.' And do you want to know the worst, the greatest disgrace? He manages not to cite Barillet once but keeps his name in the notes, like an after-thought to explain that cowardly expression 'a single artist'! After what I've told you, can you insist that there's no plot against the man?"

The principal gardener of the city of Paris contemplated his second glass of Armagnac.

"Do not make judgments too quickly, in the excitement of youth. Of course, we all know what he really was. Barillet was a new Le Nôtre, everyone knows that. But the emperor, Haussmann, and especially Alphand were more powerful in this affair than Louis XIV and Fouquet together. Alphand knows quite a lot about gardens, and he is far from through designing them for us . . . You are taking for granted many trials and tribulations, my young friend. Imagine that in 1868 Alphand had foreseen the baron's disgrace, and resolved to make his career for himself, that is for all of us. Where would we—including your father—be at present, if our boss had not known how to break off so skillfully, in order to reappear like a phoenix before the Republic?"

The Republic was my field. I loved Gambetta with my heart, and Adolphe Thiers with my reason.

"Do you mean to say, sir, that the Republic is a wench who lets herself get knocked up by the first one who comes along?"

"There you have it! I let you be the judge, Monsieur André," the horticulturist went on, with an air of exhaustion. "It's this spirit of revenge I wanted to speak to you about . . . If a man as fine as your friend can react in this manner, think how great the menace must be! Only our boss's good manners . . ."

I did not continue my attack. Combat, even for the Republic, was not in the air, but the sweet euphoria that results from a good meal.

"Besides, Barillet was through," the beanpole went on. "He'd gotten strange ideas into his head. For example, in Cairo where I had followed him, he kept on quoting a certain Baudelaire to me. A depraved character who poses as a poet, it seems. 'Sounds, fragrances, and colors correspond' he used to repeat, like someone hallucinating. I got so fed up I asked him to lend me his book. You won't believe me. *The Flowers of Evil*! As though those are the kind of plants that an honest gardener, respected by his employers, would have in mind for a square or a promenade! . . . No, as I said before, Barillet was through."

It was past four-thirty. The waiter looked like he was about to throw us out.

"It's time to get going," I said to my companions. "If we stay another half-hour, the owner will make us stay to dinner!"

We parted on the sidewalk. I felt like walking a little, like poking about, slumming on rue de Lapper where a reliable friend had once recommended a brothel to me. It was time to sow my wild oats, to rid myself of the stupid prejudices that had been obstructing my career for years: such was the lesson I had drawn from my day. What good does it do to play the honest, respectful man? That's not the way to make a name for yourself! You have to push yourself up and play elbows at the right moment!

"Can you believe that Ermens!" Ernest confided in me as the old horticulturist moved off into the gusting snow. "Did you hear how he was defending his boss! What a disappointment! . . . A real bootlicker."

He opened his umbrella in a sudden movement that revealed his anger.

"Visit me at the office. It will do me good to breathe less servile air! The air of Labadens . . . On second thought, not there. Come up to the Buttes-Chaumont. I'm there on Wednesdays giving orders to the clerks."

I had almost forgotten Ernest, Barillet-Deschamps, and this ridiculous story when, two years later, it happened that one July afternoon I had a date with a cute girl who had expressed some interest in me. I was in an excellent mood as I climbed rue Fessard, saying to myself: "Easy as pie, the girl will be in my bed tonight. A secretary temping for the Weights department isn't going to pass up a chance to make the new boss of the Measures department happy."

Since the weather was nice and my new position afforded me the time, I had arranged for us to meet at the Buttes, on the suspension bridge over the lake. From there I would be able to conduct the affair at my leisure. Depending upon the degree of vertigo the spot induced in the young girl, I would either take her up to the Rotonde for a view of Paris, or straight to the Grotto, where the shade and coolness would serve as allies.

The heat was becoming stormy. Heavy and burning like certain summer days in Paris. Leaving rue Fessard with relief, I entered the park by the gate on rue de Mexico, then took the first left. The trees had grown quite a bit since my last visit. They spread freely above the lawns, surrounded by floral clumps that looked like bouquets, and gave a pleasant cover to the shortcut I had taken. "I'll be damned," I said to myself, however, as I climbed the rocky ground. "I'd forgotten there were so many hills in the Buttes-Chaumont! Slow down, or you'll be in a sweat by the time you meet your date."

There was no one on the suspension bridge. Surprised, I consulted my watch. Ten past three. The delay was incompatible with my position. "So, my pretty one, we've decided to reverse roles?" I said to myself with some amusement, rewinding my pocket watch.

I leaned on the railing. Down below, carriages for hire were clipping around the lake, taking lovers for a spin an hour ahead of the schedule I had set for my own tryst. The parasols women were carrying sprinkled the path with pastel-colored touches like butterflies enervated by the heat. If not for the lush plant growth, one could have imagined oneself at the beach, in one of those fashionable bathing stations on the Norman coast where the chalk cliffs plunge violently into the water the way the cliff of the belvedere plunged into the lake.

"For heaven's sake! That girl has actually stood me up! It's past three-thirty and not even an excuse! . . ."

I could not get over it. I was dumbfounded by the fact that a simple secretary temping in the Weights department could have been so lacking in respect toward the new boss of the Measures department.

I was about to go drink a beer in the cafe-restaurant overlooking the lake when, noticing the poster of the Squares and Promenades, I remembered Ernest. Ernest, that fine fellow who, going by what he had told me the last time I had seen him, was not likely to have been promoted.

"Let's give it a whirl," I said to myself, nodding to a guard. "If nothing else, it will be better than having come for nothing."

Of course he knew Monsieur André, the old man protested, standing almost at attention. Imagine—he was the General Guard of the Promenades of Paris! He had a villa on boulevard de Veracruz, on the other side of the park.

"Whatever you do, don't go telling him where you got your information," the guard added, suddenly suspicious. "He misses nothing, that one! What a hell of a grip! Much stronger, I assure you, than his father's."

This portrait in no way agreed with my memory. I had undoubtedly fallen upon an idiot grown timid with age. Leaving the rotunda, the grotto, and the cascade, I headed into the undulating park, following the direction that had just been indicated. My mind had fixed itself upon a new goal. To erase my failure. To act as though Virginie did not exist, as though I had come to the Buttes not to meet her, but to visit a friend.

The master's house stood, magnificent, not far from the boulevard. Around it, the park gradually turned into a garden. Here one saw neither rocky ground, nor thorny shrubs, but parterres of roses and a virgin vine climbing the façade covered with beautiful geometric motifs designed by bricks of different shades of color. This was certainly a cut above my civil servant's apartment! But also—I consoled myself hypocritically—a heck of a lot more eccentric.

But Monsieur André was not there. Or rather, he could not be seen. Hadn't I noticed the official carriages waiting outside, lined up on the boulevard? These gentlemen, I told myself, were not about to be disturbed.

I showed my titles. They practically laughed in my face. But then they added that, since I apparently was a friend of Monsieur the Principal Guard, they would let me sit in the hall, given that these gentlemen were about to finish.

I was on edge. Decidedly the day was not going well for me. Not only had that goose of a girl dared to stand me up, but a servant was presently treating me rather haughtily. I was going to make a scene when, suddenly, the doors of the salon opened, making way for a tall man, distinguished-looking in spite of his age, who was pursued by a band of sycophants at the head of which my friend was bustling about.

I took two steps forward. Ernest, who had recognized me on stepping out of the salon, turned his back to me while continuing to behave obsequiously toward the old man.

"This is too much!" I was about to cry out. "Now that moron Ernest is going to snub me too!"

Then addressing a servant as I mastered my shame:

"Would you tell me, who is that visitor?"

"Monsieur Alphand, of course. Jean-Charles-Adolphe Alphand. The founder of the Greenhouses and Nurseries, the creator of the Squares and Promenades, the promoter of the world's fairs, the director of the Works of Paris! . . . My boss's boss, for heaven's sake!"

Pamphlet for the *Ligue française du coin de terre et du foyer*. A worker garden.

Allée Seven

As she sang, darkness came down from the trees,
and the first moonshine fell. . . . The lawn was
covered with weak condensed vapors, which unfurled
their white flakes on the tips of the grass. We
thought we were in paradise.
NERVAL, Sylvie

In making Barillet-Deschamps a second Le Nôtre, whom his old bosses, with the help of a few of his envious colleagues, threw into obscurity so that they might shamelessly take credit for his genius, we are proposing a romantic hypothesis. Or rather, an extrapolation founded on a few documents and plausible conjectures. Everything suggests, in fact, that there were two clans in the horticultural world of Paris at the end of the nineteenth century: one that claimed Barillet as their teacher and the master of the entire French school,[1] and another that wanted to see him as only one creator among many of a style called *paysager*—a "landscap-ist" style.[2] Moreover, the systematic "forgetting" with which Alphand seems to have tried to bury his collaborator has been recognized for what it was: not content with having erased Barillet from his work on the Parisian Promenades, the director of the Works of Paris did not attend his funeral and did not participate in the subscription opened for his monument: deliberate gestures that provoked in the Père-Lachaise the scandal narrated above in speeches taken, almost word for word, from a report by E. A. Carrière that appeared in the March 1, 1876, issue of the *Revue horticole*.[3]

The heritage of the Promenades was, therefore, surrounded by maneuvers, sharp words, and polemics. Which does not mean that there was no agreement upon the essential fact that a new "style" had appeared—neither "English" nor "Romantic," but "landscapist"—the form and genealogy of which were described in almost identical terms by all concerned.

Let us begin with the question of form. "The narrow allées and broken curves were followed by wide lanes and gentle and harmonious curves," explains the landscape architect Édouard André, one of the most reserved voices to speak about Barillet. He goes on to say: "Instead of simply leveling the surface of the terraces, they studied the art of remodeling the relief of the soil. The center of the lawns was dug into basins, groups of bushes rose up, and baskets of flowers, always elliptical and slightly raised, "leaned" against the trees that stood out in the forefront; the art (and name) of undulation were created."

The description was echoed by Eugène Deny, who admired Barillet-Deschamps without reservation[4] and was Jules Vacherot's teacher: "The flat soil, formed of alluvium, was reshaped; the straight and monotonous allées were replaced by allées with harmonious curves, planted with little-known essences and traced according to rules of art and perspective. Shady paths invited one to stroll beneath the leaves, enabling one to admire the flowering bushes, the lawns, and baskets of flowers; intelligently arranged clearings let one see the most beautiful points of view."

On the subject of genealogy, next. If the *Treatises* of Morel and Thouin already included some historical considerations, there was now a systematic discourse about the history of gardens that supported the "new landscapist genre." It was a fresco that intended to provide an opening to the new theory; founded upon a corpus of specific archives, it was destined to bring forth a meaning governed by the idea of progress. Alphand designed its role in the very introduction of his work, in terms characteristic of the scientific-historical humanism of the nineteenth century: "To analyze the creations of the past, to separate out the obsolete parts, and to recognize the elements that can enter modern art: such must be the object of concern of the artist who dedicates himself to the study of gardens."

And he establishes its principal lines in a dissertation that would retain its basic structure in André and Deny.[5]

First there is an evocation of antiquity, China, or Persia: instead of affirming choices, the authors establish the authority of a discourse by legitimizing the broad vision it uses to justify itself. Then comes a group of scornful remarks concerning the "primitive" art of the Middle

Ages[6] and that of the French Renaissance, judged "naïve" or "petty"[7] in comparison with Italian art, which was elevated to such a degree that the Hispanic and Flemish traditions were neglected as a result. Third, there is a global incomprehension of the baroque period,[8] considered extravagant because of its systematic antinaturalism[9] and treated with such chronological casualness that the Mollets[10] and Boyceau were evoked before Bernard Palissy. And lastly, Le Nôtre is praised with more patriotism than sincerity.[11]

But the tone of the historical analysis changes when it addresses the eighteenth century. It was no longer a matter of a dissertation in the strict sense of the word, although it was supported by a judgment that could reputedly separate the wheat from the chaff. The object had become living, almost burning, since what was at stake was the taking of a position on the notion of landscape. Passion entered into the discourse. Dufresny was praised to the skies: his unknown masterpieces had the immense merit of having a "historical" priority over English works.[12] The marquis de Girardin was also praised, as much for his genius as for the reputation he had acquired of not having yielded to Chinese "extravagances" or to the "exaggerated" taste for ruins and *fabriques*, in short to all those extravagant "follies" that a supposedly libertine era seemed to appreciate. Along the same lines, Morel, Thouin, and then the Bühlers[13] were presented as precious milestones along the path to a well-understood practice of landscaping; nonetheless, they were only qualified as precursors, insofar as the true renaissance began with the Promenades of the Second Empire.

Finally, there was the enemy, as pernicious as it seemed near, whose taste for "excess" and "sentimentality" was repugnant to these positive minds: romanticism. Édouard André could not find harsh enough words to condemn this "fad" that struck him as an offense against reason:

This mania for decoration had just produced a new failing. So true is it that beauty and simplicity are not always enough for man and that in all times the best has been the enemy of the worst. The romantic genre erupted in gardens. Simple and rural ornaments, such as cottages, wooden benches, rustic benches, no longer satisfied the need for novelty that had taken hold of draftsmen. Archaic color, which was dominant in the literature of the time, and the ferment of republicanism germinating in everyone's mind influenced even the state of gardens. Soon there was no park corner without its temple of Diana, its island of Lesbos, its grotto of Cacus. Tombs, funeral urns, inscriptions to love, to friendship, to great men and . . . even to a loyal dog were the obligatory ornaments of any landscape of this kind. The writers of the period fell into this mistaken kind of ornamentation. . . . It is hard to believe how a false idea pushed to the extreme can lead to such madness. It was then that the "terrible" style and the "melancholic" style were conceived, and the "druidic dolmens" and the "tousled ruins," which had to accompany "uprooted trees raising their tearful roots like emaciated arms," to use the expression of one of these visionaries.

This hatred of an admittedly conventional "romanticism"—for nothing distinguishes it from the universe of rubbish that Flaubert mocked in *Madame Bovary*—can be explained not only by esthetic options that made simplicity and truth the criteria of beauty, but by economical considerations. Alphand, André, Deny, and their colleagues were proper bourgeois, and, however great the artistic portions of their nature, any expense they deemed superfluous was morally repugnant in their eyes: whence the accounts they appended to their works, which appear in their *Treatises* recorded down to the last centime; whence also their absolute lack of understanding of the romantic ethos and of baroque taste.

It was undoubtedly not the first time that, in matters pertaining to gardens, economical arguments were raised to support esthetic theories: in order to support his critique of the baroque's lack of "naturalness," Dézallier d'Argenville, for example, had cited the excessive expenses incurred in order to maintain the pruning—too complicated in his opinion—of trees and clumps (in the shape of men or animals). But it was in the name of social changes, this time, that Deny and Vacherot celebrated "landscapist naturalness." The first explained: "The landscapist garden answers the needs of our society better; does it not allow us to compose, sometimes in limited spaces, a reduction of rural nature where the city dweller, leaving his occupations momentarily, comes to enjoy solitude, rest, and contemplation? Much more economical, it is better suited to the most humble fortunes, and enables one to vary the aspects and dissimulate more easily the exiguities of the site."

As for Vacherot, he was even more explicit since he clearly qualified the landscapist genre as a "democratic style." This was proof that the landscape architects were in fact interested in accompanying the changes in morals and social structure by conceiving a type of garden adapted to public promenades as well as to the more modest spaces of the private gardens, which, once reserved for the rich, were in the process of becoming a mass phenomenon.

Thus we find ourselves brought back to the thesis we put forward earlier, namely, that the nineteenth century was a period in which the legal distinction between private and public was clarified, at the same time that these two spheres were taking shape ideologically. Not that there had not been, and for a long time, gardens more intimate than the vast compositions we have focused on so far. Thus, since the Middle Ages, there had been many *courtilles* at the city limits. Sauval tells us that "from the *courtilles* of Temple, Saint-Martin, Barbette, and Boncelois, we infer that the *courtilles* were country gardens, where the bourgeois as well as the Templars and monks of Saint-Martin went to stroll and take fresh air; and likewise, from the wine of the *courtille*, a jest or proverb of times past, we learn that in planting vines in the *courtilles*, people were thinking more about contenting sight than taste."

In the same fashion, all aristocratic and bourgeois mansions of the following periods—not to mention castles and country manors—were endowed with a private garden, sometimes of considerable size, so that the same Sauval, speaking of his era this time, the seventeenth century, mentioned it as characteristic of Paris: "In I don't know how many places one sees gardens of quality, strewn with tulips, anemones, carnations, and all kinds of flowers, not to mention plants and simples, for they can be found in the faubourg Saint-Marceau and the faubourg Saint-Michel, in the Temple, in Montmartre, and in almost all the neighborhoods of Paris and of the faubourgs." It was, however—as a half-envious, half-ironic satire by Boileau reminds us[14]—a privilege of fortune reserved to nobles, the Church, or to the elite of the third estate.

Moreover, these gardens were in no way personal gardens, at least in the sense that we understand it today. For the very reason that before Rousseau the sensitive self did not exist, because it was, as convention required it to be, subordinated to a self of representation. Pleasure gardens were thus also representation—of a position in the world, a codified Eden, etc.—and not the landscape of a soul in quest of personal paradise: the mutation did not begin until the end of the eighteenth century, and would only become widespread during the course of the nineteenth century.

The best way to gauge the importance of this transformation is to compare articles written on horticulture a century later. Alongside a normal progression of the number of *Treatises*, in fact—normal with regard to the general increase in the volume of printed matter—a popular literature was growing, at times in specialized periodicals, at others in the form of columns in the ordinary press. There was material for all tastes and for all levels of the social scale: from the *Revue horticole* aimed at professional gardeners and their teachers, to the journal *Le Coin de terre*, which would be the organ of the association of "worker gardens" led by abbé Lemire, and including *La Maison de campagne*, addressed to middle-class proprietors and *rentiers*. In short, "cultivating one's garden" became a general occupation, and planting a tree oneself became a sought-after activity.

In order to reconstruct this fundamental movement that contributed to the implementation of a new social diagram, we would have to undertake a detailed portrait of the network of tensions that developed around differentiated practices—an exciting subject that we hope other researchers will pick up on, while we content ourselves with pointing out a few of its aspects. First, we want to highlight, as an example, the decisive role that two eminent and emblematic figures, the Empress Josephine and François-René de Chateaubriand, played at the turn of the century in the formation of the general taste for trees and flowers.

Back from Montboissier, I am writing these last lines here in my retreat: I must leave it, all filled with the beautiful adolescents who once hid and crowned their father within their close ranks. I will no longer see the magnolia that promised its rose to the tomb of my Floridian, the Jerusalem pine and Lebanon cedar dedicated to the memory of Jerome, the laurel from Grenada, the plane tree from Greece, the oak from Armorica, at the foot of which I painted Blanca, sang Cymodocée, invented Velleda. These trees were born and they grew with my reveries; they were their hamadryads. They will pass under another empire: will their new master love them as I loved them? He will let them wither away, cut them down perhaps: I am to conserve nothing on the earth.

There is no pose, in spite of the mythological emphasis, in this superb text that Chateaubriand wrote in November 1817 for his *Mémoires d'outre-tombe*. Misfortune had forced the unanimously celebrated author of *Atala* to sell his estate of Vallée-aux-Loups located at Châtenay-Malabry. It was a terribly wrenching loss. Slowly, the poet, with the assistance of his wife and the "most roguish of gardeners" (Benjamin), had developed this park of twenty arpents on the humid and sandy terrain of the Val-d'Aulnay that still bears its mark almost intact. Now it was to change hands. Forever.

The "beautiful adolescents" who, with Lamartine,[15] had rushed forward in a procession to breathe in the aura of the great man, would no longer have the ineffable happiness of getting intoxicated with dazzling roses, the dark mystery of the forest, the stunning trills of the nightingales! Paradise, once more, stole away, led off by a demon as accursed and seductive as the one who led to the fall of Adam: gold. Gold, which the whims of Fortune depend upon.

And how distant it already seemed, that brilliant period when François-René wrote about Combourg, remembering it with ecstasy: "I like this place, I am attached to my trees, I addressed elegies, sonnets, odes to them. . . . There is not a single one of them that I did not care for with my own hands, I know them by their names. . . . It is my family, I have no other. . . . I hope to die by its side."

Chateaubriand had already described the death of this tree under the felling ax as a terrible personal drama (that is to say in a mode fundamentally foreign to the allegorical distress of Ronsard crying over the Gastine forest). The tree had become for the romantic ethos a major symbol, "a parable of identity and vital community, the indicator of a natural order more essential than spiritual conceptions."[16]

Was it not old Schlegel, the founder of the Athenäum, who would, a few years later, write a philosophical apology in which the tree typified the vital principle of creation, thereby opposing the "infantile" idea of a gardener god to the mechanist—Voltairian—idea of a watchmaker god?

In the tree moving in all directions in the open air, with its branches, leaves, and flowers, we feel the rustling of a life; we feel that it is a living being, in comparison with the watch, as skillfully ordered as it may be, but dead nonetheless. That is precisely what is recognized by a more detailed science of nature, when it shows us the sleep of plants, their fertilization and reproduction, as in animals, but according to specific means. Yes, Nature as a whole is also such a tree of life; its leaves and its flowers are continually blooming, drawing their nourishment from the fragrant air of the sky; its branches stand up and wave about, the sap climbs up the trunk from the deep roots, and at the top of the tree invisible forces never stop their rustling.[17]

Such a vision of "energetic" Nature stands in opposition to the vision held by the previous philosophical "mechanism," which resonates, in Chateaubriand, with the central invention of romanticism: that of the "I," the suffering or happy self whose destiny has no more exact reflection than the tree planted by him. Because that tree is marked by his imprint from its first shoots onward, it is the witness of his sufferings as well as his joys, and, by its duration, prolongs the existence of the being that permitted it to develop in the first place. Man makes the tree, and the tree becomes *poiesis*. Because the tree concentrates memory, pains, and hope in its energy. Moreover, it escapes its creator, no matter how much care and love he has showered upon it, just as the vocation of the true work is to free itself of its author. Thus its destiny is that of art, which, like Paradise, can only remain a primordial dream (or *rêve*), the resurgence of a dawn forever lost, on condition of becoming a fantasy (or *songe*), for the reason that the triviality of the world betrays it.

Four years ago on my return from the Holy Land, I bought near the hamlet of Aulnay, in the neighborhood of Sceaux and Châtenay, a gardener's house hidden among the hills covered with woods. The uneven and sandy terrain belonging to this house was only a wild orchard at the end of which were a ravine and a copse of chestnut trees. I thought this narrow space might enclose my long hopes; *spatio brevi spem longam reseces*. The trees I planted there are prospering, they are still so small that I give them shade when I stand between them and the sign. One day, by returning that shade to me, they will protect my old age as I protected their youth. I chose them as much as I could from the different climates I have roamed through, they remind me of my voyages and nourish other illusions in the bottom of my heart.

Among those trees planted in the Vallée-aux-Loups the year when these opening lines to the *Mémoires* were written,[18] there was one that Chauteaubriand cherished especially—the magnolia mentioned at the beginning of the melancholy list of 1817, the exact origin of which is known to us. In the course of the year 1811, in fact, when Chateaubriand had just published his *Itinéraire de Paris à Jérusalem* with great success, and had been made a member of the Institute, the empress Josephine—or rather, the ex-empress, since she had been divorced the previous year—offered him a seedling of that lovely tree native to the Atlantic coast of the United States,[19] which was still rather rare at the time, since it had only been introduced to France a few decades before by the botanist Magnol. And we also know from the notebooks of Bonpland, the gardener-botanist-explorer Josephine had placed at the head of the nurseries of Malmaison, that this gift was not the only one of its kind: Humboldt, the learned Prussian voyager who was a friend of the writer as well as the empress, on this occasion acted as an intermediary and as an eager intercessor with Bonpland.[20]

It was in this way, then, that Josephine and François-René were brought together by a common passion for plants. But just as the writer was the bard of trees—and consequently of parks, which many preferred to gardens—so the empress introduced a passionate taste for flowers, which she had gotten perhaps from her creole origins, into a French society that had until then considered them to be one ornamental element among other possible beauties (except during the Middle Ages when they were equipped with symbolic values).[21]

With Josephine, flowers gained new attributes. Because of the care the empress took to multiply them, their fragile beauty became the feminine principle that completes, instead of opposing, the virile energy of the tree—without, however, becoming a fertility symbol. Far from any matriarchal mythology, which it would have been difficult to incarnate in a woman who could no longer bear children, the feminine principle in question here is a figure of seduction, of mysterious appeal to a fugitive elsewhere of total passion, of spiritual effusion. The blue flower sung by Novalis; the peonies, narcissuses, and celandines strewn across the poems of English romantics and American transcendentalists alike; the jonquils glimpsed by

Oberman—it is desire that suggests this floral ecstasy, and not coupling, the desire for the inaccessible encounter, for mystic communion with the beloved, which might be ruined by a single vulgar gesture, like a rose crushed by nervous fingers.

With this distinction, however. Just as the wild flowers, the simple flowers of the fields loved by Rousseau and the "neoplatonic" romantics figured an ideal quest similar to the quest of Ramon Lull or Guillaume de Lorris, so the precious and complicated alchemy—an artificial one, to tell the truth—that ruled over Josephine's floral experiments cannot be interpreted in such spiritual terms.

One might think that the mere alluring presence of a creole orchid at the heart of this bouquet would be enough to trouble this vision. The agitation of the flesh animates this passion, especially since it no longer finds any other object for its flames. With astounding and vulgar frankness, Napoleon rejected his spouse, writing her: "I have granted a hundred thousand francs for the extraordinary expenses of Malmaison, therefore you can plant what you like." And the fallen wife, who had to maintain her rank, still beautiful according to witnesses, tried to contain her hot tropical blood by intoxicating herself with flowers and botanical exotica. What could be more naively sensual in their triviality than the names the empress gave her roses? Fantastic Red, Beautiful Hébé, Touching Beauty, Virgins' Finery, Silly Laughter, Thigh of a Nervous Nymph: it was certainly not Mathilde, Asra, or Diotima who could have such improper thoughts, given that they showed themselves to be equally detached from pleasure and ignorant of the depths of the soul. Josephine was of flesh, not of mystical essence, and flowers were for her a concrete costume, a world of colors and odors that she used to compensate for a virtuousness that she found burdensome and boring—a world she plunged into in order to become one with it.

Josephine was, however, romantic in her own way—a way more worldly than interior, which would be unique to French pseudoromanticism—a trait deplored by the neoclassical architect Fontaine who, commissioned with Percier to restore Malmaison, was forced to limit his work to the castle when he would have liked to extend it to the park. In frustration he wrote: "Madame Bonaparte wants nothing that isn't in the English style, winding, full of movement, with accidents, precipices, a river, a temple like at Méréville, like at Mortefontaine, like at the Désert." And the work illustrated by P.-J. Redouté,[22] which provides the first inventory of the two hundred plant species that flowered at Malmaison, demonstrates that, long before being dethroned, the empress contributed "powerfully," as Reboul wrote in his *Mémoires, à répandre en France le goût de la culture et des fleurs* (*Mémoires, to Spread in France the Taste for Cultivation and Flowers*). Thus, alongside the roses bearing the picturesque names mentioned above, Marie-Blanche d'Arneville mentions the Yukan magnolia from China, the Chinese peonies *Poenia moutan*, the amaryllis *josephinae*, the pink locust, rare species of geraniums and pelargoniums, and even certain flowers that no longer exist today, such as the *Josephina imperatricis* and the *Lapageria rosea*.[23]

Unfortunately in 1814, when she reached the age of fifty, the beautiful creole flower died among her roses. Without mistress or maintenance, Malmaison fell into a state of neglect within months.

"In these gardens where the feet of the crowd once raked the sandy allées, grass and bramble thrived for lack of care, I made sure of it walking there, the foreign trees were dying, the swans of Oceania were no longer sailing on the canals." The words are Chateaubriand's again, describing the vanquished Napoleon tormented by memories after the irremediable disaster of Waterloo.

Faced with this brutal decay, this erasing of a park and gardens that, for fifteen years, had been in France like the resurrection of Eden, how can one not be reminded of the romantic myth of *Paradise Lost*? How can one not set these two cruel experiences—the loss of Vallée-aux-Loups and the disappearance of Malmaison—alongside the new translation that, in 1836, after abbé Delille and a few others, the elderly Chateaubriand would make of Milton's great epic peom? Lamartine, Vigny, Hugo himself would all be so haunted by it—as they were already by the tragic epic of the Empire—that they would each deliver a version of the drama in which the fallen angel—the pathetic Satan of the English Puritan—would become heroic, a figure of Prometheus beaten down by History.

Paradise lost. There is no doubt that this major theme, a constituent of the civilizations of the *Book*, even of the most ancient strata,[24] had drawn renewed energy from these exalted poems.

But we must remember that romanticism was never a dominant phenomenon in France, at least not in the German sense of absolute idealism, of an undivided project for the resurgence of the soul, for the rediscovery of the world of images that the classical spirit and then the spirit of the Enlightenment had pretended to dismiss. Too urban and consequently too worldly, too sensitive to irony—and thus to incredulity—too taken with intelligence to accept an enterprise of thinking the poetry of which seemed impregnated with a "spirit of seriousness," too impervious to a mystic heaviness linked to the earth and to village candor, too foreign to the taste for religious pathos that does not contain its own criticism, too Voltairian, or too Catholic to interpret Catholicism in Protestant terms, French society produced a version of romanticism that was lighter, more affected than really lived, and more concerned with appearances than with an interior commitment. It produced a fashion, consequently, in spite of Nerval, Quinet, and a few others, even when it pretended to pick up again, without disguise, the themes of *Werther*, Klopstock, Novalis, or of Achim von Arnim: both Parisian and provincial salons preferred the romances of Boieldieu to the *Voyage d'hiver* and the *Amours du poète*, and the grandiloquent mannerism of *Sous les tilleuls*[25] to *Henri d'Ofterdingen*.

Why should this be surprising when the myth of a lost Eden had tended to abandon its spiritual heights in order to be transformed into a bourgeois paradise in which the fall, trivially—which does not mean without drama or passion—takes the shape of adultery? Will *she* give in, or will *she* have the moral strength to refuse sin? Will the garden be the accomplice of love, or a refuge for a troubled soul? An essential part of the French novel of the nineteenth century addresses this one question. The context? The provincial park of an important figure, the most exquisite and detailed description of which can be found neither in Stendhal's *Le Rouge et le noir*, nor in Balzac's *Le Lys dans la vallée*, but in Fromentin's *Dominique*:

Even if you knew the *Trembles* as well as I do, it would not be any less difficult for me to make you understand what I found so delightful there. And yet everything was delightful there, everything, even the garden, which as you know, however, is quite modest. There were trees there, a rare thing in our country, and many birds, which love trees and could not have lived elsewhere. There was order and disorder, sandy allées following the steps, leading to gates, and flattering a certain taste I have always had for places where one strolls with a certain pomp, where the women of another era could have spread ceremonial dresses. Then obscure corners, humid crossroads barely touched by the sun, where the greenish mosses growing in a spongy earth all year long and retreats visited by myself alone all had an appearance of age, of neglect, and under another form reminded me of the past, an impression that did not displease me from then on. I sat down, I remember, on the tall boxwood pruned into seats that adorned the edge of the allées. I learned their age, they were terribly old, and I examined with particular curiosity the little shrubs that—André told me—were as old as the oldest stones of the house, which neither my father, nor my grandfather, nor my grandfather's father had seen planted. Then, in the evening, a time came when all movement ceased. I withdrew to the top of the steps, and from there I looked at the almond trees at the back of the garden, in the corner of the park. They were the first trees to lose their leaves in the September wind, forming a bizarre transparent screen against the blazing curtain of the setting sun. In the park, there were many trees, ashes and laurels, where thrushes and black-birds lived in a crowd in autumn; but what one saw from afar was a group of great oaks, the last to lose their leaves as well as to get them, which kept their reddish foliage into December when the entire wood already seemed dead, where the magpies nested, where the high-flying birds perched, where the first jays and the first crows that winter always brought to the country always landed.

Differences of place and climate aside, and notwithstanding the slight historical gap, the *Trembles*[26] might have also been called Vergy or Clochegourde. There was the same happy presence of the countryside, the same sharp sensation of the passage of time, the same mixture of styles enabling one to imagine a garden with still classical forms (pruned box-wood, steps, terraces in Stendhal, and a balustrade in Balzac) tied to a park from the Rous-seau period in which unchecked growth had done away with "enlightened" symbolics. If we have not yet reached the sensual luxuriance of Paradou[27] in which the eternal debate between flesh and the soul—that "struggle of matter and spirit" that, according to Balzac,[28] constitutes "the basis of Christianity"—takes a climactic form, the context is similar, and more than a decor: a complex of landscapes reflecting the different acts of the drama and the characters' contradictory impulses.

After a hot day night falls on Vergy, and dinner is served outdoors: "At the exact moment when the clock strikes ten, I will execute what, during the entire day, I promised myself to do this evening, or I will go up to my place to shoot my brains out," Julien Sorel swears to himself while Madame de Rênal, her heart beating with love, desires nothing so much as to have her hand taken, even as she promises herself she will withdraw it.

"Go into the garden," Henriette de Mortsauf orders Félix when she wants to hide her marital distress, marked by her husband's crises, from the one she loves. She is a lovely provincial woman with "lightly pinkish," "plump white shoulders," whose sensual and maternal generosity finds its expression in a body whose "fullness destroyed neither the grace of her figure nor the roundness required for her lines to remain beautiful, although developed." And it is in the middle of the flowers arranged in her room that—grown thin, her complexion marked by a "greenish pallor" similar to that of "magnolia flowers when they first open"—the lily of old, vanquished not by love but by its repression, receives Félix for the last time before passing away.

And so forth. One could cite many such examples. Including the heterogeneous collection of English parks, Turkish gardens, Roman ruins, savannahs filled with lions and tigers, virgin forests that Flaubert uses to describe Emma Bovary's interior disorder in a dreamlike sequence that calls for Freudian exegesis.[29] Including the cry, finally, with which Zola absolves Serge and Albine for having rediscovered the ecstasy of love: "It was the garden that had willed sin." The garden is also the principal character in *La Faute de l'abbé Mouret*, a Paradou removed from a world haunted by sin and returned to the primitive force of a triumphant nature that initiates two innocent young people to the pagan gestures of sexual fusion in a slow pantheist ascension, a "prodigious Hindu poem."[30]

Adultery, or the temptation of it, leads to madness, moral degeneration, or death. It is "sin" and condemned by a religious or social code. It is an old theme, of course, and a hackneyed one—this theme of sin tempting the weakness of man and woman through the seductive temptation of the garden.[31] There is nothing literary, however, about the examples cited, nothing that relates them to a conventional genre. On the contrary, everything in them speaks of anguish, social criticism, and the revolt against an irremediably philistine century. "Decidedly, in these times of ours, horticulturists are the only and true artists," Des Esseintes reflects bitterly, "summing up" the reflections inspired by the contemplation of the "anti-natural" flowers he has collected in his living room, transforming it into a monstrous garden. But then he immediately adds: "All is but syphilis"—words that concentrate the radicalness of *A rebours*, that *mise en abyme* of fin-de-siècle symbolism that had never ceased celebrating the garden on the pompous model of Samain, Sully Prudhomme, Renée de Brimont, or Charles van Lerberghe.[32]

For these poets, who have since been forgotten—but were highly esteemed in their time—there was no delicious poison secretly irrigating the splendid world of plants. Far from the feverish water lilies that Claude Monet painted at Giverny, and far from all anguish that was not in "good taste," their vision of the garden oscillated between the "mental landscape" inspired by Verlaine—whose "Colloque sentimental" they preferred to forget while remembering "Clair de lune" instead[33]—and the evocation of a symbolic Eden without trouble or fury.[34] Theirs was a redeeming Eden sung in disjointed yet similar voices by Anna de Noailles, the poet of native soil and the "Culte du moi,"[35] Maurice Barrès, the sententious Ruskin of *Sesame and Lilies* that the young Proust loved passionately,[36] and the social reformers of the Belle Époque, nurtured on biblical metaphors and William Morris.

Among the forty thousand words in the dictionary, there may be none that evokes more pleasant visions than the word garden. Flowers, fruits, spurting water, shade, beds of moss, birds singing. . . . It is not for nothing that Paradise was called the garden of Eden! and it is undoubtedly the nostalgia for this Paradise lost that pushes so many men, young and old, to seek happiness in the possession of a garden. When the working woman of Paris hangs a pot of reseda or nasturtiums from her window, it is a little ray of Paradise lost that comes to illuminate her hovel. And when the old serviceman and the old office worker dream of retiring to plant and graft their rosebushes and see their apples ripen, it is the old man, it is

Adam who lives in them again, as he was before the fall, having nothing to do "but cultivate and guard his garden."

Neither poet nor novelist, the man who speaks here was a political intellectual who wished to share his faith in a work of reformation he considered to be of capital importance: Charles Gide, who wrote the preface for the essay published in 1903 by Georges Benot-Lévy, *La Cité-Jardin*. In it he specifies that the "idea germinated in England under the inspiration of John Ruskin," and that it "was realized through the initiative of a few semiphilanthropic, semiesthete manufacturers, Mr. Lever, at Port Sunlight, near Liverpool, Mr. Cadbury, at Bournville, near Birmingham." He then goes on to say:

The garden city was born out of that same preoccupation that has led to the blossoming in several large cities of that charming form of charity called the work of flowering windows, or that other that brought together in Paris, last November, the first Congress of the work of worker gardens—that is to say the desire to give civilized men some of the joys of nature.

This profession of faith, which was significant for its time and shifted the garden off the esthetic and cultural terrain where we have set it so far, brings us back to social history.

Originally, contradictory ideological options aside, there was a common obsessive fear. Namely the specter of revolution announced by Marx and Engels in the *Communist Manifesto*: the dislocation of the traditional social scheme under the blows of the "dangerous classes."

From this point of view, the didactic enterprise analyzed in a preceding chapter turned out to be powerless. The gardens, zoos, and world's fairs were mainly directed at the middle class. The idea of organizing a garden oneself upon the basis of an increasingly abundant and varied popular literature corresponded to the dream of the *rentier* or of the retired person who had saved up enough to retire to the country, following the example of Bouvard and Pécuchet. But what about the *others*, the menacing swarm of the suburbs?

In creating the Bois de Vincennes and the Buttes-Chaumont, Haussmann had intended to offer the "people" spaces for leisure and hygienic reconstitution; but the Commune had shown the limits of this policy. The danger was serious, deep, and menacing in a different fashion from the endemic tuberculosis ravaging the unhealthy neighborhoods. More than a physical scourge, it was a "moral" illness stemming, according to an increasing number of observers, from the uprooting of the worker who had been projected into the confused "hell" of the cities: handed over to the labor market—in other words, having become merchandise from the perspective of liberal theory and of Marxist analysis—the worker *also* won the freedom to withdraw from the game: he could become an *Apache* (ruffian), or a pillar of Zola's *Assommoir*, or he might even join the *Bourses du travail* in order to be infected with revolutionary "poison."

Strengthened by long experience, many charitable organizations had assessed the danger some time before, and, for cynical and/or philanthropic reasons, had decided to address it with worker gardens. Thus the plans designed by Ledoux for the saltworks of Arc-et-Senans included, juxtaposed with the outbuildings, individual or collective vegetable gardens that might have been assigned to the workers for their subsistence, but also for their integration into a social order illuminated by the Masonic wisdom. Similarly, in the north and the east, the mine and ironmasters had taken care to give their personnel a patch of land, as much to make them dependent as to offer them an additional resource. But it was in the last years of the century that the "worker garden" and its organic extension, the garden cities, would become the central elements of enterprises sustained by explicit political and ideological discourses. What these discourses had in common was the vision of gardening as a moral rampart against the dissolution of society by revolutionary radicalism and the desire to promote it as an important element in the continuation of charitable practices: "assistance through work."

The intertwining of these two orders of thought—the first moral, even theological, and the second inscribed in the more pragmatic genesis of the State as providence—makes the analysis delicate: if one cuts into the heart of practices and discourses clearly linked by the "spirit of the age" with a retrospective scalpel, one risks either reducing everything to a vague Barresian mash reputed to take the place of "French ideology," or drawing too clear a boundary between the social Christianity of abbé Lemire, for whom the earth was redemptive, and the lay progressivism that would have advocated the development of worker gardens, garden cities, and school gardens only on account of their recognized social efficacy.

Where does one classify, according to this clear-cut distinction, the enterprise Georges Benoît-Lévy would dedicate his life to, which would, in the thirties, give rise to the nineteen "garden cities" of the Ile-de-France? The inspiration was Ruskinian, that is to say a mixture of spiritualism and social reformism. In fact, contrary to what has been said,[37] Benoît-Lévy's *initial* aim closely resembled that of Ebenezer Howard, the Englishman who invented the concept of the garden city: this connection can be verified by a reading of the *Roman des cités-jardins* (1906), in which Benoît-Lévy presents a young Frenchman who, after experiencing a "revelation" during a visit to the garden city of Sunrise (where, meditating upon Ruskin and Tolstoy while admiring the convivial organization of the city, he meets its founding patriarch, and then William Morris in person), manages, once back in Provence, to build a garden city in the country.[38] But, contrary to abbé Lemire's *terrianisme*, this utopian spiritualism gave nature and the earth less redemptive value than it did to work in general—which might be accomplished in factories without being degrading on that account. Finally, as political circumstances would have it, the "garden cities" built in the area of Paris[39] would not really be garden cities—since they were marvelous fragments of the suburbs, and not artificial cities surrounded by an isolating belt of countryside—and their promoter, Henri Sellier, president of the general Council of the Seine and then minister of Public Health of the Front Populaire, would be an agnostic socialist, that is to say a representative of lay progressivism.

The cleavages became deeper, however, with the institution of school gardens and the concurrent movements of worker gardens. On the one hand, there were the lay enterprises of the *Instruction Publique* and the *Assistance Publique*, on the other hand, a key project of social Catholicism that would lead to the first attempts at Christian democracy in the French mold.[40]

In the preface to his *Jardin de l'instituteur, de l'artisan et de l'amateur*, Pierre Bertrand explains:

Thanks to the happy initiative of the administration of state education and to the enlightened good will of the municipal councils, a new institution, the school garden, will spread the taste for domestic vegetable gardening and the principles of rational agricultural instruction. This type of garden will be the experiential field in which children, under the direction of their teachers, will learn about the progress realized over the past thirty years in a practical and attractive fashion, and where they will have the satisfaction of harvesting themselves the fresh vegetables and succulent fruits that they will no longer be able to do without later on.[41]

This school inspector had neither ideological nor religious presuppositions. He was concerned with "rational nourishment": the garden he hoped would become popular was strictly utilitarian, and his writing lacks Barrès's verbosity.[42] His attitude, which was neutral, or pragmatic to be more precise, is surprising in a "laureate of the ministry of Agriculture," a ministry that we know was marked by the ideas of Jules Méline during the Third Republic.[43] But it was also an attitude that appears again in a historical and theoretical work also published in 1906: *L'Assistance par le travail et les jardins ouvriers en France*, by Marcel Lecoq.

This time, it was a jurist who was asking the questions, in the name of economics and the law. How, when the "Great Depression" of the end of the nineteenth century had just completed its cycle of economic difficulties, was the government to implement a sensible policy to help the unemployed and to prevent workers' revolts? The fact is that the crisis had struck a painful blow to an industrial network that was still fragile and hardly concentrated: in spite of a rise that was on the whole regular, the standard of living for the working class remained extremely low (especially in Paris, where rents were high),[44] provoking outbursts of violence that seemed to justify the radical ideas of the revolutionary unionism of direct action. Moreover, if it had not been for the drop in the birth rate (catastrophic, on the whole), the number of unemployed people would have been stagnant on account of the funneling of savings into the "placement of fathers" instead of investment. In comparison with its two large neighbors—England and Germany—France had fallen seriously behind in economic as well as social matters: for in this regard individualism, traditional in a society marked by Catholicism and the centralization of the State, had not given birth either to a coherent collection of philanthropic initiatives, or to a structured political response (a Ministry of Labor would only be created in 1906). But what was Marcel Lecoq's verdict after making a lengthy analysis of charitable practices, of the experience of the Ateliers Nationaux of 1848, and of the risks of unbalanced competition between "free" workers and assisted unemployed workers? It was a serene *satisfecit* granted to worker gardens, devoid of any of Méline's pathetic "return to the earth": "More than any other form of assistance by work, these gardens help to awaken the energy of the unemployed, for not only does the worker find himself in the presence of work that can significantly improve his situation, but he becomes the head of a true enterprise whose success largely depends on his activity and his perseverance." The garden as the carrier of the enterprising spirit! The hero of the *Culte du moi* would have been sickened by it, for he, unlike his "adversary" Martin (a figure for the progress-hungry engineer) had thought he recognized at Aigues-Mortes, in Bérénice's garden, the "deep foundations of the universe."

Contrary to certain recent assertions founded on overly hasty generalizations,[45] it seems unreasonable to make of *terrianisme* or the "cult of the earth" a common ideological basis, characteristic of French society. The far left was critical of it, the mainstream left uninterested, while the high society of banks and salons belonged to another world. In fact—unless one assumes that Zola was quite far gone when he made the Earth (in his novel of the same name) a destructive force—a significant portion of the intelligentsia did not seem in the least interested in celebrating with Barrès the cult of a supposedly sacred soil.[46]

There remains, undeniably, a major tropism. In a still rural France, the themes of *terrianisme* were bound to have important reverberations. Either they served as currency in the political class's search for an electoral clientele; or they took the shape of a "refuge value" against anguish, in a world seized by the tornado of "progress;" or they were affected by a metaphysical dimension, heavy with a murky passion for the "redemptive glebe," or for that "feast of plants" summoned by Auguste Comte's positivist religion.[47]

This passion for the earth, a true *furor terrenus*, picked up where the *furor hortensis* dear to the eighteenth century had left off. There is no ideological-political-religious enterprise that conveys its ambitiousness—noble in certain ways, detestable in others—better than abbé Lemire's tireless work for the *Ligue du coin de terre et du foyer* ("League for a parcel of land and a hearth"), the central tool of which was the movement for worker gardens.

Lemire was the son of a peasant from rural Flanders and was influenced by Albert de Mun's "social legitimism" and the ideas on reform that Le Play defended in *La Réforme sociale* (1886).[48] Soon, however, while continuing to revere his spiritual teachers (he saw in de Mun the "heroic defender of the workers' cause") and to admire the Middle Ages because of its important social virtues, the young priest rallied to the Republic and became, by virtue of his election in 1893 as deputy of Hazebrouck, the symbol of "French Christian democracy." What were the axes of his political philosophy? Compassion for the have-nots, whose revolts he understood without approving; a hatred of the factory that turns workers into "prey designed for and necessary to collectivism"; a mysticism about the earth so complete that it caused him to maintain that only "working the earth will save the worker from physical and moral degeneration"; and a love of his native soil that made him an uncompromising patriot, but also such an anti-Semite and enemy of the "cosmopolitan bank" that he was able to support Drumont during the Dreyfus affair.[49] That is to say a complicated man, who seems altogether captivating when one considers his sincerity and his charitable work, a man who exemplified the ambiguities of the social Catholicism that would influence Péguy and Sangnier[50]—but also a rather frightening figure when one considers his fanaticism, and the indisputable role he played in the elaboration of the triad "Work, Family, Country," which would become (and has remained) the program of Fascism "in the French style."

The project for worker gardens that he sponsored (which, as we have seen, was not the only one of its kind) was not without its problems. Revolutionaries saw in it a maneuver aimed at sidetracking the legitimate revolt of the proletarian class onto a reformist and clerical terrain. Conservatives were hostile, surprised that workers, who were questionable on an ideological level, could have access to it. The search for plots of land was also problematic, even if, in

Paris for example, the railway companies (PLM and Paris-Orléans), the National Assistance, and the military authorities voluntarily offered land along tracks and on the slopes of forts. "Some men," abbé Lemire explains, "seek lost, unused patches of land for rent or sale, which nobody wants; they rent them, they enclose them, and, out of vague, sterile lands covered with refuse, they make little appetizing lots that the worker transforms into gardens." Finally, he had to overcome the incredulous sniggering of those who made fun of the miserable, even unesthetic aspect of these patches of poor land where users sometimes erected "bowers" out of planks, bituminized paper, or rusted sheet metal—structures that were pompously mocked as the worker's "country homes."

The project took off, however: 6,453 gardens in 1903, 12,081 in 1906, 15,415 in 1909, 17,825 in 1912, 47,000 in 1920, and 56,700 in 1927.[51] It had this distinctive feature: the regions with significant radical populations, such as the southwest, remained impervious to the movement, whereas, among those departments where the Christian basis remained solid, it was those of the east and north that formed the avant-garde—which was logical since they were the most industrial, and because there was an already long-established tradition of worker gardens.

Finally, there were miracles. Physical miracles such as the one related by Robert-Georges Picot to the members of the congress of 1906, in an edifying story concerning a couple of workers from Touraine: "Considered lost, they were given the last sacraments; a garden was granted them, nonetheless. For three years now they have been living there night and day and sustaining themselves thanks to the good air they breathe there."

And moral miracles—because located in the middle of the "red suburbs"—that wrested this triumphal cry from Albert Touchard:

Here and there, along the borders of Saint-Ouen and Saint-Denis, are dotted archipelagoes of Breton colonies, uneducated, almost savage populations everywhere . . . floating tribes of uprooted and malcontent countryfolk; these men live in four unhealthy, hectic, and artificial environments, the factory, the cabaret, the public meeting, the industrial city. Placing a garden at their disposal plunges them into a realer environment. . . . They were "comrades" . . . here they are men.[52]

Is this enthusiasm ridiculous? Merely the silly gushing of "good souls" convinced they know the "right path"? Undoubtedly. But it was also lasting work that brought a little happiness and comfort to tens of thousands of families on the edge of despair. Whatever a posteriori judgment we pass on the ideological influence that the *Ligue du coin de terre et du foyer* had on French society—and our own is clearly harsh, as we see in it one of the matrices of Pétainism—one ought to keep in mind that the worker gardens did have some beneficial effects.

But at the time nothing was as clear as it is today, as history had not yet done its long and tragic work of elucidation. In other words, one must remember that many of the questions that seem horribly overdetermined today, such as the earth cult and anti-Semitism, were only half determined a century ago.

Like all major human adventures, the garden combines risk and ambiguity: a painful example is provided by the story of the Jewish banker Albert Kahn, the Raymond Roussel of finance who, nourished by Bergson and seduced by Barrès, built at Boulogne-Billancourt, facing the Seine, a marvelous garden that he hoped might be a landscape of universal culture.

Maurice Denis, *The Sacred Wood* (*Le bois sacré*). Photo © Bulloz © Spadem, 1987.

The subtle smell of honeysuckle combined with the rich perfume of roses filling the tall white room, and when the June breeze rustled through the Atlas cedars with their bluish leaves, the golden spruces, the black pines of Austria, the hornbeams, the beech trees, and the oaks, a vast fragrance came in through the open window. It seemed to climb an invisible line, starting with the leap of the flowering branches and ending with the man standing before the different natural beauties he had grouped in order to create a definitive harmony.

Laid out on less than five hectares bordering on the École Maïmonide and the Baron Edmond de Rothschild's property, this pleroma was situated at 6, quai du Quatre-Septembre, at Boulogne-Billancourt, near the Saint-Cloud bridge.

At that time of year, the rose garden, which was located in the fruit garden not far from the greenhouses of the French Garden and the palmarium and the false cypresses of the Japanese Garden, gave the impression—with the elegance of its curves, the velvet softness of its petals, here slightly pink and timid, there blushing and superb, and its artful dilation and intensification—of a vital push into full expansion, within the very limitations and evanescence of its blissfully unconscious flowering.

While the man went to sit in his office, his eyes half-closed as though he were trying to preserve some strange vision, another much younger man finally rose to stand by the window: it was his turn to take in the spectacle of this garden, which formed a kind of plant archive. The old man, Albert Kahn, had been developing it since his youth, with the help of the immense fortune he had earned in the banking world where fate had cast him. Kahn, an Alsatian Jew, had known cold and hunger early on, but, endowed with an extraordinary capacity for work and exceptional financial intuition, he had become within a few years the principal employee, then senior executive, then associate, and finally proprietor of the bank. Thanks to Cecil Rhodes, the colonial administrator of South Africa with whom he had started mining diamonds, he had managed to fulfill the curious contract he had signed with the brothers Charles and Edmond Goudchaux: to increase the bank's profits, which did not surpass five hundred thousand francs at the time, to two million on the condition that he was granted a share of fifty percent.

But on this day of June 14, 1936, this man who used to invite the greatest personalities of his age to Boulogne, where he organized lunches within the framework of the *Circle Around the World*—lunches he had the elegance not to participate in—this man who had rubbed elbows with men of science, academics, politicians, and military leaders as well as writers and artists, was about to be visited by the bailiffs. Tomorrow his house would be empty, and his gardens would become the property of the state. The crisis had devastated his fortune, leaving him as poor as he had been in his youth. But, although his fall was complete and the majority of his old friends had abandoned him, Kahn seemed serene. Money had never been for him anything but an instrument in the service of a vast universal enterprise of reconciliation that he had dedicated his life to and feverishly explained to Bergson. For, as a young man, he had studied for his exams with that philosopher who, at the time, was still only a student at the École Normale and not the illustrious figure France would soon be proud of.

For all that, nothing could diminish the natural splendor, blazing with beauty, of the collection that the old man had lovingly assembled.

Facing the window, the young Élie contemplated the miracle surrounding him and, for one delicious instant, the state of his soul, as well as of his memory, gave him a brief shiver of the absolute.

Pardès: the beautiful and the divine were combined in its spirit. An image of paradise lost was realized in the lawns, at the foot of the trees.

"They were four to penetrate into the garden," he said to himself, with the memory of Maïmonedes's *Book of Knowledge* coming into his consciousness. Oh garden of knowledge! Oh Nova Hierosolyma! Jerusalem of my heart! . . . The bush of Moses, the cypress of Zion, the terebinth of Gideon, the tree of Abraham, the vineyards and orchards of Ecclesiastes . . . The breeze whispered fragments of the Song of Solomon in his ear: "I come to my garden, my sister, my bride . . . a garden locked, a fountain sealed, an orchard of pomegranates with the choicest fruits . . . nard and saffron, calamus and cinnamon, with all trees of frankincense, myrrh and aloes, with all chief spices . . . I eat my honeycomb with my honey, I drink my wine with my milk . . ."

Albert Kahn, the man Élie had always considered his spiritual teacher and benefactor, looked up. A smile brightened his features:

"My dear Élie," he said slowly, speaking with a strong Alsatian accent, "if men live with their eyes closed to beauty, it is because they do not love enough; beauty seems natural to them because they only have an abstract knowledge of it. In truth, they are *lost*. They do not feel their obligation to go toward it and even to install it."

"Yes. You taught me that our duty is to say yes to life and to participate in the movement that projects us toward the mystery of our end. Thanks to you, I endeavor to orient this torrent according to my conscience."

The confused sounds of Paris could be heard now and then in the background, like the droning notes of a distant organ.

Élie thought of all those obscure hearts who had abandoned their power to think in order to raise yellow, red, blue, green *golems* of metal, forgetting that science gives us the secret of physical operations, but of life it can only give us a translation in terms of inertia. Thus they not only naively confuse the beautiful, the essence of which is spiritual and divine, with the useful, but they also lack intuition, a form of sympathy capable of introducing us into indefinitely continued creation and the reciprocal copenetration that is the domain of life.

As he turned back to contemplate the garden and the lively birds flying across it, he felt that everything happened as though a deep current of consciousness had penetrated matter, leading it to organization and multiplicity, with this particularity, however, that the vital current does not confine itself to a single course, but follows different directions or deviations and may even flow backward. Leaning over further, he began to observe the roses climbing the arches, taking on solid and geometric forms in order to adorn them with a kind of strange dance.

"I have just finished reading the book by Darwin that you recommended, on the movement of climbing plants," he said, turning around. "Fixity is, in fact, not the characteristic that enables us to decide upon the difference between a plant and an animal. And although it is true that a plant is generally immobile by virtue of the fact that it takes its nourishment on the spot, it can sometimes move. The consciousness of the plant cell is not so asleep that it can never wake. The chlorophyl function is the culmination of the vital impulse in the plant."

The old man smiled again and spoke: "Everything is living, my dear Élie. Everything is living: mark my words. Between a plant and an animal, between an animal and man, there are only differences of degree, for differentiation is not a negation but a creation. The evolutionism of Darwin or that of Spencer is to conceive of variations as due to exterior and accidental causes. Evolution, however, does not occur in a unilinear homogeneous series, but virtually, according to heterogeneous terms that actualize it along a ramified series."

Élie continued to look at the flexible branches of the rose garden from which clusters of flowers in full bloom radiated.

The atmosphere of serenity reigning in the room invited one to seek the infinite under the finite appearances of the vegetal microcosm offered there. Élie was experiencing its metaphysical essence; it did not escape him that some very intimate part of his being maintained itself in this part of the universe.

That the blond arborescence trembling against the wide sky should figure, once again, that sweet, lost time and place, and that the Arch of Alliance should rise under the arch of Sekem! From the Hesperides: the fields of martagon lilies and fragrant origanum. From Egypt: the heliotropes, fireweed, and hollyhocks watered by Iris's tears. From China: the open peonies. From Japan: the azaleas. And from Persia, to the east of the Great Seleucia: the tree of light and life, spreading its crystal roots over the ground and its fruit of ambrosia in the air.

Intoxicated, he let his eyes roam over this new garden of Eridu where Eden, the tree goddess, ruled. Eden! With King Manosher, he imagined participating in the creation of these closed places strewn with rare essences, where all the scattered beauties of the earth were assembled. Eden! Whence flow the four rivers of the world, taking different paths and watering kingdoms and countries. Eden! Paradise! Image of the divine world for which we languish infinitely, like the Sassanids who, so they say, hung clusters of golden grapes above their beds in winter. Eden! Oasis of Al Djannel vibrating with the murmur of the eternal river.

He had gone this far in his exquisite rambling when it occurred to him that, among natural forces, there is one whose truth has not always been recognized: that life, like consciousness, creates something at every instant. What quantity of human energy had been put to work to create this paradise?

The young man looked at Albert Kahn who was dozing in the heat. His arm on the desk, his legs stretched out, he had let his eyelids close once again.

"So much work!" Élie murmured.

The old man looked up, struck the table with his right hand, tanned and muscular, to signal his amused approval.

"Certainly, my child," he said, "certainly. Nonetheless, Selam is not the Jardin des Plantes! For me botany has never been the main thing, but a representation of the solidarity needed between human societies. Our dear Bergson once said that 'It is through art, at least as much as through the sciences, that peoples manage to understand and love each other.'"

There was a gust of wind; the branches heavy with roses trembled. A woodpecker began pecking against a fir with dull, clear sounds; nearby, fat blond bees persistently danced around the deep and perfumed calyxes.

Soon the sound of a trumpet blowing rang out on the Saint-Cloud bridge, breaking the silence violently.

Albert Kahn, half asleep and far from the evening din, suddenly remembered a party given long ago in this place.

The night air is filled with Debussy's *Nocturnes*. The Colonne Orchestra is set up on a raised floor near the Palmarium: *Clouds, Feasts, Sirens*. There is a vapor of music trembling around the trees, a vast, shimmering shawl strewn with violet irises and black petals exuding languid perfumes, in the light of intertwining dominant ninth chords. All Paris is present. Rodin, Catulle Mendès, the Charpentiers, Bergson. Is that Léonide Blanc sitting near the tea pavilion? I see neither Barrès nor Paul Adam. They undoubtedly did not want to run into Péguy. Stéphane Mallarmé, dreamy-eyed and looking very tired, has left the rue de Rome in the company of a few friends.

During the intermission, Émile Dujardin converses with Paul Marguerite. Judith Gautier serves coffee. Attracting much attention is Nina de Villard, dressed in a gown of gray pearl cashmere, which is attached in the back with a belt under a bow of green velvet to an apron of braided green silk simulating striped fabric. On a pedestal table there are a few issues of the *Centaure*, the *Revue indépendante*, *Vogue*, and the *Symboliste*. The heat was as langorous as today, but there was a dense crowd in the garden. Men in formal dress smoking cigarettes. Very beautiful women, with sapphires cut into tablets, emeralds, and brilliants sparkling around their necks, cameo rings on their long fingers, and, covering their fair chests, large *perle-noire* medallions, jewels from Froment-Meurice, and white silk fans from Edmond Morin. I can see their light gold hair glinting; it is almost white and looks as though it were painted by Odilon Redon, Gustave Moreau, or Puvis de Chavannes. Everywhere images of Salome, Helen of Troy, Leah, Galatea, Pasiphae, Cleopatra, Esther, Delilah, Iseult, and Mélisande, dressed in sumptuous dresses enriched with precious stones, or half naked. The unreal souls of the pink and white flowers in immense bouquets flow into the women's souls, and the women's souls flow into the flowers', eager to rest in a celestial and mysterious sky.

Ah! These *Nocturnes* under the stars, these beaches of impressions captured by an immemorial intuition that makes the voice of all nature rise, as though at its source, reminding us of the inspiring commotion whence the music rose. There is, in the pleasure of the immediate, the turmoil of the *Reflets dans l'eau* or of the *Jardins sous la pluie*, which, like the variegated play of light in Monet's *Water Lilies*, open upon the secret alchemies of the infinite.

But the crowd has grown noisier: Richard Wagner's *Parsifal* is the topic. With Rodin I made the pilgrimage to Bayreuth. They are talking about *Parsifal*, *The Ring*, *Tristan*—especially *Tristan*. Dujardin and Mendès are having a lively discussion about the supreme wedding of love and death, of quintessential and magical chromaticism and magic, of the ineffable beauty of the *leitmotive*. "Claude Debussy in person has said what a high opinion he has of the prelude of the third act of *Parsifal* and of the entire episode of Good Friday," someone said. "Yes, but the *Mariage des roses* or the *Vase brisé* by Franck," another responded, "the *Mélodies* of Fauré, and his music for *Pelléas*."

I withdraw from the terrace. Outside, the weariness of the hour is expressed in the pale and powdery appearance of the *Centaurea candidissima*, while the *Obelia* valiantly holds on to the harsh blue of its dry flowerets.

I go join my guests again. A young woman with a strangely ingenuous face, wearing a knotted item of turquoises and pearls with a small matching buckle, is reciting Mallarmé's poem, "Des Fleurs": I can see her sky-blue gown trimmed with a diagonal strip of black velvet. I dream. Every sound comes back to me *quasi parlando* when I listen to Fauré's *Prometheus* and Déodat de Séverac's *Héliogabale* played, one by the brass, the other by the instruments of the Catalan *cobla*, under the open sky at the arena of Béziers. By the unexpected and troubling grace of the beautiful Rachilde, I am surprised to find myself wiping away a tear: at the height of ecstasy, the heart grieves, the exquisite becomes mortal and, on the moss of the vast, dark park, lovers listen to the furtive staccatos announcing the hunters of King Mark.

Here now, accompanied by Huysmans, is the dashing, young count Robert de Montesquiou-Fezensac, in whom I recognize my dear and chimerical Des Esseintes. My heart fails me before so much beauty, so much superhuman perfection animating face and body. I call my chauffeur, wanting to lose myself in the black night and wake tomorrow in a chaste and limpid dawn, along a beach washed by the tide, Cabourg perhaps or Honfleur.

. . . Albert Kahn had a dreamy look. In truth, what had he known of life's pleasures? Time had passed very quickly, filled with work, late nights, and receptions. At the age of thirty-five he had already met the greats of this world, those in possession of beauty and love as well as those who lead wars. But a crash had wiped him out very early on—the crash caused by the pain of living, which breaks more cruelly than the material bankruptcy he was now experiencing.

There had been the meeting with Bergson, and the nocturnal philosophy lessons. Then his *élan vital* was suddenly broken in a sinister cracking that struck body and spirit when he was only thirty-five years old: an ailment the neurologists had called neurasthenia, attributing it to organic and dynamic disorders, but Kahn, alone, knew its true cause and history. Just as the social and material success he had achieved rested only on his fragility. An immense success, great fragility. And in this garden exhaling an overly suave perfume, he had lost himself, just as he was losing life every day a little more.

The swallows crossed the space of the window in pursuit of insects, crying out and beating their wings like little scythes of black light. Below, the part of the Vosges forest where he had seen the straight and slender trunks rise seemed asleep in the hairy ferns, guardians of silence and immobile dancers among the blocks of blue sandstone.

Again he saw the arrival of the trains with their wagons loaded with firs fresh from his native country, which he had ordered. Unloaded there, on the platforms, they fed a deep nostalgia at the bottom of his heart.

The old Albert Kahn rose, seized by a very strong emotion. Élie, who held a grant from the foundation Travel Grants Around the World and had won his deep affection, looked at him and said in an anxious tone: "Are you ill, dear teacher?"

The old man smiled: "No, not exactly, my child. I was daydreaming."

"It's very hot. I am going to get you a glass of water."

"Go on. You are a real *Lebtob*."

Élie left the room hurriedly while the old man slowly walked over to the sofa to lie down.

"We are not free," he said to himself, with the strange and painful impression of always having known that. "We are not free. I could not do otherwise. I had no choice."

The more he thought about it, the clearer it became: Albert Kahn was born Jewish and poor and, in order to survive and succeed with his project, he had been forced to forget he was Jewish and to become rich. He went over those years he had been fascinated with Maurice Barrès who he still claimed—before and in spite of everyone, including those who had praised him while he was living but belittled him now—was one of the greatest stylists of his time. "Beautiful ideological garden, all animated by one who is no longer . . . ." Albert Kahn recalled the *Garden of Bérénice* in whole fragments: "Come to Aigues-Mortes, to the narrow garden that does not see the sea. The closed walls, the Constance tower that now only has to keep memories."

Not content with having made Barrès one of the founding members of the Circle Around the World, he had created with him the National Assistance in September 1914, basing it on the Sacred Union. He, Albert Kahn, at Maurice Barrès's side! The man of the "spiritual families of France"! Barrès the anti-Israelite! The false patriot who, with Maurras, Adam, and Daudet, had a few years before incited part of France to celebrate instinct, the knowledge of roots, the earth, blood, and the dead—making consciousness pass through supposed absolute knowledge, identifying Law and the State, without even realizing that he was mumbling the philosophy of that "loathesome German," Hegel! Barrès who, without proof, accused the Jewish officer Dreyfus, pretending that our thoughts translate "very old physiological tendencies," claiming that he was speaking in the name of "French morality" and "French justice," and getting tangled up, contemptuously, in the terrifying logic of racism!

How annoying this overexcitement was! Albert Kahn felt at that moment like those pious Jews who were often interrupted by enemy attacks while building the second Temple: they fought with one hand while holding a trowel in the other to raise the house of God.

The house of God was that garden where the maples and river elms of the Japanese Garden now muted the low-angled light along a path of sand and gravel bordered by exotic plants that the Emperor of Japan had personally sent to Albert Kahn. The Japanese houses and the red bridge built by Japanese workers appeared, sparkling in the beginning of the sunset reddening this distant scene. There were also areas of singular retreat that seemed on the edge of mystery.

Eminent figures had crossed these places: Lépine exclaiming over the Japanese inventions, the poet Rabindranath Tagore admiring the roses of the rose garden designed by the French landscape architect Duchêne, accompanied by the Countess de Noailles and the hellenist Maurice Croiset, Jaurès, Chamberlain, Anatole France, Israël Levi, Clemenceau, Poincaré, the pasha of Marrakech, Painlevé, the maharajah of Kapurthala, Joffre, and Lyautey coming to breathe in this mad oasis, apart from the tumult of the world.

It was still hot, and Albert Kahn was happy to see Élie, who came back into the room with a tall glass of fresh water.

"Still pensive?" Élie said in a slightly anxious tone, offering him the glass.

"Still pensive, Élie. So many things have happened in my life. So many things, meetings, events, thoughts. So many truths and errors."

"What errors?" Élie murmured.

"Those one cannot avoid making, those one should not make."

"What do you mean?" asked the young man, sitting down on the only chair in the room.

Albert Kahn was quiet for a long moment. Outside, the pinks and greens had begun to melt into a delightful mixture above which a dying star was already shining. Élie was ardently hoping to reach an opening of the universe. But, at the same time, with a strange and anguishing emotion growing in his throat, he felt a need to return to the open window, to look at *Sélam*—the term Albert Kahn preferred to use to designate his gardens, which were almost not his gardens anymore. The sun was setting over Paris. *Sélam* was still in the light, although Élie could measure the decline of the sun with his eyes.

In this alternating calm and anxiety, Albert Kahn began to speak to Élie, who had come back to sit beside him. The old man's voice, muted but charged with strong emotion, sometimes created a whistling sound.

"Dear Élie, yes, I too have foundered in seductive errors. I believed what I wanted to believe. I believed in a kind of universal benevolence. *Sélam* is the Hebrew *shalom*, peace, and the noble Oriental greeting: 'Peace, joy, and happiness to those who are far and those who are near.' *Sélam* was to have been the garden of my soul, Élie. But I forgot the Just to raise it to the reality of a pure symbol where it cannot be recognized. My desire was to gather in this place the scattered beauties of this world in order to try to know the penetrating secret. But a rose would have sufficed. A single rose, if one knows how to look at it, suffices to make a garden. The essence of all pleasures is metaphysical and partakes of mystery. A rose is an epiphany. A single rose, Élie. But it was only a short time ago that this illumination penetrated my spirit. Look, my gardens will die just as I will die. For everything that has been is mortal, and to live is to accept our mortality. All the same, I would like to speak to you about a subject more serious than my death or the death of my gardens. I am referring, of course, to the death of liberty, and with its death, the repeated martyrdom of our people. Élie, I can already hear the mad music of carnage that they are trying to drown out; it is coming from the other side of the Rhine, as you know. I see the sad parody of this terrible dementia not only in my own loss but in that of Europe in which, however, I continue to believe and hope, because of the ideas of democracy and liberty it has invented. But Europe is now springing toward the good in order to destroy it, forgetting the fig tree of Israel beneath which our people praise invisible God with songs like the war drums of Babylon or Tyre or the cymbals of the pagan jubilation of Sidon or Nineveh, making a barbaric cacophony. I tell you, Élie, my son, watch out for the war songs to come. Watch out for them and, just as our fathers twice saved the Law, which is the divine word of the holy Book, from the sack of Jerusalem, and then from the collapse of the Roman world and the Nordic and barbarian invasions, get ready to know the hideous face of brutality. Watch out."

Albert Kahn fell silent. The sun could no longer be seen on the horizon. Only the suave odor of roses still hung in the air.

Élie looked at the old man without speaking. Without speaking, he rose, taking the glass left on the table, and disappeared.

Albert Kahn was almost completely stretched out on the old sofa, his eyes open on a distant, inaccessible landscape that seemed to be moving closer and closer.

Élie came back very soon and gave him something to drink.

In truth, it was calm in the room, in the garden, and in their hearts.

Talking seemed to have calmed the old man and the younger one was calmer for having listened. Albert Kahn continued, however:

"Please understand," he said, "physical, moral, and spiritual suffering has operated many changes in me. The time of vanity is passed, and it has been a long time since I got intoxicated on the intimate and infinite perfume of strange flowers in their unreal halo of symbolist philosophy. Now it is for me only a bastard resurgence of forms of the sacred. Slowly, I, the slave, left Egypt. I renounced the idols to honor that unique Law that makes the universal radiate. The universal . . ."

Here the old man's discourse was interrupted. His arms stretched along his body, his legs straight, he seemed to have suddenly fallen asleep on the sofa. For a long time Élie contemplated this man he loved. Then he went back to the window once again in a state of perplexed melancholy.

A system of lights set up in the trees made it possible to visit the entire property at night and, as always in this delightful season, lovers were strolling two by two through the garden, each part of which lit up, then fell again into obscurity, according to the rhythm of their progression. Located next to the Golden Forest, the Blue Forest rustled its nocturnal gown nonchalantly; arrowheads, bastard acorus, buttercups, rushes, purple loosestrife, water lilies, clover, and water plantain were the flora of the ponds.

Upset by the old man's words, Élie nonetheless felt his taste for life return as he breathed in the beauty of this natural world in which the moon, above the lights, illuminated the rushes and reeds rising out of the pure waters.

He credited Judaism for the creation of that Law that separates the just from the unjust and upholds the right of the weakest against natural forces that he could see only helped the strongest to rule, even in this garden that fascinated him so. He was certainly aware what kind of night could brutally put out the day in order to hide the blackest crimes. He had in him a similar prescience of the worst that might happen, razing the ground in a desire for blood that would release a cloud of human smoke. But when he heard the clear laughter of a woman walking along a barberry hedge, he could not stop himself from wondering which path, lit up by fireflies, she had come out of, which magic copse, which silvery stream had begotten her, which rose had lent her her adorable complexion. There was in the night air a divine beauty in complete harmony with the immanence of this world. And, remembering Nietzsche, he told himself that asceticism is only a ruse to preserve life. He feared Nietzsche's *Zarathustra*, but he liked his aphorisms—that manner of openwork thinking under the deflection of momentary light, with the mocking humor that bounces from rock to rock, above ecstatic disillusionment and supposed terrestrial disgust.

Albert Kahn was sleeping. Élie turned off the lights and left the room.

Behind the Sailboats (*Derrière les voiliers*), etching by Denise Le Dantec, 1978. Photo © collection Le Dantec.

Allée Eight

*In the Middle Ages, European unity rested upon a
common religion. In modern times it has given way
to culture (to cultural creation), which becomes the
realization of the supreme values through which
Europeans recognize, define, identify themselves.
Today, however, culture is also giving way. . . . Thus
the image of European identity is receding into the
past. European: one who has a nostalgia for Europe.*
KUNDERA, The Art of the Novel

During the night, between the thirteenth and fourteenth of November, 1940, abandoned by
everyone in his big house empty of furniture, Albert Kahn was dying amid indifference.
Who, in these distressing times, was going to worry about a poor, eighty-year-old Jew who
had been foolish enough to engulf his fortune in the pursuit of a wild dream that history had
just rejected in a bloody move? Who was going to care about his project of "universal
reconciliation" through art and culture? Or his concern for making "individual interest har-
monize with the collective spirit"? Words of another time, words empty of meaning. The
democracies seemed to have been conquered: the Nazis had occupied Europe, the Jewish
people were experiencing a holocaust. A world had crumbled and, as for the only friend the
only man could still have counted upon, Bergson, he too was dying, dying and as desperate
as the companion of his youth.[1]

Heine's terrifying prophecy had been fulfilled.[2] The barbaric gods of ancient Germany had
been resuscitated and the people of Europe forced to play the second act of their suicide.
Death, Mort, Mavèt, Tod, Muerte, Smérte, Morte . . . The same sinister bell tolled in each
language, announcing the death of men, death of humanism, death of Europe, death of art,
death of the novel, of painting, music, poetry, and architecture—death of the garden.

Death of the garden: the idea will surprise those who reason in statistical terms, according to the obtuse logic of "human sciences." For the statistics indicate that the total amount of planted but not agricultural space has not tended to decrease in France today—on the contrary. The number of households owning a house—and thus a lawn—has increased with the standard of living whereas, in the city and "housing schemes," the support of "green spaces" has become a reflex.

But we know this, for example: the dizzying increase in the sale of records, far from entailing a progression in musical life as it has been understood in Europe until now—that is, the passionate support of the "elites" for the musical creation of their time[3]—has been accompanied by its disappearance. And Milan Kundera is justified in noting that in Russia "hundreds and thousands of novels [are published] in huge runs and with great success," whereas "it has been about a half-century since the history of the novel stopped in the empire of Russian communism."

Michel Deguy has—with painful relevance—called this disaster an "apocalypse of culture" through the effect of the cultural product. It is a phenomenon that has occurred with the involuntary complicity of the avant-gardes: it would, in fact, have been strange if the art of gardens had been kept out of this self-destruction that was signaled, as early as the twenties and thirties, by a semantic mutation: the words "green space" (espace vert) were gradually substituted for garden.

The green space is a concept born with urban planning, that is to say the will to master scientifically the urban explosion of the late nineteenth century. Before then, people spoke of "urban art," using everyday words: street, square, building, monument, promenade, park, garden. But beginning in 1910, a specific language came into being, the result of a theoretical effort of rationalization aimed at regulating the disorganized fluctuations of the modern city by cutting up the territory according to the segregationist technique of zoning.[4] In this context, the green space has most often appeared as a residue, the "negative" effect[5] of the built structure and of traffic patterns—when it is not conceived, even more vulgarly, as a vegetal makeup applied as a last resort. In short, in losing its name, the urban garden was deprived of any positive force other than hygienic. No more geography: the green space is not a place, but a portion of undifferentiated territory whose limits are decided within the abstract universe of the plan. No more history: the green space makes fun of context as well as tradition. No more culture: the green space is only a green arranged according to the sole "rules" of convenience; art is either dismissed from its domain or reduced to "packaging."

Atopical, achronic, anartistic, the green space pays no attention to layouts, proportions, mineral or aquatic elements, to landscape or geometrical composition. It is a vegetal nothing devoted to the purification of the air and to physical exercise. The emotion resulting from a stroll through "beautiful nature" is not its purpose, which resides instead in the cold perfection of its concept.

This reduction of the garden to a green might, however, not have turned out to be catastrophic: after all, it was only a matter of a linguistic mode, a piece of a technical discourse in the process of being codified. But, unfortunately, it ran into the most powerful tendencies of the plastic avant-gardes between the wars: the condemnation of ornamentation, cubism, neoplasticism, and abstraction. The clash took the form of a fusion inscribed in the desire of these movements to break with tradition, by inventing the visible of modernity.

This explains the violence of the attacks led by the *Congrès internationaux d'architecture moderne* (C.I.A.M.) against "culturalist" urbanism[6] and the garden cities. Several paragraphs of the Athens Charter are dedicated to vilifying Ebenezer Howard's invention, which was relayed in France by Benoît-Lévy. "Enough fussing over context and landscape" was the essence of Le Corbusier's message; and enough petty utopias, too. What was needed was big, straight, "free," fast: a city where the ground would be—as in the *Project for a Contemporary City of 3 Million Inhabitants*—an immense green space as flat as a table, crossed by highways and strewn with "Cartesian" towers carried by piles.[7]

Nothing, then, was more foreign to modern taste than the undulating complexity of the notion of landscape. Advocates of the series, of standards, of progress, and of geometric simplicity, the "moderns" could only see it as elitist affectation, that is to say as a bourgeois anachronism. Thus they set to repudiating it upon the occasion of the Exposition des arts décoratifs of 1925.

We know from its witnesses that this exhibit was prepared in a fever by the moderns, who saw it as an occasion for decisive manifestos. Roux-Spitz's summaries as well as the catalogue commentaries are formal: the rule was to run counter to the landscape architects by means of the "sharp and precise lines" of cubist geometricism. The brothers Paul and André Véra had shown the way in their own garden in Saint-Germain-en-Laye and in the Parisian one of Jacques Rouché, by advocating the return to the geometric pruning of trees and clumps and by insisting upon the architectural rather than the landscape aspect of their creations.[8] But the propositions of Le Corbusier or Mallet-Stevens for the 1925 exhibit were very provocative: Le Corbusier's "garden" for the New Spirit Pavilion was a roof-terrace, and Mallet-Stevens's work included "schematic trees executed in reinforced concrete by the Martel brothers."

The public was scandalized and offended, of course, and rejected their projects.[9] But in truth, this cubism and this abstraction expressed the essence of the new climate and would end up by clearly imposing themselves upon the cultural elites; the anemic landscape school, on the other hand, was incapable of meeting such challenges.

Its most talented and representative master, J.-C.-N. Forestier,[10] had kept his distance for more than fifteen years: called to Spain after his work on the Champ-de-Mars (1908) where he had created regular gardens, he composed the park of Maria-Luisa in Seville and the Montjuich park in Barcelona before going to Lisbon and Havana. Undogmatic in his ideas, open to cultural diversity, he was the most brilliant representative of the "mixed" style that his colleague Jules Vacherot, chief gardener of the World's Fair of 1900, had implemented with him in the Champ-de-Mars and theorized in a precise fashion. Moving away from both the classical style, in which "nature is enslaved and subjected to the needs of the composition," and the romantic style, in which nature is "copied and idealized," "mixed or inventive" art was, according to Vacherot, the kind "that results from the personal initiative of the artist and in which the natural elements have only second priority." Consequently, it rested on two principles: "unity in the whole and variety in the details."[11]

A few learned works and a lovely profession of faith were not enough, however, to hide the fact that this school inspired by Alphand was shut up in academicism: an eclecticism similar to the spirit of the Beaux-Arts[12] that, in Vacherot, was betrayed by the use of the adjective "mixed," which his successors would soon replace with "composite."[13]

Born out of the bourgeois expansion in a milieu animated by the embers of Saint-Simonism, this school had remained essentially bourgeois. Bourgeois, that is to say terrorized, in these years after the Commune, by the idea of the *new* assimilated to the specter of the Revolution. It had proven itself incapable of breaking, even after Alphand's death, with a code marked by the vision of a technocratic engineer indifferent to the individual site.[14] While the symbolists sought in Nature an alchemy of "correspondences," while the impressionist painters planted their easels in the countryside to wash their eyes and paintbrushes in light, while a double revolution was taking place in the notion of landscape, the official "landscape architects"—the only ones able, it goes without saying, to get public commissions—remained enmeshed in their "stylistic" disputes. Blind to the dazzling interior light of Odilon Redon and to the luminous ecstasies of Renoir. Foreign to the great and thrilling discovery of an *elsewhere*, which would carry Gauguin and Segalen toward the *Immémoriaux*, take Cézanne to the Sainte-Victoire Mountain, and plunge Monet into the aquatic bedazzlement of his garden at Giverny.[15]

Such blindness could only beget defeat in the face of the strong convictions of artists as brilliant as Mallet-Stevens and Le Corbusier. From then on, the "landscape" school that had come out of the ambiguous meeting of Alphand and Barillet had no existence outside a bitterly antimodern rehashing. Bitterness and intellectual confinement prevented the only encounter that might have allowed, toward the mid-twenties, the erection of a barricade against functionalist geometricism: the encounter with surrealism which, in a superb text by Aragon,[16] had offered a "modern" source of support and, even better, the occasion to rethink the landscape in the light of the Freudian discovery of the unconscious.

What is the point of dreaming about a rendezvous that never took place? Relegated to the department of old-fashioned things because excluded from the debate on modernity, the landscape garden disappeared from plastic and architectural thought. Even worse, in the thirties, after the war, when the *hard-french*[17] was building massively, without any apparent feeling, the *grands ensembles* or housing schemes of the suburbs and the first "new cities," it became a register of recipes, of "tricks of the trade" at the service of its mortal enemy, the green space, with the purpose of "animating" it.

The garden's suicide was consummated. The victory of technique had struck art down, as Heidegger had announced. And the heirs of the avant-gardes, dismayed, had no other solution than to become either "collaborators with modernity"[18] or the uncertain apostles of an "ambiguity"[19] that the modern movement in architecture had—in its passion for "progress" understood as the production of a meaning—hoped to eliminate.

How can one rebuild, when the ground itself has been destroyed? How can one create a new foundation for the garden, when the being of man seems to have imploded? Putting the "moderns" on trial does not free one of their lesson.

Carried by the *Manifestoes* to cutting truths, and by a theoretical arrogance generating blindness, the work of deconstruction undertaken by the "moderns" led to the destruction on the theoretical level of the being of man and, consequently, of the enigma that Western art had tried to explore since its inception. But this work of mourning was in no way the effect of a morbid fantasy that avant-garde thinkers, artists, and revolutionaries offered themselves as a mysterious luxury. They were the lucid, desperate, or rebellious witnesses of the suicide of Europe, the death of humanism and of culture—even if, in this last case, their revolts prepared the way for the totalitarianisms that would not have come into being without the great collective slaughter of 1914–18.

In other words: the proclamation of the "return" of a "subject" that the perverse "moderns" supposedly tried to suppress is only a sinister mystification, if by this one means to say that all the tragedy of the era could have been avoided on the sole condition that rebellion and revolution had not permanently upset the fragile equilibrium of democratic societies that had been evolving "of their own accord" toward a political, economic, and social better-being. Or, better yet, if there was a return of the "subject"—once the great holistic ideologies had also been deconstructed[20]—this return was essentially problematic, in its mode of appearance as well as in the configuration of the individual recomposing himself within it.

This difficulty goes back to the garden. For, contrary to architecture, whose mode of being depends upon its presence—and thus upon its silence as well—the art of gardens has certain similarities to narration, which presupposes a representation of the individual. Scenes arranged, as in a novel, like so many stages in the path of a specific being in *experimental egos*:[21] such is in fact the art commanding the organization of gardens—with this difference, however, that the mechanism of the drama, unlike the novel that uses a whole range of tones, is based upon a single tone, but one with infinite resonances: the confrontation of the given and the artificial, of nature placed in relation to the effort of culture.

Most landscape architects of today—at least those who, in the heart of a narrow and confined milieu, would like to refound the landscape in the cultural context of postmodernity—would probably accept this definition as a point of departure. Which does not mean that their agreement goes beyond that.

Some, whom we will represent by Bernard Lassus, propose to reactualize the tradition of Dufresny[22] by following a similar approach to that of brute art and conceptual art. Advocating a minimal intervention that would result from a mastery of the "ambience," then of the "immeasurable," their conception of landscape has found an important echo in England and, by way of certain ecological themes, in Germany.

Trained as a painter, but involved with architecture through family tradition,[23] Bernard Lassus executed during the sixties a group of plastic experiments and reflections that led him to a radical criticism of modern architecture's neglect of relations and transitions.[24] His study on the "inhabitants–landscape architects"[25] as well as his experiments with color[26] led him to a theory of landscape as perceptible *structure*. A structure that is essentially flimsy, more arachnid than strongly expressed, reduced to a few nothings that carry meaning, like the half-steel, half-concrete bridge stretched over the wide road cutting through the park of Istres: the metal gate that disappears into the greenery is brightened up by a few stylized butterflies, while the arch above the road figures a massive rock. There is here a desire for something *flou* or fuzzy "in opposition to the pseudo-rationality that, in the name of efficiency, has denied the perceptible approach and, at the same time, stifled the landscape"[27]—a desire one finds again in his *Jardin des retours* conceived in relation to the old *Corderie royale* of Rochefort, built by Blondel in 1666. In this regard, Jean Duvignaud speaks of the "diversion" of a building that has no function today, through the extremely discreet use of plants and perspectives on the Charente, and through the naming of the areas: Garden of the Navy, Garden of La Galissonière, Garden of Bégon.[28] Thus, according to Pierre Donadieu, an ecologist involved with the project: "More than a finite space, B. Lassus creates a substratum, the condition for the emergence of representations, images, sounds, and odors. Form does not come first, it is induced by the articulation of intentions, both a matrix that cannot be bypassed and the suppleness of becoming, places of the ephemeral and the durable, proximity of the visual and the tactile."[29]

It goes without saying that such restraint provokes controversy. The same that accompanies minimalism and *arte povera*. How can one speak of a work when the landscape architect voluntarily locates his intention on the fringes of nonintervention? Is this subtle poetry or mystification? As for the English critic Stephen Bann, he settles the matter without hesitation: "Lassus is almost the only one, in an obvious crisis, to propose viable conclusions."[30]

At the opposite end from this "ambiguity," Michel Corajoud wishes to stand without reserve in the domain of the work: the work in which culture imposes itself on nature, in which landscapes are deliberate formal creations.

Corajoud, who is also a professor at the school of Versailles, has the ambition to reconstitute a "lost knowledge" involving Le Nôtre as well as Morel, by inscribing it in an esthetic that affirms the site, and not in a semiological abstraction. A man of matter and truth, he thinks about the nature of soils and possible vegetation before making a choice. For this designer, who was linked at the beginning of his career to the "neorationalist" architects of the A-U-A[31]—especially Henri Ciriani with whom he worked on the Villeneuve in Grenoble[32]—the experience of the layout and of geography is essential; as a passionate creator who is annoyed by affectation, pretense, and "the accumulation of objects, even innovative ones,"[33] he entered into an intellectual communion, through projects conceived with the architects Henri Gaudin, Roland Castro, and Renzo Piano, with the philosopher Michel Serres who opened up for him a space of fringes, swamps, slanted geometries, and ramified paths that create networks of tensions comparable to those of acupuncture. Thus his project for the Jules Verne park in Amiens—which was rejected, unfortunately—composed a group of landscapes inspired by *The Mysterious Island, Twenty Thousand Leagues under the Sea,* and *Five Weeks in a Balloon* using the concrete language provided by a marshy site and a plant with a thousand possibilities, bamboo. The poetry of the work was at the opposite end of the spectrum from the anecdotal vulgarity of a Disneyland. This demonstrates how the formalism he has often been accused of does not stem from a will for power or a nostalgia for the classical garden, but from an ethics refusing falsehood and the abuse of the concept, albeit "immaterial."[34]

We have talked about Lassus's perceptible "minimalism" and Corajoud's poetic "formalism." But we need to refine these categories by analyzing the projects more precisely and, better yet, by situating the originality of other landscape architects, key figures such as Jacques Simon, Gilles Vexlard, and Alexandre Chemetoff. We must also question the actual structure of command where a new type of amusement park is tending to emerge: that in which the promoters are no longer interested in offering visitors a voyage to the heart of the (reconstituted) marvels of nature or history, but of recreating, by means of technological miracles, an imaginary universe known by all.[35]

We must conclude, however. Conclude this book, dedicated to the most romantic of the visual arts, with a visit to the north of Paris, where an attempt has been made to invent a new mode of landscape narrative inspired by cinematographic narrative techniques: the Parc de La Villette.

The history of this grandiose project has been told several times.[36] It will, consequently, suffice to recall that, after many ups and downs and an international competition, control of the operation was given to Bernard Tschumi, an architect with a cosmopolitan background, since, born in Paris, he studied in Switzerland before teaching in London, then New York.

The problem was dual. Philosophical: how was an urban park to be defined today, in an era that Jean-François Lyotard has called postmodern, when the West seems to have lost its points of reference—those "great narratives" upon which its humanist conception of man was founded? Formal: how was a park, without being overwhelmed to the point of disappearing, to be composed in relation to architectural masses, one of them as impressive and rigid as the City of Science and Indusry designed by Fainsilber, the other as complex and refined as the City of Music conceived by Christian de Portzamparc?

Bernard Tschumi seems to have found the solution in a hyperconceptual problematic inspired by his reading of Barthes, Deleuze, or Derrida,[37] formalized in a language that is less vegetal than technological.

A square framework superimposed on the site without any clear relation to it and high-tech architectural "Folies" on the summits are the starting points for a group of "sequences" formed by transitional lawns, game areas, roller-skating paths, "limping" allées (on one side a row of adult plane trees, on the other a row of young trees), ground covers marked out by spotlights, all leading from one "thematic garden" to another, each one of these having been entrusted, like the construction of the "Houses," to a different team: Water Garden (Alain Pélissier, with Peter Eisenmann, John Hejduk, and Fujiko Nakaya); Garden of Gardening (Gilles Vexlard, with Jean-Max Albert and Dan Flavin); Energy Garden (Alexandre Chemetoff, with Daniel Buren, Bernard Leitner, and Markus Raetz); Garden of Games (Ettore Sottsass and Martine Bedin, with Tony Cragg); Calm Garden (Kathryn Gustafson, with Rebecca Horn and Hulrich Ruckriem); etc.

Moreover, the fountains, as well as the lighting needed in a park including several restaurants and large cultural centers open late into the night,[38] will call upon lasers as well as programming.

This admittedly ambitious complex presents itself as an anticipation. The anticipation of a twenty-first century in which courtly gardens, "ramparts of hams and flasks," esoteric dreams, princely perspectives, follies of rockery and foliage, landscapes of the soul and of reverie would be forever stored on the dusty shelves of antiquities, to make room for a technical universe streaked with currents and strident moves, with jostling images and "information" chains.

A page will have been turned then. The world will have become clip, as in the films of Beneix or Besson.

Unless the grass goes mad.

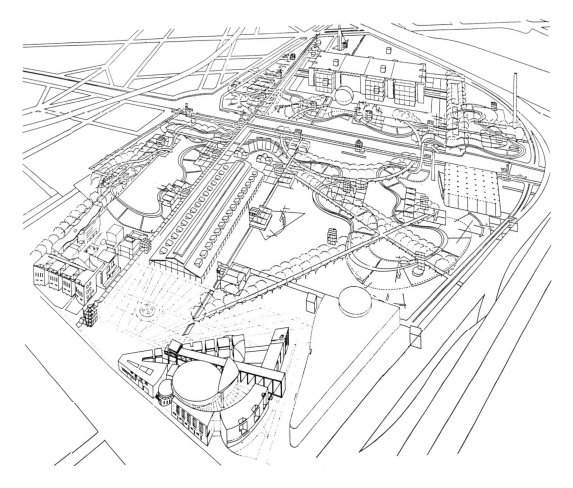

Bernard Tschumi, aerial view of the
Parc de La Villette. In the
foreground, the Cité de la Musique
by Christian de Portzamparc.
In the background, the Cité des
Sciences et de l'Industrie by
Fainsilber.

Michel Corajoud, project for the
park of Sausset, Seine Saint-Denis.

Bernard Lassus, the front garden
(detail), project for the new city of
Isle-d'Abeau.

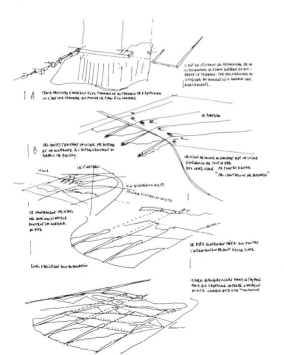

Here I stand, amazed, on the figurative road of mystery: in the first twist, behind the castle of water, after the gray back of the last housing project, when everything meets the wind, when the Amazon casts its waters into the Seine, in the alhambra pavilion.

The mind gets lost in the tragic avenues lined with cancerous elms where tranquility is broken by backfiring motorcycles ridden by groups of children. Greetings to the Zone! I hear echoes of a foreign tongue, and then another language that is the same because, shining mirror, I have set foot in one of those suburban Babels where the lawns of *Home Sweet Home* shine with the hair gel of disco dancers.

Here one came out, a half-century ago, on the rue du Point-du-Jour. Remember: the Billancourt Bridge over the river, the metal guardrails wet from the mist of the breathing masses; the wait; the hoarse cry of the siren like a terrible queen mother, who, out of breath, lures them to plunge through the automatic passageways toward the modern Tartars. Ten hours in this mental labyrinth where ideals become attached to superstitions like nightmares to dreams. And red, yellow, blue, and green sparks spring up from the crucibles, then fall back down in a rain of radium, melting, in the evening, on the sweating foreheads of night.

I move forward through the nets of false pearls of the lovely, listless weather of eternal nature. Nature—*rediscovered*.

My feet pass over an accumulated esthetic of pretense and trompe l'oeil. The Virgin is a comely gipsy with castanets on her fingers; hanging from her flowered skirts are three kids with jet-black eyes carrying waltzing wicker baskets. They are followed by a handsome young smurfer with a red silk scarf around his neck, who leaps and dances as he throws kisses to the crowd.

Having come from Beaubourg, the thief in the yellow T-shirt flees as fast as he can on Mouna's motorbike. Magnificent, he flees between darkness and light—between East and West.

And everything around me takes on an exotic air. Under the feeble light of the wrought-iron lamps, Snow White wears a dress trimmed with lace of scallop shells, her hair is of sandstone and the seven dwarves are made of gravel and cement. A little farther on, the Tahitian woman in a red bikini with the green peas has climbed down from the poster on the wall across the way. The two women look at each other without laughing; it is the sun that gives them their smug and insolent expression. A wedding in chrome, over there, on the façade, in the grass and dandelions. The painted horses have a splash of indigo to drink. A sand-colored lion shakes his immobile mane, renouncing the massacre.

I have left a poppy on a shell-breast. I have caressed the Tahitian's splendid ass. I have picked bouquets of flowers with petals of cracked dishware. I have crossed Africa and the Amazon twice. I took a detour through the Galapagos Islands on the back of gigantic turtles made of newspaper and glue. I have taken all the trips I have never taken. I have loved all the women I have never loved.

Enter! Enter my Thebaid, and do not say there are too many blue flowerets: they are only violets with stems of brass, and, on the ground, there are doe tears shaped like tiny beads of pearly pebbles, like the champagne froth of waves on the sea . . .

It sometimes happens that I sit down on this chair, preferably at sunset. I look at the colored birds of the façade. My image blurs in the reflections of my Eden.

The mica is slowly consumed in the river of darkness rising from the hedges.

I let myself go to the heart of the melodious pitch pine where other nostalgic thoughts, other webs of constructions are produced, labyrinthine and broken into separate sequences like a dream with infinite directions—singular, contrived stories rising in my mind on the occasion of an unusual circumstance or an unforeseen similarity.

It is still sunny. Now is the gentlest moment. The Phrygian melilots shine brighter than the stars of Sirius, and worry hangs over the rockery like gold pieces strewn on a green Deauville or Baccarat carpet. The pumpkins, squash, cantaloupes, and staked-up melons, superb, enormous, obese, are, depending on how you look at them, brilliant Turkish turbans, the children and grandchildren of Cucurbitus I, well-fed and well-off bourgeois, fairy tale carriages, or shining, magical Venetian lamps hung at the four corners of space—on the edge of the fallow land where I hear the regular, solitary, meditative sound of the hoe, plied by some modern Fiachra toiling under the pink and gray shroud of the dusk engulfing him.

It is the hour when the poet rises, intoxicated with his trip to the Hesperides, without ever having studied the way. Everything is a miracle in this garden of love. And the body that thought it was confined expands and exults in this happy disorder coming to life. Fruit hangs on the branches like succulent, close kisses. Vertigo! Was it then I who dreamed in this place? Lovely place, so adorable under your vaporous veil of light, remember my dream. Cradle the boat of my body. Lovely place of pure illusions, keep me in your power.

Now he is going back, cutting through the fields, under the immense clear blue of the sky, in the air saturated with freshness where nature, both calm and diligent, greets him with the proud reserve of a recently ennobled peasant; the grass, strewn with marguerites and pink clover, is perking up at this moment, full of sap, and moths flutter about enviously with the breeze that is chasing the dust from the road.

Am I the old man of Tarentum? Alcinoos? or the man of Corycus? Priapus, Vertumnus, or Pomona? The lover of tulips?[1] The gardener of Kirchhorst?[2] Simeon plowing Mount Sinai? Augustin stealing pears from his father's garden?[3] Bouvard or Pécuchet?

I have picked up the newspaper. Once more, the sun has made the wall before me crumble. A large absence has occurred in my memory. Light has filled the calyx of the roses. A kind of haze has come into the air.

I have pushed my chair back to a sheltered area in order to contemplate the spectacle. Chandeliers are going up and down the steps of pink marble, going to the square of water, on the side of the quincunxes, to the left, on leaving the house. Out of reach, a mute orchestra resonates in the shaded perspective.

I quench my optical thirst. I see the water through crystal. I take a broken mirror out of my pocket; it lights up with marvelous periodicity to the colors of all crimes. A young man in a blond wig begins to cry out on entering the maze of mounds, balustrades, terraces, statues, fountains, and always-green copses. "Do you like Nature?" someone asks. "Alas! you do not know what you are asking" (I answer) "for if you had any friendly feeling for me, as you would like me to believe, I would distress you, instead of diverting you."

Oh vast love of pretense! Art transforms, and haunts, and makes strange. Night has not yet fallen, but the sky has already hung out its cadmium jewels before the blinking eyes of the gillyflowers. Phoebus plunges his horses into the abyss of Iberia, and in that place where the halo of an immense melancholy is growing, where a topiary esthetic rules in which roses and lilies are only the elements of an austere grammar, I accept the despair of height—the vermilion gardenia with a red that is the mathematics of a red deeper, more fugitive, more mysterious, and even more cruel.

At this point, however, it may be enough to try to read beauty into what was mutilated and will carry away the fatal tempest of terror. I have put my newspaper down, lifted my eyes to the sky, seeking in the clouds the gentle divinities of pastorals. And I return to my garden where, simple and beautiful, nature agrees with the free rhythm of my reveries. At dusk, when they cover themselves with humid carpets of moss, the woods, parks, and gardens exhale infinite tremors. And the strongest and widest periwinkles are blue, veined with mother-of-pearl, less obscure and more mauve, enchanting the heart with a peaceful joy leading to the highest meditations on goodness and truth.

I stand up.

The last rays of light are falling in the strange menagerie around me, where a few giraffes without spots and moles without eyes move about. The cry of the woodpecker on the elm is more cutting when the breeze is soft. Illusion has regained its rights. Art is a great sun in the night. It rises, mastering marvels and ravages, attacking presumptuous innocence. What mad desire has given rise to this venerable and tranquil park where two lovers stroll? The imaginary is coupled to the real under the sky like vine branches to the vine, or like those illusory lovers intertwined under the leaves.

Illusion has regained its rights.

And imagination searches the horizon for some mysterious sign that might satisfy its unbridled taste for beauty.

The perfume of an unknown flower haunts me. The strange flora of the giant artichokes can be seen standing in a distant garden. The parterres are strewn with bowing crystalline hyacinths and azure blue chokeweed. A lady's-slipper crowns the tiny *fabriques* of tuff and porcelain, which the goddess's flight marked with bloody spots. Each clump conceals a dozing cat with shifty, golden eyes and false agaric fur, ready to bite. At the aeronautic center of the cherry trees, a many-colored torpedo loses its tail. A heart-shaped arrow sticks out like a question mark from the foot of a tree. It is in this place of confusion that I first felt the amorous impulse take shape in me. A burning movement was born with the laughter of a young woman under the threads of virgin vine; it turned into a tremor in a jumble of hollyhocks and flame-launching suns projected into the night.

Open up, roses of pleasure! one cannot leave the city merely by crossing the bridge—dance halls, sleazy dives, trembling lilacs of our mental suburbs!. . .

Writers, poets, enter the crooked gardens of your *follies*! It's Sunday: the path ends with a flowering gate where I lean on my elbows and watch Nana dance in her lover's arms.

I pretend I am taking off my hat which the wind of the Arts has not stolen from me when I run into Rose dressed for a ball under a street lamp adorned with periwinkles and columbines. The man hugging her frail body is wearing a white sweater with blue stripes. Artists, to your paints! It is one of Auguste Renoir's oarsmen: I recognized him from his sly eyes, his lovely red mustache, and his large build.

Here we are among excellent beings and things . . . Honoré de Balzac's elderly daughter has given up the shabby flower beds and stupid borders: she dances on her runway to the stars, far from the *petty lawns*.

Immobile and smiling, taking little steps in the grass, Miss Suzanne Leenhoff, a Dutch pianist and the future wife of Édouard Manet, strolls along the shores of the Seine on the island of Saint-Ouen; as she advances, the shores turn into a garden; a little farther on, one sees three men fishing in an idle boat.

Wednesday December 4 [1872], My dear Zola, Mssrs. Pissarro, Sisley, Monet, and Manet request the pleasure of your company at dinner on this Wednesday the 11th. 7 o'clock. Café Anglais. R.S.V.P.

Rendezvous with the painter in his garden at Gennevilliers which is chock-full of flowers newly imported into Europe—*Do you remember the day we saw a bouquet of peonies by Manet at the hôtel Drouot? The pink flowers, the very green leaves, painted in paste and not in glaze . . . There was something quite wholesome about it,* Vincent wrote Theo.

At Giverny, the master, Monsieur Monet, receives us. We cross a little bridge lacquered green.

The Seine is very blue—*The water doesn't have that color? But excuse me, it does, at certain moments, just as it has scabby reflections.* Return to the garden in the country home of Nittis in Saint-Germain-en-Laye. The air circulates under the trees; the women are half lying down in the grass; Madame Monet has traded hats with Madame Manet; Claude is leaning toward the fire-red tulips, a watering can at his feet, while chickens from the farmyard come and go . . .

Oh this fruit! the mouth of a woman—of women! To drink from these lips, to dive into a tall dark head of hair, to caress silky golden curls . . .

La Goulue is dancing with the Cheese Girl at Bougival, by the water. Boneless Valentin dances with rubber limbs.

I see here the terrible beauty of those who were goddesses for a few years, and who remain, spinning and bewildered by the violence of their pleasures, in the immense shadow of the suburbs where one can barely glimpse a bit of greenery in the background, an old wicker armchair, a mangy dog one calls to, an old romance—the refreshment of earthy drunkenness, a few roses, a few forget-me-nots, a few resedas. Yes, FORGET-ME-NOT.

Fences, trellises—a few branches of virgin's bower and honeysuckle, sometimes an audacious branch of button roses, hang outside: these are the gardens of the suburbs.

And it is at this moment that a limping fallen woman with disheveled, moon-colored hair and a rumbling stomach puts out a soup plate of milk for the tomcat in the tender lilac grove. The old couple next door closes the shutters, superstitious about the phases of the moon.

The dilapidated vegetable gardens, dear to Huysmans, by privilege, sometimes have a short stairway leading down to the Oise or the Marne; their walls are garnished with pieces of broken bottles or powdery wild radishes springing up from between the badly stacked bricks—resembling the garden walls at Yonville-l'Abbaye where Charles and Emma Bovary have just climbed down from the Swallow (their carriage). It seems they have moved in . . .

Idle, a little bit of wind, in the fading light, gives a last sweep to the loose steps in front of the villas of brick and millstone facing the abandoned gardens, haunted by vague linden trees, clumps of laurels, boxwood, and spindle trees.

One can hear in the distance the last sounds of people on a spree: Waiter, one more Armagnac! A solitary young woman raises her cloudy eyes. Her delicate shoes are powdered with white nettle; her silk blouse is torn.

Such is the creature you may meet. Frightened, she flees as soon as you try to sketch her slightest motion under the blinking light of a summer star.

Wake up, phantoms, oh my fellows, with your old, tender, and crazy gestures. Seek sustenance in these gardens crowded with stocks, languishing, lost, and abandoned under the moon.

I have approached a clump of roses.

Die Ros' ist ohn' Warum, sie blühet weil sie blühet,
Sie acht 't nicht ihrer selbst, fragt nicht, ob man sie siehet.

The rose is without why's; it flowers because it flowers,
It does not make a problem of itself, does not ask if one sees it.[4]

Paris–Ile Grande–Paris, 1985–1986.

FROM BREUIL TO ESSART

1. Colomban, an Irish missionary, went to Gaul, founding around 570 the abbey of Luxeuil on the ruins of Roman baths. The abbey was tied to the Rule of Saint Benedict: *Regula sancti Benedicti vel sancti Columbani*. He died in Bobbio in 615.

2. "*Fieg* in modern Breton or *Fiakr*; *Fiach* or *Fiachra* in Irish." Peager, *Prénoms bretons* (1975), p. 26.

3. Note that Hildegard, a monk of Saint-Denis appointed bishop of Meaux by Charles the Bald, in writing his *Life of Faron* around 870, did not hesitate to attribute to the Scots—that is to say to the Irish— the origin of monastic life.

4. *Revue Celtique* 29 (1908):285.

5. Regarding the problem of defining the medieval marvelous, one should consult Jacques Le Goff, *L'Imaginaire médiéval* (Paris, 1985).

6. See Jacques Dubois, "Un sanctuaire monastique au Moyen Age: Saint-Fiachre-en-Brie," *Hautes Études médiévales et modernes*. Centre de Recherches d'histoire et de philologie de la IVe section de l'École pratique des hautes études, V, 27 (1976), including 372 pages and a map.

7. The *courtilliers* were in charge of the *courtils* or small enclosed gardens. The *préoliers* took care of the "*prés*" or little pastures. The *verdiers* were responsible for the orchards, or were officers of waterways and forests. The *treillageurs* built trellises with laths or poles placed parallel or crossed in different directions in order to form fences, bowers, espaliers, etc. The *maraîchers* were in charge of cultivating large areas called *marais*, which produced vegetables. The *floresses*, daughters of *Flora*, goddess of flowers and gardens, took care of flowers.

Allée One

1. Pierre Riché, *Éducation et Culture dans l'Occident barbare* (Paris, 1962).

2. Georges Duby, *Le Temps des cathédrales* (Paris, 1976), and *L'An mil* (Paris, 1967).

3. This last fact is worth noting: besides the notoriety of the abbey founded by Saint Colomban, who turned it into a center of monastic learning, we know that the gardens were one of its major elements. The proof is the famous plan, commented on so many times, that associates *hortus*, *herbularius*, and *fruitier* with the convent buildings. The orchard also served as cemetery.

4. "These two notable species of adorable flowers signify for the Church for ever and ever the supreme honors that the crown of Roses gathered in the blood of martyrs, and that the Lilies wear in all the brilliance of their white chastity."

5. A monastery such as those presented in medieval iconography and in the account books of the late Middle Ages, and by a few ancient plans—such as that of the fortified garden within the canon's priory of Saint Augustine, which has recently been excavated in Plessis-Grimoult in Calvados. Or such as the *mote du jardin* or "garden lump" of the abbey of Jumièges, designated by the expression *Hortulus vulgo Thabor*, figuring Mount Tabor (site of the Transfiguration of Christ), which served as a belvedere in the garden.

6. Song of Songs 4:12, from *The New Oxford Annotated Bible* (New York, 1973). Fountain of Life and image of the female genitalia, symbolizing the Virgin's chastity, which is echoed by "The bird sang in the Beloved's garden" of the song of Blanquerna by Ramon Lull, the Catalonian visionary.

7. There is no doubt about the Oriental origins of the game of checkers; however, there was also a Celtic game that required a checkerboard, mentioned, for

example, in the *Dream of Maxen*, one of the stories in the Welsh *Mabinogion*: the object in question was a *Gwyddbwyll*, which can be translated as "intelligent wood."

8. A compilation can be found in the work by Sir Francis Crisp, *Mediaeval Gardens* (London, 1924; New York, 1966). See also John Harvey, *Mediaeval Gardens* (London, 1981).

9. The same can be said, for example, of those country homes or *gloriettes*, mentioned in seigniorial accounts and found in numerous iconographic representations.

10. *The Romance of the Rose*, trans. Harry W. Robbins (New York: E. P. Dutton, 1962), p. 5. The following quotations from the poem are also taken from this translation.

11. " All my companions call me Idleness; / A woman rich and powerful am I. / Especially I'm blessed in one respect: / I have no care except to tress and comb / My hair, amuse myself, and take mine ease. / My dearest friend is Mirth, a genteel beau, / Who owns this garden . . ." (p. 13).

12. Spice, in the original, is *espice*, which appeared around 1150 in the *Voyage of Charlemagne*: taken from the Latin *species*, "species," that is to say "species par excellence," "(stimulant) foodstuff," "medicinal drug." The ancient Greeks were acquainted with cinnamon, then pepper. See *The History of Plants* by Theophrastus, published in the fourth century BC; during the first years of the Christian era, naturalists and doctors, both Greek (Dioscorides, Galen) and Latin (Pliny), mentioned ginger, cloves, and nutmeg, come from a distant and mysterious Orient. But dur-

ing the Middle Ages, after the barbaric invasions and the Arab conquest, their source was no longer known. Arriving in Gaul via Genoa and then via Venice, they were thought to have a supernatural origin; apothecaries sold them by the ounce.

13. Venetians called pepper "the grain of paradise." It was the most valued and expensive of spices—"as costly as pepper" was the saying. The pepper referred to here is malgueta.

14. Zodary, or camphorated saffron.

15. The trees mentioned include the laurel, pine, and mulberry, as well as the pomegranate, nutmeg, almond, fig, quince, peach, medlar, olive, and date.

16. The influence of the Crusades upon the evolution of Western gardens was, however, more imaginary than botanical: when they returned, the Crusaders, such as Robert d'Artois—a companion of Saint Louis—brought with them no new varieties of fruit trees or ornamental plants, but visions of marvelous gardens.

17. "No single thing which in that dream appeared / Has failed to find fulfillment in my life" (p. 3).

18. See the quarrel with Christine de Pisan who saw misogyny in this, while Jean de Meung wrote: "To make oneself Lord of one's wife / Who should not a Lady be either / But one's equal and companion."

19. Regarding Jean de Meung's conception of nature, one should recall that, like Alain de Lille, he was opposed to the Dominicans, the "guardians of orthodoxy," and laid the foundations of a secular constitution of nature, announcing the rationalism of the Renaissance.

Allée Two

1. Alongside the *Arbolayres* that treat trees one finds the *Books of Simples*, treatises on vegetal drugs and pharmacopoeia that question the "virtues" of plants or their evils, undoubtedly in reaction to the *Antidotaries*, "confections," "electuaries," "opiats," and salves that, combining numerous ingredients, remained inaccessible to the poor. The monastic garden contained a

medicinal section because of the rule of charity creating an obligation to the needy.

2. The floods seem to have been due to a lowering of temperature that brought on a swelling of Alpine glaciers.

3. Peas and broad beans; but a harmful substance contained in the flowers and fruits of the broad bean led to outbreaks of illness.

4. Jews were accused of having poisoned wells: see, for example, Machaut's prologue to his *Jugement du Roi de Navarre*, where he returns to these accusations.

5. On the evolution of agrarian techniques, see Bertrand Gille, *Histoire des techniques* (Encyclopédie de la Pléiade), and Jean Gimpel, *La Révolution industrielle au Moyen Age* (Paris, 1975).

6. These miracles were grounded, we should add, in the new intellectual start in the area of technology and agriculture inaugurated in the eleventh century: to call it, as Gimpel does, an "industrial revolution" is certainly an exaggeration. But we do think, *a contrario*, that Le Goff's insistence on the slowness of evolution and the rudimentary character of technologies does not provide an explanation for the sudden growth of the cathedrals. (See "La vie matérielle," in *La Civilisation de l'Occident médiéval*, Paris, 1964.)

7. Abbess of Hohenburg on Mont-Sainte-Odile, who wrote a *Hortus deliciarum*.

8. In the book *De vegetatilibus*, chapter *De plantatione viridariorum*.

9. One ought to keep in mind that the twelfth century saw the beginning of urban growth with the appearance of the *bourgs* or market towns, representing an extension of the city and the religious establishments into *quartiers* at the heart of a new monetary economy whose expense caused the development of crafts and commerce. The period also saw the emergence of a "bourgeois" who was now manager and no longer laborer.

10. Charles Joret, *La Rose dans l'Antiquité et au Moyen Age* (Paris, 1892).

11. Mikhail Bakhtin, *Rabelais and His World* (Cambridge, Mass., 1968).

12. These outdoor feasts, which included a banquet and musical entertainment on a flowered meadow arranged for the occasion, could serve as a prelude to hunting; see Roblot-Delondre, "Un 'Jardin d'amour'

de Philippe le Bon," *Revue archéologique* (Paris, 1911), a study of a painting of the Flemish school exhibited at Versailles.

13. It has disappeared since. Relying on the miniatures executed in the fifteenth century under the direction of J. Mielot for the *Épître d'Othea* by Christine de Pisan, M. Charageat, in his *L'Art des jardins* (Paris, 1962), suggests that the park of Hesdin, with its rivers and *bosquets*, announced the "landscapist" genre.

14. The expression comes from Edouard André, *L'Art des jardins* (Paris, 1879).

15. *Archives des ducs de Bourgogne*, published by De Laborde, pp. 268–71.

16. E. Bourassin, *Philippe le Bon* (Paris, 1975).

17. Joret, *La Rose dans l'Antiquité et au Moyen Age*, p. 50.

18. Henri Sauval, *Histoire et recherches des Antiquités de la ville de Paris* (1724). Note that the Hesdin estate of Philip the Good came almost a century after Charles V's gardens.

19. From Saint-Foix, *Essais historiques sur Paris* (London, 1755).

20. See the monograph by Leroy de La Marche, which cites Bourdigné: "There [in Aix] they began to plant, to graft trees, to build *tonnelles*, pavilions, orchards, galleries, gardens." Special mention is made of the *roues* (wheels)—that is to say round baskets or flower beds—bordered by *clisses* made of wood.

21. Sauval wrote: "In the same Hostel Saint-Pol, in 1398, Charles VI had planted in the garden of the Champ-au-Plâtre 300 bunches of white and red rosebushes; 3 groups of *bourdelais*; 375 groups of *marêts*; 300 lily bulbs; 300 German irises; 115 pear grafts; 100 common apple trees; 12 apple trees of Paris; 1,000 cherry trees; 150 plum trees and 8 green laurels, bought on the Pont-au-Change."

22. The Gothic garden's power of creation, we must admit, does not seem to have been comparable—for lack of a botanical art equal to that of the master masons—to the creative power of architecture. Evidence of the gap between the magnificence of the cas-

tles and the relatively crude character of the gardens that accompanied them is suggested in several plates of the *Riches heures du duc de Berry*.

THE DREAM GARDENS

1. The sentence (in ancient Venetian) essentially means that he would have liked to find a pretext to throw out this embarrassing evidence of failure.

2. This aspect of Alberti's work, too often neglected, has been highlighted by Werner Sombart, *Der Bourgeois: Geistesgeschichte des modernen Wirtschaftsmenschen* (Munich and Leipzig, 1913), then by Max Weber in his classic study *The Protestant Ethic and the Rise of Capitalism*. The comparison of Alberti's treatise on the family with those by Defoe and Benjamin Franklin suggests to these scholars that the ethic of modern capitalism had already been formed in fifteenth-century Italy, but was suppressed and would only reappear during the Reformation: a thesis that might in many respects also be defended on the spiritual level.

3. *Les Jardins du Songe* (Les Belles Lettres, 1976).

4. Maria-Theresa Casella and Giovanni Pozzi, *Francesco Colonna: Biografia ed Opere* (Padua, 1959).

5. Ballad written by Andrea Marone of Brescia, a humanist friendly with Cardinal Giovanni de'Medici, son of Lorenzo and future Leo X. It appears in the introductory pieces of the Aldine edition (E. Kretzu-

lesco-Quaranta, p. 32) and can be compared to this dedication to the Duke of Urbino by Leonardo Crasso, the silent financial partner behind the *Poliphilo* and a humanist in his own right: "What you find there is not meant to be spoken on street corners; but comes from a philosophical culture, is drawn from the very sources of the Muses, expressed in a magnificent language, and deserves the gratitude of men of science."

6. Here we beg to differ with the thesis upheld by Emanuela Kretzulesco-Quaranta for the simple reason that it proves to be untenable. One cannot in fact maintain that the monk from Treviso, who was without a doubt Aldus Manutius's interlocutor, was none other than the prince of Palestrina who had taken refuge among his Dominican friends—even if traces of the latter have been lost. Maria-Theresa Casella and Giovanni Pozzi have in fact established, by means of the conventual registers and of a story by Bandello that features our monk, the existence of a Fra Francesco Colonna of Treviso, monk without vocation, a colorful and quarrelsome character, a big talker and a womanizer, who was evidently quite different from the noble figure of Prince Francesco.

Allée Three

1. This is very understandable given that this text does not in the least possess that primordial value attributed to it by a certain tradition, as it was born from a return to antiquity experienced as the necessary source of all art: in our opinion, its importance stems from the fact that it is unique of its kind rather than from any content codified by an "architect" without singular genius.

2. Examples can also be found in the *Carnets* of Villard de Honnecourt.

3. The case of the reliquary should not lead us astray for, although the object itself may be movable, the space that makes its meaning remains immutable—interior.

4. Signed by Jean Martin, the Huguenot humanist celebrated by the poets of the *Pléiade*: we are also indebted to him for his translations of Vitruvius, Serlio, and—Alberti (of which certain plates were executed by Jean Goujon). But the case of the *Hypnerotomachia* is more problematic: he himself (to arouse curiosity perhaps) attributes it to another, who might then be the polygraph-alchemist Jean Gohory.

23. Reprinted in Osip Mandelstam, *The Complete Critical Prose and Letters*, ed. Jane Gary Harris, trans. Jane Gary Harris and Constance Link (Ann Arbor, 1979), pp. 53–60.

5. The *Hypnerotomachia* being—we think, as does E. Kretzulesco-Quaranto—a major conduit for the interpretation of the Fontainebleau iconography.

6. If their exact attribution remains obscure, the Huguenot ties between Martin and Goujon seem established, if only by their likely collaboration on the publishing of Alberti's *De re aedificatoria*.

7. Traces of which have just been discovered.

8. "Before the king entered the city, he spent one night at Poge royal (Poggioreale), which is a country house that the king Ferdinand and his predecessors had built, which is such that the lovely speech of master Alain Chartier, the subtlety of master Jean de Meung, and the hand of Fouquet could not speak, write, or paint it. It sits rather far from the city, as far as Tours is from Plesseix, and from the door of the city to it, one goes by big paths and alleys on all sides. It is surrounded by orange trees and rosemaries and by all other fruit trees in winter as in summer in such great quantity that it cannot be estimated. The said garden is closed with walls in a square, and is so beautiful that I could not write it in a man's life. Around this house are the beautiful fountains, the aviaries full of birds of all kinds and so strange one cannot imagine. On the other side there is a beautiful park with large animals in abundance, the warren for rabbits and hares, the other warren for pheasants and partridges, and it seems that all has been made by human desire. For neither according to my wish nor to that of living man could anything more happen to

human nature. I think that all the happiness of the preceding kings was there." In *Carnets et bulletins de la grande armée d'Italie* (Paris and Nantes, 1986).

9. In *Recepte veritable* (1563).

10. The book of the *Voyages de Jean de Mandeville* has had a curious fate. Written in French at the end of the fifteenth century by a Norman gentleman who had been forced to take refuge on the continent, its German translation was the object of continual new editions until the eighteenth century, while its English translation has become a classic—in fact Joyce in *Ulysses* made a pastiche out of it, as a key moment of early English literature—while its original French version has been almost completely forgotten.

11. With this added feature: the labyrinth was a major theme of Gothic esotericism.

12. See, for example, the *préaux*, which permitted the invention of artificial meadows.

13. On this point see Keith Thomas, *Dans le jardin de la nature* (Paris, 1985).

14. It goes without saying that this is a formula. Partial, in both senses of the word, as they all are. For this "plastic ambition" was also the continuation of Gothic flamboyance, as of the influence of the masters from Flanders, "so numerous in Paris at the end of the sixteenth century"—an influence that has been rightfully emphasized by V.-L. Tapié, *Baroque et Classicisme* (Paris, 1972).

Allée Four

1. As a Florentine humanist, Alberti also aimed, explicitly, at the reasonable realization of this agreement: his esthetic *Treatises*, beginning with *De re aedificatoria*, had their moral, social, and economic continuo in the *De familia*.

2. The Flemish school, in particular.

3. There was a time when critics so underestimated them that they were almost ignored. This neglect was facilitated by the fact that the gardens of that period have all been, if not destroyed, at least completely remodeled following later conceptions. However,

more recent studies (Sten Karling, Hazelhurst, Michel Conan) have helped bring them to our attention once again.

4. The expression comes from Montaigne, who uses it in a positive fashion.

5. As defined by Michel Foucault in *The Order of Things*: homotopia can be read as a homogeneous vision of space subordinated to a geometric grid identical in all points, that is to say controllable; whereas "heterotopia," more sensitive to "places," would proceed by *discriminatio* and *convenentia*, that is to say by

working on elements one by one, then placing them in an appropriate relationship to their boundaries.

6. Especially in his great work (admirable in many respects), *Art and Architecture in France, 1500–1700,* where the master words are "advance" and "delay" in relation to the only two models that truly interest him: the classical Florentine Renaissance, which was its implicit predecessor, and the French classicism of the age of Louis XIV, which is the object of a genealogy.

7. *L'Architecture à la française* (Paris, 1982).

8. The adjective is necessary, for it goes without saying that only a ridiculous gallocentrism could deny the essential influence of the Italian lesson.

9. The line (*"le trait"*) is the group of geometrical procedures enabling one to evaluate in advance the cut of the stone according to its position in the projected edifice (stereotomy).

10. The Italian art critic Federico Zeri has in effect suggested distinguishing the Renaissance proper, the principle of which was rationality and the center Florence, from the *pseudo*-Renaissance, or obscure Renaissance still linked to the Middle Ages, whose main center in Italy was undoubtedly Siena (*Renaissance et pseudo-Renaissance*, French translation, 1985).

11. Weren't a number of their collections called *Mélanges* (*Miscellanies*) or *Fricassées*?

12. In the description of his "delectable garden," however, Palissy recommends the presence of a hill; not in order for one to be at the top like Alberti, but in order to be at the bottom, where one could obtain fresh running water.

13. *Les Cinq Sens* (Paris, 1985).

14. The *Poliphilo*'s success in French was largely due to the fact that it could be read as a continuation of the *Romance of the Rose.*

15. In fact, most of them were far from being unpublished, since the researchers (E. Droz and A. Piaget) who, in 1925, assured their reprinting, sometimes

attributed most of the pieces to "old masters" who had long been dead.

16. "Ces larges rains, ce sadinet / Assis sur grosses fermes cuisses / Dedens son petit jardinet?" ["Those broad loins, that mons veneris / Sitting on fat firm thighs / Inside her little garden?"]

17. In Greek, φυσις = nature-rocket.

18. Especially since the baroque itself, including the plastic arts, remains an essentially fleeting category; see Claude-Gilbert Dubois, *Le Baroque: profondeurs de l'apparence* (Paris, 1973): "The fundamental nature of the baroque is to diversify itself, to metamorphose like Proteus, to be elusive like the flames and water that poets love so much."

19. *Histoire du costume en Occident de l'Antiquité à nos jours* (Paris, 1965). The *canons*, adorned with lace and ribbons, were worn above the knee. The *rhingraves* were a type of breeches. This ornamental profusion was so provocative that—without any success, moreover—"sumptuary edicts" aiming to regulate it would be issued in 1633.

20. The labyrinth, however, was partly eclipsed in this period due to the fact, according to Claude Mollet, that many gardeners no longer knew how to plant them correctly or how to design them with correct proportions. Which suggests that, contrary to a certain simplistic vision that tries to see in the Renaissance and the classical period an increasing mastery of forms and techniques, "progress" is not univocal.

21. In spite of the remarkable work by Franklin Hamilton Hazelhurst, *Jacques Boyceau and the French Formal Garden* (Nashville, 1966).

22. Thus we learn through Peyresc's *Correspondance,* in a letter addressed to Rubens in 1622, that Boyceau was part of a group of experts appointed by Marie de Medici to appraise the series of cartoons by the Flemish master, *The Life of Constantine,* and that Boyceau supported them so ardently that he convinced everyone of their worth. The same source informs us that Boyceau was the Parisian mentor of one of Rubens's

best students, Abraham de Vries, who did a portrait of his protector, which has unfortunately been lost.

23. Jacques de Nemours would be the editor of Boyceau's *Treatise* but would die prematurely.

24. Let us add, however, that certain specialists remain cautious in their opinion of Boyceau's career. Thus Michel Conan, in his postscript to a later edition of André Mollet's *Jardin de Plaisir*, saw in him a gentleman-intendant who was more of a theoretician than a designer: a character resembling the philosopher-musicologist Marin Mersenne who, in spirit of his treatise, *L'Harmonie universelle*, was never a composer himself (Mersenne, incidentally, was also a friend of Peyresc's).

25. Hamilton Hazelhurst's valuable study is not ambitious enough here, in our opinion. Lacking a sufficiently broad vision of the general history of intellectual circles, it remains limited to the garden and does not attempt to make the connections that we believe important.

26. On the theory of mimesis and its evolution in Western art, see the useful work by Bernard Lamblin, *Art et Nature* (Vrin, 1979).

27. Entitled *De la composition et ordonnance des jardins, et des choses qui servent à leur embellissement* (the first book, a general one, has no title, and the second concerns trees).

28. For those who may be surprised by these references, let us mention that the Peyresc and Du Puy circles, frequented by Boyceau, were at the center of the philosophical controversy of the period. This con-

troversy opposed, both to Aristotelian scholasticism and to Campanella's "enchanted naturalism," the "philosophical mechanisms" ("phenomenological" for Gassendi, "metaphysical" for Descartes, "physical" for Hobbes—Mersenne being at the center of these polarities). See in particular Robert Lenoble, *Mersenne et la naissance du mécanisme* (Vrin, 1943) and G. Mongredien's paper, "L'influence sur le milieu contemporain," *Pierre Gassendi* (Paris, 1955).

29. Let us make the following clear: we are not assimilating *clôture* and *fermeture*, in love as we are with medieval architecture, which strikes us as being in many ways more "open" than certain contemporary architecture that uses the supposedly immaterial wall screen. As we perceive it, transparence is in no way synonymous with porousness.

30. It goes without saying that the parallel between Boyceau and Malherbe should not be taken too far. Not only because Malherbe always insists on closure (*clôture*), but more importantly because the baroque/classical caesura will always remain ambiguous in the art of gardens, including in Le Nôtre's work (see below).

31. The presence of these terms suffices to show the influence, alongside the Italian, of the Andalusian gardens. And the fashion, in the first half of the French seventeenth century, was "furiously" Spanish.

32. We borrow this long quotation from the afterword that Michel Conan wrote for the new edition of *Jardin de plaisir*. Let us compliment this scholar whose erudition is equaled only by his passion to share it with others.

Allée Five

1. An "admirable formula" quoted in a letter by Maldiney, according to Ponge in *Pour un Malherbe* (Paris, 1977).

2. In 1667, Colbert and Louis XIV, scrapping the project they had ordered from Bernini for the eastern façade of the Louvre, chose Perrault's colonnade: a gesture that has traditionally been interpreted as the

end of a period of hesitation and the advent of French classicism.

3. Jean-François Maillard, *Essai sur l'esprit du héros baroque: le même et l'autre* (Nizet, 1973).

4. The fountain builder Claude Robillard, the mason Villedo, the master gardeners Trumel and La Quintinie, among others.

5. Fouquet visited the site so often that he developed a fever there, according to the guest-witnesses at the feast of Vaux.

6. F. H. Hazelhurst, *Gardens of Illusion: The Genius of André Le Nostre* (Nashville, 1980). The best French study on Le Nôtre is still the one by Ernest de Ganay.

7. *Versailles: lecture d'un jardin*, research report by M. Corajoud, J. Coulon, and M.-H. Loze (1982). Besides demonstrating the use of the "golden section," the consideration of certain "irregularities" makes it clear that Le Nôtre took advantage of accidents and previous layouts (Boyceau?), and did not start from a tabula rasa, as interpretations in strictly classical terms pretend.

8. Let us remark that Le Nôtre had, regarding his colleague (whom it seems he had presented to the king) a qualified opinion: see his remark, reported by Saint-Simon, about the *bosquet* of the colonnade of Versailles that Mansart executed in his absence (his visit to Italy in 1679 with Bernini): "You have made a gardener out of a mason; he has given you an example of his trade."

9. Gaston Bardet, *Naissance et méconnaissance de l'urbanisme* (Paris, 1951).

10. Which may be roughly translated as *Rough Project for an Attack upon the Events of Encounters of the Cone with a Plane* and *Lessons of Darkness*. The work seems to have treated—the manuscript has never been uncovered—the method for the drawing of shadows. Its astonishing title is borrowed from one of the major genres of baroque religious music through which Sernisy, Marc Antoine Charpentier, Couperin, etc., became famous.

11. The same can be said for Le Vau, to whom we owe the main baroque building of Paris (the Institute) and the Oval Salon of Vaux.

12. It is worth remembering here Georges Perros's marvelous aphorism in *Papiers collés*: "In the age of Mozart, everyone wrote music like Mozart, except Mozart."

13. Maldiney's "admirable formula," quoted above—"Classicism is only the tautest string of the baroque"—seems to us written for Le Nôtre.

14. A. J. Dézallier d'Argenville is not to be confused with his son who published—among other things—a *Dictionary of Gardening*.

15. Le Blond created the gardens of Peterhof, designed for Catherine of Russia: with André Le Nôtre's cousin, Claude Desgots, whose (reconstituted) work can be admired at the castle of Champ-sur-Marne, he was the best continuator of the French classical tradition that would dominate the taste of the European, including English, aristocracy until the middle of the eighteenth century.

16. Cited in the margin: M. Cato, M. T. Varro, Pliny, Columella, Palladius.

17. Cited in the margin: Boyceau and Mollet. Note that Boyceau's *Treatise* continued to be studied, since it appeared in two successive editions during the first fifteen years of the eighteenth century.

18. "The others who have written of agriculture apparently found the subject not very worthy of their pens," he continues. "Some speak of the size of the fruit trees, of the cultivation of vegetable gardens, of the botanical garden and the property of simples; the others of the management of fields, the duty of a good father, laborer, and farmer, of the vine and harvests, of fishing, of hunting, and the manner of cooking and making all kinds of jams." (He cites, in this order, La Quintinie, François the Gardener, L. Ligier, the Solitary Gardener, the Botanist Gardener, J. B. de Tournefort, the Florist Gardener, Liebaut, and de Serres.)

19. His scholarship would be demonstrated by later treatises of natural history (*Conchyliologie, Zoomorphose, Lithologie*).

20. La Quintinie (1626–1688), gardener of the royal vegetable and fruit gardens, had published two large volumes dedicted to his art under the title *Instructions pour les jardins* (1690).

21. "In the past, the allées, contre-allées, and palissades were given a thousand extravagant forms, which
are still much in use in the gardens of Italy (Frascati,
Tivoli) and of Spain (Aranjuez, Buen Retiro); men on
horseback, boars, deer, dogs, making an entire hunt in
short, were formed there. Others carved pyramids,
obelisks, and balls, with volutes that continued to the
end of the palissades. . . . This fashion still persists in
Holland (Loo, Honflardick, Soesdick) and in Flanders, where these bizarre designs are more sought
after than in any other country. . . . The English (St.
James, Hampton Court) and the Swedish (Yacobdal,
Droiholm) follow our manners more in their gardens:
we have sent them some of our designs, which they
have executed fairly well; and in addition, they have
brought over architects and French gardeners who
have left some of their productions. . . . These trinkets
are no longer in fashion in France. A noble and grand
simplicity is preferred."

22. From 1713 to 1716. In 1728 he also took a trip
to England where, we are told by the author of his
éloge ("praise") published as the introduction to the
1780 edition of his *Conchyliologie*: "It seems clear that
he did not fail to visit the wonderful houses that decorate the area around London. The lords, who stay
there for long periods, adorn them with a magnificence that makes them in certain respects hardly infe-
rior to the country homes of the monarchs."

23. "Makes Nature yield to the miracles of Art." The
poem is quoted in Allée Four, above.

24. An astonishing detail: Boyceau was already making variety an integral part of his program. Moreover,
he had something to do with the drawing of the Tuileries. And it would also be in the name of "variety"
that the "Anglo-Chinese" party would end up by pre-
vailing over a symmetrization that was considered
boring.

25. It should be said that these bourgeois-philosophers were often of aristocratic origin.

26. Jean Ehrard, *L'Idée de nature en France à l'aube des
lumières* (Paris, 1965); G.-L. McCann, *Le Sentiment de
la nature en France dans la 1ère moitié du XVIIᵉ siècle*
(Paris, 1926); B. Tocanne, *L'Idée de nature en France

dans la 2ᵉ moitié du XVIIᵉ siècle* (Paris, 1978); Daniel
Mornet, *Le Sentiment de la nature en France de J.-J.
Rousseau à Bernardin de Saint-Pierre* (Paris, 1907);
Roland Mortier, *La Poètique des ruines en France*
(Droz, 1974); Georges Gusdorf, *Naissance de la con-
science romantique au siècle des lumières* (Paris, 1976);
Keith Thomas, *Dans le jardin de la nature* (Paris,
1985).

27. The anecdote is related by Lesage in *Le Diable boiteux* (the devil speaks to Don Cléofas of the people
that would have to be handed over to the prison for
the insane): "I also want to send an old boy from a
good family, who no sooner gets a ducat than he
spends it, and who, unable to go without coins, is
capable of everything to have some. Fifteen years ago
his laundress, to whom he owed 30 pistoles, came to
claim them, saying that she needed them in order to
marry a valet who was seeking her hand. You therefore have other money, he said to her; for where the
devil is the valet who will want to become your husband for 30 pistoles? Oh! but, she answered, I also
have, in addition to that, 200 ducats. 200 ducats, he
replied with emotion! a plague on you! You only have
to give them to me, I'll marry you, and we'll be quits.
He was taken at his word, and his laundress became
his wife."

28. One can see in him a forerunner of romanticism,
like the preface writer of his *Oeuvres choisies* in 1830,
or even of surrealism.

29. In the preface to his *Amusements sérieux et
comiques*.

30. "Not knowing how to handle either a brush or a
pencil, he made up for it by taking from different
engravings parts of still lifes and landscapes, which he
cut up and then disposed and fixed next to each other,
so as to compose a subject with a design traced only
in his imagination."

31. Édouard André, however, in his *Art des jardins*
(1879), states that "the park of Mignaux (Poissy) still
shows visitors today the traces of its author's hand."

NOTES

32. Marin Marais's *Suite d'un goût étranger* develops a sequence of gardening motifs: *Les Fêtes champêtres*, the *Tourbillon*, the *Labyrinthe*, the *Arabesque*.

33. See the work of Philippe Beaussant.

34. Lesage's *Le Diable boiteux* and *Gil Blas* were absolute "best-sellers."

35. An important role was also played by a few others whom we have already mentioned. We should add to the list: Carmontelle, Bergeret, and Pierre-Adrien Pâris.

36. See Sigmund Freud about the *wait*.

37. In his *Essai sur les jardins* of 1774.

38. The actual Parc Monceau designed by Carmontelle and Blaykie, then remodeled by Alphand and Barillet-Deschamps.

39. Although he had known Girardin for many years, Robert does not seem to have participated in the *creation* of Ermenonville, but seems to have limited himself to painting a few landscapes.

40. Unless at Retz. This famous "Desert," which also was almost destroyed—but where Olivier Chopin de Genvry is today rebuilding the *fabriques*—was the work of de Monville, grand lord and high dignitary of the Masonic lodge like the duc de Chartres, the promoter of the Parc Monceau. It is probable that Retz functioned as a route of initiation.

41. *Dans le jardin de la nature* (Paris, 1985), a work that sins by erudition, even though therein lies its

value and charm: those garlands of citations that can prove everything, and the contrary.

42. Which would have been paradoxical in an era that tried, on the contrary, with Kant, to make a careful distinction between one and the other (see *The Critique of Judgment*, §43).

43. See, in a number of other texts of similar spirit, this passage from the *Lettres cabalistiques* of the Marquis d'Argens (quoted by Ehrard): "Nature is the stumbling block of geometricians; as long as they are getting lost in their imaginations, they think they know the most beautiful things; but as soon as they try to apply to real qualities their imaginary points and surfaces, all the reality of their Art vanishes. The famous Gassendi recognized most rightly that mathematicians and especially geometricians have established their empire in the land of abstractions and ideas, and that they stroll there completely at ease, but that if they wish to pretend to go down into the land of realities, they will soon find insurmountable resistance."

44. "Ville, campagne, jardin," chapter 6 of *Naissance de la conscience romantique des lumières* (Paris, 1976).

45. "Jardins contre nature," *Traverses* (October 1976). The pertinence and beauty of this article cannot be sufficiently applauded.

46. The expression comes from Louis Corpechot, *Les Jardins de l'intelligence* (Paris, 1912).

Allée Six

1. The marquis had served the king as a captain during his exile in Lorraine.

2. In his remarkable treatise, *Théorie des jardins ou l'Art des jardins de la nature* (first edition 1776, and second, with an important additional preface, 1802), the architect and landscapist Jean-Marie Morel, who was undoubtedly one of the more important and prolific minds of his time (and also one of the first to acknowledge his debt to Dufresny) claims to have designed the main part of Ermenonville. The allegation would be contradicted by the marquis de Girardin who, without denying tha Morel had been

consulted, maintained that Ermenonville was his personal work—a thesis that seems to have been corroborated by many of the marquis's drawings.

3. Ermenonville was developed over a period of twenty years and has been described in detail, several times (see the one-volume reprint of Girardin's treatise, *De la composition des paysages*, followed by *Promenade ou Itinéraire des Jardins d'Ermenonville*, with a substantial "postface" by Michel Conan, Paris, 1979). Moreover, unlike Méréville or Retz, for example, one of its major components—the park proper, with the Island of Poplars containing the (empty) Tomb of

Rousseau, Arcadia, the grotto with cascade, and several *fabriques* including the most famous Temple of Philosophy—are accessible today and in a satisfactory state of preservation, which is not the case of the Prairie or the Desert.

4. Fragonard and Hubert Robert were old friends of René-Louis de Girardin: it was in their company, in fact, that he had once visited Italy.

5. Let us note, however, that although he was fair with his people, the marquis was not any less strict: in the village he was nicknamed *Père la tapette* under pretext that, when the time came to encourage his gardeners to work harder, he did not hesitate to use a switch (a taste for corporal punishments inherited from his anglomania?).

6. Manuscript in the Bibliothèque de l'Arsenal, quoted by André-Martin Decaen in *Le Marquis de Girardin, dernier ami de Jean-Jacques Rousseau* (Paris, 1912).

7. *Paradise Lost* (1670) was translated into French six times during the eighteenth century (by the abbé Delille, in particular). But it was at the beginning of the nineteenth century, as Robert Mallet has remarked, that its influence became truly important. See Mallet, *Jardins et Paradis* (Paris, 1959).

8. Augustin Thierry's *Considérations sur l'histoire de France* gives us a few clues about this triple confrontation, situating the debate of the years 1820 and 1830 on the "primal scene" of the French nation: is it principally Gallic, Roman, or Frankish?—a debate that goes back to the legitimacy of this or that current in incarnating the principle of the French nation.

9. The individual who is, according to Gusdorf, the main invention of romantic humanism.

10. The myth should be understood here in its two meanings (more complementary than contradictory): as an affabulation meant to delude in order to gain adherents; and as the fundamental postulate and motor of the democratic hypothesis.

11. "In France-Comté, the more walls one builds, the more one's property bristles with stones stacked on top of each other, the more rights one acquires com-

pared with one's neighbors. Monsieur de Rênal's gardens, full of walls . . . " And further on: "Luckily for Monsieur de Rênal's reputation as administrator, an immense *supporting wall* was necessary for the public promenade . . . "

12. The opening of the Tuileries was apparently only secured *in extremis*, at least according to Charles Perrault: "'Let's go, Colbert said to me, to the Thuilleries, to condemn its doors; this garden must be kept for the King and not eroded by the people who, in less than no time, will ruin it entirely.' The resolution struck me as rather harsh and unfortunate for all of Paris. When he was in the great allée, I said to him: 'You would not believe, sir, the respect that everyone, down to the lowest bourgeois, has for this garden. . . . It will be a public affliction not to be able to come here anymore to walk about, especially since at present one can no longer go into the Luxembourg or the garden of the Hôtel de Guise.' 'Only idlers come here,' he answered. 'The people who come,' I answered him, 'are sick, and in search of air; they come to talk about business, marriages, and all kinds of things that are more appropriately discussed in a garden than in a church where, in the future, rendezvous will have to be held. . . .' Colbert made a tour of the garden, gave orders, and spoke no more about closing its entrance. I got much joy, in this way, from preventing this promenade from being taken away from the public."

13. An inventory of which can be found, at least as pertains to Paris of the seventeenth century, in the work by Marcel Poète, *La Promenade à Paris* (Paris, 1913).

14. See Walter Benjamin, "Paris, Capital of the Nineteenth Century," in *Reflections* (New York, 1978) and, of course, "Passagenwerk."

15. The fact that this appreciation was made by an English traveler gives it all the more weight; for it is known that, when it comes to parks and gardens, London has always been endowed the way no other European capital has.

16. Tivoli—the old Folie-Boutin (named after its old owner), located on the present site of the Saint-Lazare

station—was the prototype, at the time, of the amusement park. It was, moreover, directed by one of the members of the Ruggieri pyrotechnist dynasty.

17. Quoted by Guy Barthélemy, *Les Jardiniers du Roy* (Paris, 1979). The idea of transferring the rest of the menagerie from Versailles to the Jardin des Plantes had been formulated as early as 1790 by Bernardin de Saint-Pierre, who was at the time the administrator of the now national Jardin du Roi. But it was the wild lyricism of Lakanal's intervention before the Convention, on June 10, 1793, that obtained from the people's representatives a vote in favor of a law promulgating the creation of a museum of natural history in a form that has changed little since that time.

18. The zoo of Loo would, moreover, be pillaged— "requisitioned" for the Republic—by Andreé Thouin, the chief gardener of the Museum who had become commissioner to the armies in the north at the time of the offensive at Pichegru in Holland.

19. One can find a juicy survey in the already quoted work of Guy Barthélemy, the subtitle of which is *Petite Histoire du Jardin des Plantes de Paris*.

20. See this passage from *Discipline and Punish*: "The first of the great disciplinary operations is therefore the constitution of 'living tableaux.' . . . The constitution of 'tableaux' was one of the big problems of the scientific, political, and economic technology of the eighteenth century: to establish gardens of plants."

21. The subsequent editions of his *Conchyliologie* were thus presented as a "Natural history of shells from the sea, from fresh water, and terrestrial and fossil shells. With a treatise on zoomorphism, or the representation of animals that inhabit them: a work in which one finds a new method of dividing them (with plates in line-engraving representing more than 2,000 testaceans drawn from life, accompanied by extended descriptions and remarks on each family, with several systematic tables and foreign nomenclatures)."

22. Monsieur de Latte, life member of the Société Royale des Sciences of Montpellier, in an *Éloge de M.*

d'Argenville, dated May 5, 1768, which appears as the preface to the 1780 edition of *Conchyliologie*.

23. Starting in the early 1740s, d'Argenville was a member of several royal scientific societies and, shortly before his death (1758), the Académie de La Rochelle chose him to succeed Réaumur.

24. Flaubert made no mistake here. All of his "modern" work (in contrast with *Salammbô* or *La Tentation*), which was conceived as an "assessment of the nineteenth century," was an attempt to bring this latent truth into daylight. Does it not begin with *Une leçon d'histoire naturelle: genre commis* (1837), parodying the popularizing articles in the press, in order to end with the description of the desperate and ridiculous enterprise undertaken by Bouvard and Pécuchet, meant to give life to the didactic verbosity overwhelming them?

25. Member of several Academies, including the Académie des Beaux-Arts, he was curator of the Louvre and would be named general director of the Empire's archives in 1857.

26. These examples have been remembered by Michel Vernes in a remarkable article, "Paysages de la mémoire: sur la mise en scène de l'histoire dans les jardins paysagers," *Traverses* (January 1986).

27. The school of Barillet-Deschamps, which will be discussed further on. Barillet himself created the gardens of 1867; Laforcade those of 1878 (the Trocadéro); Deny would participate in the development of the garden of 1889 (the Champ-de-Mars); Vacherot in their renovation for 1900.

28. The Parc Monceau (which was recast) and the totally new parks of Montsouris and the Buttes-Chaumont.

29. Théophile Gautier.

30. An explicit trace of this democratic spirit can be found in the book by Jules Vacherot, who claims to have been inspired by Barillet-Deschamps, and who was the chief gardener of the world's fair of 1900. See *Les Parcs et jardins au commencement du XXᵉ siècle*

(Paris, 1908): "For a few years now," he explains about the landscape garden invented by his master, "this genre has been taking such a development in France that one could call it the democratic style."

31. The expression is Gaston Bardet's: we know that one of Haussmann's major aims was to make barricades impossible by widening the line of fire.

32. A century later, Pompidou would describe the automobile as the measure of the new urban modernity.

33. Haussmann's *Mémoires*, vol. 3, p. 173.

34. *Les Promenades de Paris*, original edition Paris, 1867–73, reprint, Princeton, 1984.

Allée Seven

1. The proponents of this thesis included Jules Vacherot, *Les Parcs et jardins au commencement du XXe siècle* (1908): "Barillet-Deschamps was a renovator of the landscape genre called the English garden, which had, under his impulse, grandiose applications. He is one of the rare artists who, after Le Nôtre, by designing and planting gardens, won a reputation approaching that man's undying fame, and who has been transmitted to us only by still existing creations, by the opinion of his contemporaries, and by his students, as Barillet-Deschamps left no written work that might, in these times of ours that are so quick to forget, remind future landscape architects of him."

2. Thesis upheld, on the contrary, by an old collaborator of Barillet's, Édouard André in *L'Art des jardins* (1879), in which he affirms that this "new genre" had "since then been attributed to a single artist" (and in a note: "Barillet-Deschamps who perfected it, but did not invent it").

3. That issue contains the exact text—which we have only sketched out—of the speeches made by Vilmorin, Ermens, and Lepère.

4. Deny saw in Barillet a "man of altogether superior talent, as well as a refined researcher." In *Jardins et parcs publics* (1893).

5. The structure we describe is thus a kind of "average" of these three *Treatises*.

6. "Gardens, in the Middle Ages, hardly deserved to be considered artistic creations" (Alphand).

7. "Looking at the plans of Fontainebleau that Androuet du Cerceau left us, one recognized that the little tormented parterres, the symmetrical and narrow allées, the borders of thick boxwood, the many pretty statues, basins, and aviaries, and abundant water were the main attractions. The whole cut into petty divisions, but kept up with care" (André).

8. Which was understandable, of course, at the time these works were written.

9. "He [the gardener] sought, not to obtain an original creation, but to reproduce an established type; he dreamed of a conventional nature, lined up, leveled, corrected, transformed, pruned, deformed; he was in a way challenging nature, and trying to reduce it with scissors. These procedures, in spite of so much effort, only gave rather poor results; and there is no reason to be surprised. One does not rise up with impunity against the truth that rules nature and also, although still too rarely, human intelligence" (Alphand).

10. André calls Claude Mollet's *Treatise* "a little naive," and Alphand calls embroidered parterres "puerile."

11. Regarding Le Nôtre's gardens: "However, a few parts have kept the petty aspect of previous compositions. The parterres often have dry forms and complications in the layout that are completely useless. The planting of these parterres, with shrubs or flowers, does not have all the richness intended. The borders are spindly; the allées, too multiplied, are not justified. . . . The trees of the allées are subjected to a pruning system of disputable grace" (Alphand).

12. "At the time when William Kent began his first works, that is to say after his return from Italy, more than forty years had passed since a Frenchman had tried his hand at this genre or drawn up plans for

Louis XIV, which were not executed for lack of money. The honor of this creation thus fell to Dufresny, and not to William Kent" (Deny).

13. Creators of the Tête d'Or park in Lyons.

14. "Paris est pour un *riche* un pays de cocagne
Sans sortir de la ville il trouve la campagne
Il peut, dans son jardin tout peuplé d'arbres verds,
Recéler le printemps au milieu des hyvers
Et, foulant le parfum de ses plantes fleuries
Aller entretenir ses douces rêveries."
["Paris is for a rich man a land of plenty
Without leaving the city he finds the country
He can, in his garden all filled with green trees,
Harbor spring in the middle of winters
And, pressing the perfume of his flowering plants,
Go entertain his sweet dreams."] (Our emphasis)

15. "It was in the month of May or June. Châtenay was dazzling with roses. The Vallée-aux-Loups, darkened by its leafy forest and resonating with its nightingales, resembled the avenue of a mystery" (Lamartine, *Souvenirs*).

16. Georges Gusdorf, *Fondements du savoir romantique* (Paris, 1982).

17. Friedrich Schlegel, *Philosophie de la vie* (1828). Cited by G. Gusdorf, *Fondements du savoir romantique*. This statement should be compared with Roland Barthes's "What is the most painted object, during the entire course of human history? Without a doubt, the tree" (*Le Texte et l'image*, 1986).

18. The text dates from October 4, 1811.

19. This is true at least for its most widespread variety, the *Magnolia grandiflora*, which could thus remind Chateaubriand of his stay in America (whence the allusion to his "Floridian").

20. Anecdote reported by Marie-Blanche d'Arneville, *Parcs et jardins sous le Premier Empire* (Paris, 1981).

21. "The symbolic idiom of flowers died with the Middle Ages" (Huysmans, 1903 preface to *A rebours*).

22. P.-J. Redouté, *Le Jardin de la Malmaison et les plantes rares cultivées à la Malmaison et à Navarre*.

23. One should not conclude from this enumeration that Paris had in this way caught up with London or Amsterdam. See, for example, this remark Bonpland made upon visiting London a few months after Josephine's death: "The nurseries of Hammersmith are the most beautiful, the gardens of Kew seem the richest of Europe, in two hours' time I found more than 30 plants that are not at Malmaison."

24. *Pardès* was the Persian word for garden, as well as the origin of the word paradise.

25. This best-seller by Alphonse Karr has been forgotten today but deeply moved the youth of the 1830s and 1850s. *Sous les tilleuls* seems to present all the ingredients of German romanticism: the inevitable meeting of the hero—Stephén—with his beloved—Magdeleine—in Mr. Müller's superb garden; the exalted kiss in the shade of the trees, the vows sealed by the *Vergiss-mein-nicht* (forget-me-nots); all combined with a course on hyacinths and the different varieties of linden trees. But the whole is ruined by an excess of posing that seems fabricated, as though, upon crossing the Rhine, the quest for the absolute had turned into a melodrama or a stiff vaudeville.

26. The *Trembles* are on the Atlantic coast, whereas Verrières is in Franche-Comté, Clochegourde in Touraine, and Paradou in Provence; moreover, *Dominique* was written in the 1860s, that is to say at the time of the action of *La Faute de l'abbé Mouret*. But its universe, which evokes Fromentin's youth (the 1840s), is much closer to Stendhal and Balzac than to Zola.

27. Zola left, in addition to a mass of charged descriptions, a plan of the Paradou including a classical garden adjoining the burned castle (basin, fountain, parterres, straight and perpendicular allées, grotto, statues), an orchard, a small wood, meadows, a thick forest, a desert of rocks and springs given over to brushwood.

28. *Lettres à Madame Hanska*.

29. "One saw some of them [English ladies with blond curls] lounging in the carriages, gliding by in the middle of the parks, where a greyhound leaped before the team that two small postilions in white

trousers were driving. . . . And you were there too, sultans with long pipes, swooning beneath the arbor, arm in arm with the *bayadères, djiaours*, Turkish sabers, Greek bonnets, and you especially, pallid landscapes of dithyrambic lands, which often show us, all at once, palm trees, firs, tigers on the right, a lion on the left, Tartar minarets on the horizon, Roman ruins in the foreground, then kneeling camels—the whole framed by a well-scrubbed virgin forest, and with a big, perpendicular ray of sunshine trembling in the water, where, in the distance, swimming swans stand out in white flecks against a background of gray steel."

30. Huysmans, in *A rebours*.

31. This sin that the two medieval lovers of the *Roman de la poire* would commit in the orchard after having communicated through its fence for a long time.

32. Cited among others for the single reason—an important one!—that they were set to music by Gabriel Fauré.

33. "Nocturne jardin tout empli de silence
Voici que la lune ouverte se balance
En des voiles d'or fluides et légers . . ."
["Nocturnal garden all filled with silence
Here is the open moon balanced
In fluid and light veils of gold . . ."]
(Renée de Brimont)

34. "C'est le premier matin du monde.
Comme une fleur confuse exhalée de la nuit,
Au souffle nouveau qui se lève des ondes,
Le jardin bleu s'épanouit."
["It is the first morning of the world.
Like a confused flower exhaled by the night,
The blue garden blossoms
To the new breath rising from the waters."]
(Charles van Lerberghe, "La Chanson d'Ève")

35. The third part, one should note, is entitled "Le Jardin de Bérénice."

36. A work that Proust translated with the help of his mother.

37. See Françoise Choay, *L'Urbanisme, utopie et réalités* (Paris, 1965): "Without participating in any way in the culturalist spirit and communitarian vision that characterized the city of Ebenezer Howard, the garden city of Benoît-Lévy is a kind of green and hygienic city for breeding, aimed at obtaining from the workers who live there the best possible yield."

38. "Like at Sunrise, it was decided to create an isolating belt of fields; a site would be reserved for the factories, sheltered by the mountain and on the shores of a little stream of water that would put them in contact with the port; then there would be residences layered in tiers down to the sea, where public buildings would be built and municipal buildings placed on a boulevard running along the coast."

39. They would gather 25,000 housing units organized on 19 sites that were not completely autonomous urban developments, like the city of Hampstead built by Unwin at Letchworth in 1919. Eight of them—the best preserved—were presented in an exhibit in Paris in late 1984. But the best thing to do is to visit them at Champigny, Châtenay-Malabry, Drancy, Gennevilliers, Le Plessis-Robinson, Le Pré-Saint-Gervais, Stains, or Suresnes.

40. Which, under the joint influence of the Anglo-Saxon bishops (Gibbons, Manning) and Leo XIII's encyclical *Rerum novarum*, had just been won over to the Republic.

41. From the 1906 edition. The subsequent editions (1912, 1921, 1922) would be entitled *Le Jardin moderne de l'instituteur*, etc.

42. "The worker, the amateur in effect, whose house is devoid of a garden, generally can, in return for relatively low annual dues, rent on a long-term basis, or buy, the 3, 6, or 10 ares of land he will need from horticultural societies, towns, and philanthropic associations."

43. After becoming the head of the Ministry of Agriculture (where he created the *Mérite agricole* before imagining a protectionist policy), then seeing his government fall (it had opposed the retrial of the Dreyfus

case), Méline used his temporary retirement to write *Le Retour à la terre*, then *Le Salut par la terre*.

44. "134 households out of 1,266 only have, once the rent has been paid, 400 francs a year. Some live on 0.20 francs a day, while a kilo of bread costs 0.25 francs, a kilo of meat 1.50 francs, and a kilo of sugar 0.75 francs. None of the households studied has 1 franc a day per head." (Dusmesnil and Mangenot in an inquiry concerning the XIIth arrondissement, 1898.)

45. See B.-H. Lévy, *L'Idéologie française*. For example: it was understood that the "magnification" he proposed was interesting insofar as it designated a blind point, repressed in the unconscious of French antifascism.

46. Except through snobbism, which also affected the salons, and even Jewish bankers (see below). Thus it is rather touching to see Marcel Proust succumb to Thoreau's sirens: Swann at Walden Pond, that would have been truly chic!

47. "Subjectively envisaged, Plants acquire a noble destination as the definitive foundation of Humanity's elementary existence. As such, they become the necessary ministers of the Great-Being who respects in them the principal agents of his material providence," etc. (with as many capital letters). From A. Comte, *Système de politique positive*. One can understand why one of his main disciples, Émile Corra, congratulated himself, around 1934, that "Hitler's Germany had instituted an annual harvest holiday" (*La Fête des Végétaux*, posthumous work, Paris, 1935).

48. See the study on this subject by Jean-Marie Mayeur, *Un prêtre démocrate: l'abbé Lemire (1853–1928)* (Paris, 1968). One can also read, concerning the worker gardens, the 1904 defense by one of the movement's leaders, Louis Rivière, *La Terre et l'Atelier. Jardins ouvriers*, and the university thesis, although hagiographic, by Paul-J. Bacquet, *Les Jardins ouvriers et le terrianisme* (Paris, 1906), with a preface by abbé Lemire.

49. "Enemy of foreign invasion," proclaimed abbé Lemire at the Christian Democratic congress in Lyons (1896): "On this subject I am in agreement, I can see, to the depth of my soul, with the men who have come to this place , in agreement with Drumont, with Delahaye, with Guéron, with the brave young people of *Free France*, with the father of the workers, our beloved Harmel, with the abbé Garnier." In *L'Enquête* by Dagau (1899), however, while maintaining his hostility toward "Jewery," he promises not to "take part in anti-Semitic agitation."

50. The affectionate ties, at the beginning of the twentieth century, between Lemire and the "young people" of the *Sillon* founded by Marc Sangnier were well established—even if Sangnier's later evolution would tend toward increasingly radical democratism.

51. As a comparison, one should note that in 1920 "170,000 gardens in industry are counted: 88,000 depend upon the mining companies (70,000 of which adjoin houses), 60,000 depend upon the railway companies." That is to say a ratio, in terms of surface, of 5,500 hectares to 1,670 (figures quoted from J.-M. Mayeur, *Un prêtre démocrate*).

52. Quoted from J.-M. Mayeur.

Allée Eight

1. Born in 1859, that is to say a year before Kahn, Bergson would die a few days after his friend, on January 4, 1941.

2. The one given in *On Germany* (conclusion of the chapter: "From Kant to Hegel").

3. Which has little to do with rock, in spite of what some may say.

4. To each function (work, rest, entertainment, etc.) corresponded a zone, and vice versa.

5. "Negative" in the photographic sense. Furthermore, the language of urban planning has also used the concept of a "planted free space." "Free"—that is to say without any determined function.

6. This is the designation given to the group of currents (mainly central European—Sitte, but also Weber—and Anglo-Saxon) that, rejecting the concept of modernity as rupture, tried to think of it as continuity.

7. Project of 1922. Which cannot be understood without this aphorism: "The city will be transformed little by little into a park."

8. Thesis explained by André Véra in *Le Nouveau jardin* (1912).

9. The organizers of the exhibit even tried to hide Le Corbusier's proposal behind an eight-foot-high fence!

10. After studying at the Paris polytechnic, Forestier (1861–1930) completed his education at the École forestière before being named curator of the Promenades de Paris. He was also an urban planner.

11. Jules Vacherot, *Les Parcs et jardins au commencement du XXe siècle: École française* (*Barillet-Deschamps*) (Paris, 1908).

12. Not to be confused with the universalist aims of the Kahn gardens.

13. In his Introduction to the collection of photographs by H. Saint-Sauveur, *Les Beaux Jardins de France* (Paris, c. 1925), R. Ed. André, professor at the national school of horticulture at Versailles, speaks of the "mixed or composite" style, meaning a combination of existing styles.

14. Dominated by a desire for unification, the squares described by Alphand in his work are (like Haussmann's buildings) types that could be reproduced with variations, and not the expression of a site.

15. One will undoubtedly be amazed—and rightly so—by this single allusion to an essential work. But the composition of our book imposed the cruel choice between Giverny and the Kahn gardens. A dilemma we resolved by choosing the lesser known of the two gardens.

16. "Le sentiment de la nature aux Buttes-Chaumont," in *Le Paysan de Paris*, 1926.

17. The expression is taken from Bruno Veyssière (the review *A. M. C.*, June 1986), who designates with that term the singular version of the "international style" produced by French architecture after the Second World War: that is to say the fusion of a neoclassical modern rationalism, formally more related to Auguste Perret than Le Corbusier, with the industrial techniques of heavy prefabrication.

18. See Milan Kundera: "All those who extol the racket of the mass media, the idiotic smile of publicity, the forgetting of nature, indiscretion raised to the ranks of virtue, must be called *collaborators of modernity*" (*The Art of the Novel*).

19. See the book by Ventury, *Contradiction and Complexity in Architecture* (New York, 1966), translated into French under the title *De l'ambiguïté en architecture*.

20. "We call holistic an ideology that valorizes the social totality and neglects or subordinates the human individual": Louis Dumont, lexicon from his *Essais sur l'individualisme* (Paris, 1983).

21. We are borrowing this concept from Kundera, who prefers it to that of *characters*.

22. The Lassus studio, in the landscape school of Versailles, carried the name of Charles-Rivière Dufresny.

23. One of his great-uncles was the colleague of Viollet-le-Duc who restored Sainte-Chapelle.

24. In 1977, Lassus would speak instead of "common denominator" and "delayed contrast" (see *Les Jardins imaginaires*).

25. Presented at Claude Lévi-Strauss's seminar at the Collège de France.

26. "A pinkish air." By introducing into the heart of the flower a Bristol paper, which became colored through reflection, Lassus intended to show that a tulip is also a "volume of light."

27. B. Lassus, quoted by Franco Zagari, *Abitare, il verde 4*, October 1986.

28. Michel Bégon, intendant established at Rochefort in 1688, gave his name to the begonia. As for his

grandson Roland-Michel de La Galissonière, he introduced the "gallissoniensis" magnolia into France, as well as several other American arboreal essences.

29. From the magazine *P + A* (*paysage et aménagement*, landscape and development), May 1985, dossier on B. Lassus.

30. "Le Destin paysager de Bernard Lassus" (study unpublished at this time).

31. Urban planning and architecture studio of Bagnolet. It was, during the seventies, the French center of progressive architecture, intending, with Paul Chemetov citing Habermas, to pursue "the unfinished movement" of modern rationalism in architecture.

32. Park in the Arlequin quarter.

33. See the dossier for the park of Amiens: *L'Ile mystérieuse*, chapter 1, "Sens dessus dessous: l'idée directrice."

34. For example, this passage from the dossier for Amiens: "Without the swell, the sea would only be an abstraction. Bamboo speaks the same language. And because it does not lie, this transposition is thus possible: the 'mysterious island' of Amiens has no need of the water because it is in the middle of a bamboo field."

35. The Disneyland of Marne-la-Vallée, but also Schtroumpfland, and the Mirapolis of Cergy-Pontoise.

36. See, especially, François Chaslin, *Les Paris du Président* (Paris, 1985).

37. Tschumi quotes Barthes's definition of sequence in *L'Analyse structurelle du récit* and Deleuze's definition of centering (*cadrage*) in *Image-mouvement*. As for Derrida, who participated in the team that included Eisenmann, his concepts of *archi-écriture*, *archi-trace*, and *différance*, which are both "spacing (and) temporization" (*Marges*), have also been reflected upon by Tschumi.

38. The concert hall of the new conservatory, the great hall, the Zenith, the present theater.

GARDENS OF GRASS AND BRILLIANCE

1. La Bruyère, *Les Caractères. De la mode*, 1638.

2. Ernst Jünger, in *Jardins et routes*, 1940, quoted by B. and L. Kayser in their recent and beautiful anthology, *L'Amour des jardins* (Editions Arlea, 1986).

3. A. de Musset, *Sur trois marches de marbre rose*.

4. Angelius Silésius, *Le Pèlerin chérubinique. Description sensible des quatre choses dernières* (I, 289).